BRUTAL

THE UNTOLD STORY OF MY LIFE INSIDE WHITEY BULGER'S IRISH MOB

KEVIN WEEKS

and Phyllis Karas

ReganBooks
An Imprint of HarperCollins *Publishers*

Fifty percent of Kevin Weeks's gross proceeds from all the sales of this book will be shared among the families and fiduciaries of the victims who submitted claims against Kevin Weeks's bankruptcy estate.

Photograph Credits:
All insert photographs courtesy of the author's personal collection, except:
Pages 1 (bottom), 4 (top), 7 (bottom) by Doug Grad; pages 5 (top), 8, 10, 12 are handouts from the police; pages 3, 6, 11, 14 (bottom) courtesy of *Boston Herald*; pages 5 (bottom), 9 (bottom) by Phyllis Karas; page 7 (top), 9 (top) by Alexa DeGennaro; page 13 by Constance Flavell Pratt; page 14 (top) by Jane Flavell Collins; page 15 (top) by John Tlumacki, courtesy of *The Boston Globe*; page 16 courtesy of the Federal Bureau of Investigation.

HarperCollins books may be purchased for educational, business, or sales promotional use. For information please write: Special Markets Department, HarperCollins Publishers Inc., 10 East 53rd Street, New York, NY 10022.

FIRST EDITION

Designed by Kris Tobiassen

Printed on acid-free paper
Library of Congress Cataloging-in-Publication Data has been applied for.

ISBN-13: 978-0-06-112269-9
ISBN-10: 0-06-112269-6

06 07 08 09 10 WBC/RRD 10 9 8 7 6 5 4 3 2

I DEDICATE THIS BOOK TO THE FOLLOWING PEOPLE:
THE TWO PEOPLE THAT I AM PROUDEST OF,
MY SONS KEVIN BARRY AND BRIAN MICHAEL.
THE PERSON THAT WAS THE BEST PART OF MY LIFE AND
MY BEST FRIEND, PAM, EVEN THOUGH I WASN'T ABLE
TO REALIZE IT AT THE TIME.
MY BROTHERS AND SISTERS,
WHO BELIEVED IN MY GOOD SIDE.
MY FRIENDS WHO STAYED WITH ME THROUGH
THE WORST TIMES.
AND, LASTLY, TO THE FEW MEN IN LAW ENFORCEMENT—
DAN DOHERTY, STEVE JOHNSON, THOMAS DUFFY, TOM FOLEY,
BRIAN KELLY, AND FRED WYSHAK—WHO WERE STRAIGHT
TALKERS AND ALWAYS PLAYED IT DOWN THE MIDDLE.
KEVIN WEEKS

TO SHERRY AND TOM BOWMAN
AND JOY AND TOM GLENNON,
WHO SO GRACIOUSLY SHARE
THEIR SPECIAL DAUGHTERS.
PHYLLIS KARAS

CONTENTS

FOREWORD

BY BILL WEEKS

The reader of this book faces a quandary: how to deal with the violence, brutality, and amoral behavior of the characters and at the same time see how deceit, and wrong perceptions of what constitutes success, led my brother Kevin to become entwined in a life that is beyond the comprehension of "civilized" people.

You may not be able to comprehend how a father could be prouder of a son in crime than two sons who succeeded in other endeavors, but then you were not raised in an environment where violence was not only prized, but encouraged. You might not understand how his brothers cannot and would not condone the acts that were committed but love their brother in spite of his actions. You cannot understand how razor-thin the difference between taking the right or wrong road can be when you are caught up in an environment that is not within your control and in which you can only strive to survive with some sense of identity and self-worth.

The streets of Southie were tough, but not as tough as the apartment at 8 Pilsudski Way. There violence reigned supreme. What do you do when the streets are safer than your home? It was better to go out and take a beating (although mostly you were inflicting one) than face the consequences of failing. And you could win and still fail—you didn't win by enough, the other person wasn't bloodied enough or got up too soon after the punishment was inflicted. Do nothing, and you got a beating. There was a malevolence that permeated the air we breathed. We were the primary targets of it, and there was nothing we could do but survive it. And survive it we did, each in our own way and with any and all means and tools that we had within us and whatever external support system we could devise and utilize.

So one grew up inured to violence. It was a fact of life, nothing to get excited over. In fact, the absence of it was not necessarily a good thing, as you just wondered when it was going to occur and if you would be ready for it. It preyed upon your mind. It was actually easier to take the beating than to worry about when it was going to happen. Not *if* it would. That it would was never in question.

My brother Jack and I got out how and when we could. The train ride to Cambridge was in fact a ride to another world, one that was as alien to the people left behind as their world is (or should be) to you.

Kevin was not as lucky. You might feel that it was unthinkable that his parents would not want him to escape and better himself. But then you could not think in the terms that those who are supposed to be most influential in a child's life saw the world.

The desire to control and dominate was uppermost. And the standards that were in place revolved around your "street presence." Education had no street presence. It was not tangible in that it did not make you tougher, better able to fight, more feared by those around you. Sure, it was something to talk about, but you couldn't use it in the same way that you could a pair of fast fists. Smart was good, but having the ability to beat someone senseless! Now *that* was real power. Education was often talked about in the apartment, but always with the implied threat that if your marks weren't acceptable, be ready to give your soul to God because your ass belonged to our father. It seemed that it was just another excuse (as if one was needed) to justify the violence that would be visited upon the failing student. And A's weren't acceptable.

It is in a way unfortunate that all the brothers were good with their fists. If we hadn't been, maybe Kevin's life would have taken a different twist. Most of our ability to fight came from withstanding the blows that our dad would throw at us. We aren't talking about slapping here. You had to be able to take a pretty good shot early on. Hell, you could get punched for blinking too much—true!

Kevin ended up following in his older brothers' footsteps. Because we were able to fight, he had to as well. And he had to be better—that was also a rule—you had to outdo whoever preceded you. Kev was and is tough. But he is toughest in the streets, where there are no refs to make sure that the rules are followed, no bell to end a round, and definitely no decisions given on points. An incident occurred when he and Jack were arguing in the apartment in front of our parents. Jack, not wanting to continue the disagreement in front of them, asked Kevin to step outside. Kev said, "Sure," and let Jack lead the way out the door. Jack had taken only a step or two when Kev suckered him, dropping him to the floor. Kevin felt no remorse, as he had been drilled to never give any opponent an advantage. The interesting thing is that our father was not upset, but rather proud that one son would cold-cock another!

So Kevin's story is that of a smart, affable kid who was encouraged to make wrong choices. James "Whitey" Bulger got him at the age of eighteen, but he had been schooled in the ways of the streets since he was old enough to make a fist.

They say that you can take the kid out of Southie but you can't take Southie out of the kid. That is true. You are always from Southie wherever you go. People from Southie do not, when asked where they are from, say "Boston." They say "Southie." It is a fact that you do not run away from, do not deny, and are not ashamed of. There are many negative stereotypes that are laid on people from Southie—racists, thugs, ignorant, and so forth—and Southie has always been a convenient place to look down on and feel superior to. But there are a great many good and decent people who hail from there and continue to dwell in that peninsula jutting into Boston Harbor. One thing that so many people not from Southie could never comprehend is the camaraderie that was so evident. In a way it was like a big unruly family, with internal feuds and bickering, but a united front against anyone not of the clan. As they say, when you are in a foxhole, you hope that the person next to you hails from Southie—you know he will have your back.

And like any family, Southie always had its black sheep, usually a whole flock of them. The blackest was Whitey Bulger. He was incredibly violent in a neighborhood that normally took violence in stride. Jimmy brought it to a different level, and Kevin found himself attracted to it. Kev was already a student of the art, and an excellent one at that.

Fighting teaches you to not think about the punch, just to throw it. There are times when you connect and knock someone senseless and not realize immediately that it was you who threw the punch. You are trained to react. In effect, a fast muscle twitch occurs before your brain has the time to process it. You see and react without thought. If you are conditioned to this since you are old enough to walk, you can become extremely formidable and dangerous. Where other people are working themselves up to throwing that first punch, you are already walking away from the bleeding, unconscious person on the ground. That is Kevin in action. When confronted with a threatening situation, immediate violence without remorse or fear occurs. He was invaluable to Jimmy. Smart, fearless, loyal, and without many of the internal constrictions or self-limiting awareness of society's proper behavioral characteristics, Kevin found his niche in the world.

He led the good life, in the style of *Goodfellas*—money, street respect (all that really counted), and the knowledge that everyone knew who you were, knew the power you held, and understood the consequences of crossing you.

Pretty heady for a young man. Hell, it would be heady for any man who was raised knowing that the streets were what counted. In terms of the street, he was a success.

One day in the late 1980s I was in a board of directors' meeting at the company I worked for. One of the directors asked another if he saw the article about Weeks on the front page of the newspaper over the weekend. He replied that he had and another gentleman also said that he had read the article. As they spoke they realized that they had each seen a different paper and the Weeks in each of the three articles was a different brother, Jack in the *Worcester Telegram* for a political campaign that he was heading up, Kevin in the *Boston Herald* regarding a difference of views with law enforcement, and myself in the *Middlesex News* for taking a proactive stance on sewers for areas of the town for which I was a selectman. The first director looked at the other two and then turned to me and said, "I guess you all come from a family of high achievers, no matter what you're into." Kevin was a very high achiever in a field that does not tolerate failure very well.

Kev is sorry for only a few things in his life. He loves his sons mightily and rues the things that he did that lost him his wife Pam. He followed the rules of the streets all the way, and it cost him almost everything. Sure, he enjoyed the fruits of his labor, but at the end he was almost relieved when the law was finally able to put a stop to it all. He never complained about the time he spent in prison. It seemed to actually give him the time he needed to assess his life and contemplate his future. Not his next career or where he would live, but what was meaningful in life and how he wanted to interact with those who mattered most to him.

He is not that different in personality than when he was our little baby brother, still affable, still with a quick smile and a quip, still with an alertness and an inquisitiveness to everything around him. He has tamped down the violent side, keeping his hands in his pockets and not making fists as readily as before.

But I wouldn't suggest that you get in his face. You can only expect him to be so nice!

AUTHOR'S NOTE

For the more than twenty years that I was associated with James "Whitey" Bulger, despite the fact that we were together nearly every day for hours at a time, I was unaware that he was leading a dual existence. While I knew he was paying FBI agents for information, I had no idea that he was also an FBI informant, that he was giving the agency information it could use to take other players off the street. It shocked and infuriated me, along with everyone else in the South Boston mob, when I learned this fact in the spring of 1997, more than two years after Jimmy was already on the lam. While I've never had the chance to discuss the situation with Jimmy, I have my own theory about why he became an FBI informant.

Jimmy returned to the streets from his nine-year prison sentence in 1965, at age thirty-six. Nine years after that, around the time when I began to work with him, he had already made his arrangement with the FBI. His informant file was officially opened on September 30, 1975. His handler was FBI agent John Connolly, who grew up in the South Boston housing projects a few doors down from the Bulger family. Stevie Flemmi, who Jimmy had teamed up with in 1974 and had immediately become involved in serious crimes with, had been enlisted as an informant in the mid-1960s. Stevie's FBI handler was H. Paul Rico, who had kept him out of jail for a 1968 car bombing. I have never felt that it was a coincidence that Jimmy became an informant a year after he started working with Stevie. I don't think Jimmy had a choice. I believe he was given an ultimatum: Either you cooperate or you're going down for crimes committed.

However, the fact that I didn't know, and never even suspected, that Jimmy was an informant is yet another indication of the man's brilliance. John Connolly might have been a good checkers player, but Jimmy was a master at chess and outplayed Connolly at every move. A master of manipulating people and turning them to his way of thinking, Jimmy turned out to be the one in control of the informant–handler relationship.

Looking back at the years I spent with Jimmy, unaware that he was an informant, I can now see that there were mysteries I did not comprehend, scenes I did not notice. But it is important to note, when reading my story, that many pieces did not fall into place for me until after I finally learned the truth about my closest associate.

KEVIN WEEKS
Boston, Massachusetts
March 2006

ONE
GROWING UP
IN SOUTHIE

By South Boston standards, my childhood was surprisingly normal. I grew up in the Old Colony Housing Project, the fifth in a family of six kids, with two older brothers, two older sisters, and one younger sister. The odds were good with a family of six in Southie that one would run afoul of the law. I was that one.

Our apartment on 8 Pilsudski Way, apartment 554, was about 1,200 square feet, with four small bedrooms, a parlor, and a kitchen. My parents were in one bedroom; we three boys were in the other. My older sister Maureen had her own bedroom, and Patty and Karen shared theirs. I was born on March 21, 1956, and, at fifty, am two years older than Karen, who is the youngest of the six of us. Billy, at fifty-eight, is the oldest. All eight of us ate dinner together in the kitchen. While I never saw my mother without the crutches her arthritis made necessary, she made sure there was more than enough food for all of us to eat. Our clothes might not have been brand-new, but they looked fine. I never remember wanting for anything.

My father, John, changed tires for a living and later worked for the

Boston Housing Authority. The most he ever brought home was $160 a week. He grew up in Brooklyn, joined the army as an infantryman during World War II, and was a professional boxer, a middleweight. He had been pretty good at it. A throwback, a big puncher, he was the type of guy who would take two of your punches just to land one of his. He'd also trained boxers. He was twenty-six when he married my mother, Margaret, who was from Boston. My maternal grandparents came to Boston from Ireland, while my father was Welsh and Irish.

My father had a real bad temper and was always in a bad mood. He ran our house strictly. We all went to bed early and got up early. He was very physical with all of us. He'd slap the girls, but he'd punch the boys. He was quick with his hands, but you never knew why or where they would strike. He could hit you on the head for no reason at all, saying, "That's for nothing. Now do something." Or he would give you a crack, saying, "That's in case you did something and you got away with it." Not only did he hit his kids, you never knew when you would see him in the street fighting a neighbor. With us, he was a strict disciplinarian who often went over the line in his forms of discipline. By today's standards, he might be arrested for the way he handled his six kids. As a result of the beatings I got from him, I never touched my own sons when I became a father.

My mother had a hard life. She was in constant pain from her severe arthritis and had numerous back and knee operations. Both my parents were voracious readers, and books and school were important parts of our lives. Until grade four, I went to the Michael J. Perkins School, right in the Old Colony projects, at the top of my street. For grades five and six, I ventured a little bit farther, to the John Andrew School in Andrew Square. For the next two years I was at the Patrick F. Gavin School on Dorchester Street. All of these were public schools.

Our family was a close one, and every Sunday all six of us kids went to nine o'clock Mass at St. Augustine's. Jack, whom we all called Johnny while we were growing up, is four years older than me. He was an altar boy. I wasn't cut out for that. Back then, Mass was still in Latin, and that had no appeal for me. When we got home, we had to tell our father what the sermon was about and the color of the priest's vestment. He wasn't religious, but he made us go. My mother stayed home, and the priest used to come to the house once a week to give her communion.

But even more than books and religion, my father made sure that boxing ruled our family life. From as far back as I can remember, I boxed. Whether we wanted to or not, my brothers and I boxed. Every night we would move the furniture in the parlor and the three of us boys would box in the living room. My gloves were hand-me-downs from my brothers and were practically bigger than me. My brothers wouldn't seriously bang on me till we were older, but Johnny and I always boxed in our bedroom, as well as in the parlor. From the time I was eight and he was twelve, right up until he left for Harvard, Johnny would be Muhammed Ali and I would be George Chuvalo. Chuvalo was the Canadian heavyweight champ who used to take a lot of punches but would never quit. That was why I liked him. And when I boxed with Johnny, I would take a lot of punches from Muhammed Ali, but like Chuvalo, I would never quit.

As a kid, when I wasn't boxing, I was on the swim team, traveling to meets all over New England, or playing basketball or Ping-Pong. It was fun to get out of the house to travel to swim meets. In high school, I was a diver for the swim team. I enjoyed the exercise, but, like with every sport I did, I always tried to win.

Every summer, from ages seven to seventeen, I left the city and went to Boys Club camps down the Cape or all over New England. I was usually sent for two weeks, but most summers I wanted to stay for a longer period of time so I'd get some kind of a job there, teaching swimming, or working as a counselor or lifeguard, or whatever I could do to extend my time in the country. But I was also happy living in the city. Southie was a great community to grow up in. I had a nice group of friends in the Old Colony projects, and we all played street hockey, football, and baseball together. We always stuck up for one another. In the fall, we'd make huge piles of leaves and jump in them for hours at a time. In the winter, we made giant igloos out of snow and ice. Before forced busing and the integration of the housing projects, Southie was a safe, happy place to raise a family. We never locked our doors, and the most serious crime was a fistfight. Or a parking ticket, which most likely got thrown out when you went down to the courthouse. After all, they were all working people and a ticket was a day's pay. The neighborhood police had walking beats and walked the streets and knew everyone. Families like the McCormicks, the Faiths, the Holmeses, the Naves, and the Kuzmichs all knew one another, too, and watched out for each others' kids. It was a different world then. Everyone had two parents at home. Single parents were unheard of.

Sure, some kids had run-ins with the law, but in the end nearly all of them turned out to be legitimate people. I wouldn't have traded my childhood in Southie for anything. I believe we got a better sense of life there than we would have received in the suburbs. We learned to appreciate the simple things in life, like a broomstick and a pimple ball, one with semiround bumps on it, for when we played what we called half-ball. There were few black kids at the Old Colony projects and maybe one at South Boston High. Growing up, I did have one black friend, Mikey Blackimore, who lived in the D Street Projects. He was a good kid, but all my other friends were white. Southie was predominantly Irish, probably 50 percent then, with 25 percent Italian, and the Polish and Lithuanians splitting the other 25 percent. There were a lot of Irish-Italian married couples. They made beautiful babies. But not too many years after I grew up there, forced housing integration changed everything, as did the demand for the waterfront, which pushed up the prices and the large influx of drugs, like OxyContin and heroin.

Growing up, I never drank or did drugs. Nor did my friends. We'd known one another all our lives and had our fights and stuff, but we'd get over them quickly, even if our parents didn't. They wouldn't speak to each other for months after we'd solved our problem. If one of us did something wrong, all another parent needed to say was, "I'm going to tell your mother," and immediately we'd say, "I'm sorry." Today that same kid would say, "Go fuck yourself, lady." And grab her purse at the same time.

But I knew from early on that there were a lot of tough kids in Southie. And I learned that you didn't always have to win when you fought there, but you had to stand up and be counted. You didn't have to be the toughest, but you needed to be able to protect yourself if you were challenged. We all fought. We never thought about it. We just did it. There were lots of nice kids out on the street who were tough with their hands. There were good people who worked hard and played sports and were happy-go-lucky, but that didn't make them any less tough to fight.

There are tunnels that lead from one area of the project to the next. My father didn't like kids to hang out in them and make noise, so whenever he heard them in the tunnel, he'd send one of us boys down. He'd always send the one closest in age to the kids making the noise. That way if there was a fight, it would be fair.

There was never a day, however, that my father would spare the rod. One day when I was seven, I talked back to him and then raced into the bedroom. In the room, Johnny and I had bunk beds, with me sleeping on the bottom bunk and Billy on a folding cot. When I dove under the bunk bed, my father went down on his knees and stuck his arm in to grab me. I was always doing things with my tool box, which I kept under my bed. I opened it, grabbed my small claw hammer, and smashed it hard on his hands. I broke two of his fingers and split them open. My father went berserk and threw over the entire bunk bed, both mattresses and box springs and all. He was a brute, with huge shoulders and arms. He dragged me out and beat me.

Afterward, my mother came in and said, "What were you thinking?"

"I knew he was going to beat me," I told her. "So I got him first." I knew even then that I didn't have to win every fight, but I had to try.

For no reason, one Saturday afternoon when I was eight, my father told me to go into my room. "You ain't going out," he said.

"I didn't feel like going out," I told him, and went into the room. I was in there playing when my sister Patty, who was two years older, walked in.

"How come you don't want to go out?" she said.

"I'm using child psychology on him," I told her. I'm sure it didn't work that day, but it was worth a try.

While my brother Billy was always calm in the way he handled things, I was more like our father. When something happened to me, the first thing I thought of was punching. Like with our parakeets, Salt and Pepper. One morning when I was nine, we found Pepper lying dead on the bottom of their cage. The two birds were always fighting, so we figured that Salt had killed Pepper during the night. The next morning I came walking out of the shower, and hadn't realized that Salt had gotten out of the cage. All I knew was that an object was coming at my head. I threw a left hook and killed Salt in midair. My mother was bull because Salt was her pet. I felt bad because we had all liked the bird, but that was just the way I reacted to things.

A few years later, when I was eleven, I was in the house playing cowboys and Indians with guns. My father was playing against us kids. Since I was still small, I could put my feet on both sides of the hallway wall and climb up to the ceiling. My father walked by and didn't know I was there. I shot him with a toy pistol, yelling, "Bang, bang, you're dead."

He was using a baseball bat as a rifle, and when I jumped down, he flicked the bat at me. "Don't ever shoot your father in the back," he told me. When I walked into the bedroom, Johnny started yelling when he saw my face. My father's bat had hit me above the left eye, as well as just below it. I ended up going to Boston City Hospital and getting thirty-one stitches, fourteen below the eye and seventeen above it. My sister Maureen was working as a nurse in the Emergency Room at the time. Johnny Woods, a black man who was Billy's boxing trainer, was also at the hospital, working as a security officer. Johnny knew my father well and put me on a gurney and wheeled me right into the ER.

When the doctor came out to see me, he had to inject Novocain into the cut around my eye. It was painful and I yelled. When my father heard me scream and then saw my eye swell, he punched the doctor and knocked him right out. The next thing I know, I'm lying on one gurney being stitched up by a second doctor, and the first doctor is lying on the gurney and they're bringing him to. Johnny Woods grabbed my father and rushed him out of the ER room so they could work on me. Afterward, my father took me out for an ice cream sundae.

When I was twelve, I got into a two-hour fight with one of my best friends, Mikey McCormick. By the end of the first hour, a crowd of about two hundred neighbors, including my father and my brother Johnny, had formed a circle around us. Mikey, who weighed about thirty pounds more than me, was bleeding from my punches. But neither one of us was going to quit. We'd fight for a while and I would keep on punching and then he'd get his hands on me and we'd wrestle to the ground. Then that would be broken up and we'd both get up and start fistfighting again. My brothers always said that I wouldn't quit, no matter how much I got hurt. It was true, even though Mikey wasn't hurting me as much as I was hurting him. That day I got the better of Mikey, but there were plenty of days when he got the better of me.

When one neighbor, Mrs. McCannell, whose daughters were the same age as me, started rooting for Mike in a loud, obnoxious way, I threw a punch on purpose that missed Mikey, but hit her in her stomach. She doubled over and my father yelled to her, "That'll teach you to keep your mouth shut."

Finally, the parents decided it was enough and the fight ended. Mikey never would have given up if our parents hadn't stopped it. When I got home, my father gave me an open-handed slap across the mouth that hurt more than anything I'd suffered in the fight. "What's that for?" I asked, holding back my tears.

"For hitting a woman," he told me. "Don't ever hit a woman again." I didn't cry, because if I did, my father would crack me again and say, "What are you crying for?" The next day Mikey and I were friends again, but our parents didn't talk to one another for two weeks.

The only time I saw my father cry was the day Pee Wee died. Pee Wee was a beautiful black cocker spaniel given to me on my first birthday. The two of us grew up together. Even when she got old and had bad arthritis, she followed me everywhere. One morning before school, around seven, when Pee Wee and I were both thirteen, the two of us were heading to Argus Bakery on Mercer and East Eighth streets. A guy drove around the corner, but the sun got in his eyes and he didn't see us and hit Pee Wee. Right away, he got out of the car and went over to pick up the dog. I was crying hard but I still cracked him, punching the man in the mouth and splitting his lip. He had killed my dog and I was so mad. But he was a decent person. He took a blanket out of his trunk, gently picked up Pee Wee, put her in his car, and drove the two of us to our apartment. He got out and my father came down, but the dog looked dead. The man was sorry and understood why I had hit him. My father took Pee Wee to the Animal Rescue League, but there was nothing they could do. I went to school, but I was crying, so they let me out early. We ended up getting another dog at the pound, but I never forgot Pee Wee.

When I was fourteen, I got tested through a program at the South Boston Boys Club, which was doing some sort of a survey. The test showed that I had an IQ of 145. My brother Johnny had an IQ of 150. My father didn't get overly excited over those scores. When I was in the sixth or seventh grade I came home with a report card of all A's and one

B. My father gave me a beating and said I wasn't applying myself. It wasn't because he cared that much about my education. He was just in a bad mood and my report card gave him a convenient reason to beat me.

As great as it was growing up in Southie in the 1960s, there were some genuinely scary times. Like the November night when I was thirteen and walking home from swim practice at the Boys Club, which was on West Sixth Street. It was around eight-thirty and I was with Richie Faith, who was ten at the time. We were walking through the Old Colony projects, heading toward Patterson Way and Ninth Street, when a guy suddenly jumped out of the bushes we were cutting through and tried to grab Richie. When Richie took off, screaming and running down the street, the guy came at me. I picked up a ten-inch pipe, probably part of a metal fence, that was lying there, and as he came at me, I hit him with it. He fell down, but I kept on hitting him until he staggered and took off.

A few minutes later, Richie, his father, Bill Faith, and my father and my brother Johnny all came running over to where I was. Richie had run up to his house a block and a half away and told them what was going on. When they got there, I was standing there, still holding the pipe. "Are you all right?" my father asked. I nodded, and he looked around and saw that there was blood everywhere, all over me, all over the ground. "What happened?" he asked. "Where did the man go?"

"I don't know," I said. "I just took the pipe and kept on hitting him."

My father kept looking at the blood and said, "Jesus Christ, there's so much blood. You must have killed him."

My father took me and together the five of us followed the trail of blood across the street and toward the schoolyard. The trail just ended abruptly in the middle of the street, so they figured the guy must have had a car or something that he got into and took off. Then they took Richie and me home. When we got to our house, I got cleaned up and ate, and we all talked about what had happened. Then my father told me to go to bed. I was lying in bed in the room I shared with Johnny and could hear my parents talking in the next room. "The little bastard has no fear," my father was saying to my mother. "I worry about him, Peg."

The truth of the matter was, I had been scared to death. My father wanted all of us kids to be able to take care of ourselves, but he meant with our hands. He wasn't big on weapons. If I hadn't had the pipe, I would have used my hands, but the outcome probably wouldn't have been so good for me. And I hadn't had the option to run like Richie did. I certainly hadn't wanted that scene to happen that night. I would have been happy to have walked home with no problems, eaten a peanut butter sandwich, and gone to bed. But since it happened, it was a good thing the adrenaline had been flowing and I was able to keep hitting the guy until he took off and left me. I was also lucky they were doing the fences over and I'd been able to get hold of that metal pipe. I hadn't been a hero that night. I had just used my natural instinct to survive.

Another night, my brother Johnny, who was sixteen at the time, was also coming home from the Boys Club when he saw a car parked on West Sixth Street with its lights off. As Johnny walked by, he could see that the guy inside the car was exposing himself. Johnny opened the door and started punching him. Then he kicked in the headlights of the car. This was in the late 1960s when there were weirdos all around. It seems like this stuff is more prevalent today, but maybe it's because people just didn't talk about it much when I was growing up.

My father had certainly made sure that all three of us boys were able to use our hands to take care of ourselves in the ring as well as in the street. He never trained us in boxing or put us through the paces like learning how to jump rope and hitting the heavy bag and the speed bag. But at home he made sure we had good wind and good footwork and knew the basics, like how to throw a jab, a straight right hand, and a left hook. The biggest thing he did for my boxing was to get me up at six in the morning to go for a run. His rule was simple: If you don't run, you don't box. So from age twelve on, I woke up at six every morning, 365 days a year, regardless of the weather, and began the day with a three-mile run, usually in the park near Old Colony. Then I would get ready for school. My brothers ran, too. It was the best way to build up your wind.

Billy, who was eight years older than me, was the purest boxer of all of us, a completely natural boxer who won more than 108 fights. For each of his amateur fights, which he fought all over the country, he made about $25, which was enough to pay for his gas, tape, wrap, and stuff like that. Billy was so good no one could even touch him. He outclassed everyone.

Billy was offered a $17,000 contract to go pro when he was eighteen, a huge amount of money in 1966, but he wanted to go to college. That same year, Sugar Ray Robinson saw him fight in the New England tournament. Fighters came from all over New England to fight in that tournament, which was held in the old Boston Garden. Then you fought all your fights in one night, and could end up fighting as many as seven fights in one night if you kept on winning. Today, fighters fight one fight a week. After Billy won that tournament, Robinson went into the dressing room and spent forty-five minutes talking to him about boxing. My father and Billy's trainer, Johnny Woods, were there, too. Robinson told Woods that Billy was the best amateur fighter he had ever seen.

Billy also won that tournament the next two years, as well as the Golden Gloves Open Division in Lowell for three years. Two of those years he was awarded the outstanding fighter award in both those tournaments. Billy had the perfect temperament for boxing. In the ring, he was always in control of himself and his emotions. My father was proud of Billy and rarely missed one of his fights. I went, too, and also used to watch him spar at the local gyms like the Baby Tigers gym on Washington Street, near Boston City Hospital, or the McDonough Gym in South Boston on East Fourth Street, ironically right behind the South Boston District Court. A large number of good fighters came out of South Boston, but Billy was one of the best.

Johnny was a great boxer, too, and won twenty-nine amateur fights. But unlike Billy, he didn't have the disposition for boxing. He'd get mad in the ring, which was never good. Then he would lose his composure and try to hurt the other fighter. He would turn violent, like he was fighting in the street. I had a violent streak, but when I was boxing I didn't forget the fundamentals of boxing. You just never got mad in the ring.

I would never be the pure natural boxer that Billy was, but I won my fair share of matches. I have excellent hands, which is just part of my physical build. I also have big shoulders and big arms and was considered the heaviest hitter of the three of us. Being able to punch hard was a big advantage in the ring. I was a boxer-puncher. I could box, but I could also hit hard. I had good instincts and loved the sport. And I started early. When I was six, I won the Boys Club boxing championship, and at seven the South Boston Baby Gloves tournament. Baby Gloves was always held on St. Patrick's Day, and everyone in Southie would come to watch us fight three rounds. Before I was sixteen, I also won the Silver Mittens and fought in the Junior Olympics.

And I always wanted to win. Out of my seventy-eight fights, I only lost two. One was to a kid from New Bedford. I took the fight on a week's notice and lost. But three weeks later, I fought him again and won. The second loss was at the Boston Club, when I was eighteen and fighting in the New England tournament. I made it to the finals and lost. I wore either purple-and-gold or green-and-white shorts, and the other kid had on white shorts with big red hearts. I didn't take it seriously when I saw him come into the ring. He caught me with a left hook and dropped me in the second round. I lost by a split decision and never underestimated an opponent again.

Butchie Attardo was my trainer after the Baby Gloves tournament, while Red Corrigan trained me and James "Stretch" Walsh was in my corner during my boxing career. As an amateur, I won a lot of tournaments, including the Golden Gloves at seventeen as a 139-pound lightweight.

Like my brothers, I boxed in tournaments all over New England. The only time I remember the three of us fighting in the same ring was in the McDonough Gym for the Golden Gloves in Southie when I was ten. That night we all won in our weight divisions. Other times, Billy and I also won numerous outstanding boxer awards, which we were awarded after winning multiple fights in one night. Between my brothers and me, we must have won a couple of hundred trophies, for boxing, basketball, baseball, and swimming, all of which served as dust collectors on Pilsudski Way. They're all gone now.

My father went to a few of my bouts, but my mother never did. She didn't like fighting. I got a little money for my fights, but the most was $200 for an amateur fight. There was so much I liked about boxing: working out and getting in shape, matching my skill against someone else's, going to the gym, breaking a sweat, and just plain getting out of the house.

I was nervous before every fight, with butterflies in my stomach. But the second I got in the ring, it was just me and my opponent. I never saw or heard the crowd and just focused on the fight. Most of the time we didn't talk about the matches. You were friends with some of the fighters, so you fought and then shook hands. You might fight the same guy two or three times. I never had my nose broken, but I did end up with two or three black eyes. My hands and thumb were broken a few times, and my fingers never healed correctly.

When I was seventeen, a couple of people wanted me to turn pro. I met Emile Griffith, the one-time middleweight champion of the world, who had come to town to fight Joe DeNucci, who later became Massachusetts Secretary of State. I was at Connolly's Gym at the time, training to fight, when Griffith's trainer, Gil Clancy, had Kevin Dorian, Beau Jaynes, and me sparring with Griffith for a week. After the week, Gil Clancy wanted to take me to New York to train and turn pro, but my father wouldn't let me go. I was a junior at South Boston High and wasn't really disappointed. The three of us also sparred with Ken Buchanan, three rounds a day for a week, when he was getting ready to fight Roberto Duran, the lightweight champion of the world.

I stopped fighting for a few years, but in 1982, at age twenty-six, I got back in shape and started to fight again. Then I was getting $250 just to show up, but at the end I couldn't get any fights. People didn't want to fight me. I weighed 167 pounds but was trying to get back to 156. Johnny Pretzie, who had fought Rocky Marciano, and Tommy MacNeil, who had fought Floyd Patterson for the heavyweight championship of the world, were training and managing me then. Even though I was a super-middleweight, I took fights against heavyweights, giving those guys fifty extra pounds against me, just to get a fight. I ended up getting three Friday-night fights at the IBW Electricians Hall in Dorchester and won all three. Then I stopped fighting and went onto other things.

But back when I was still in school, boxing was sometimes even connected to my schoolwork. My favorite teacher was Vincent Borelli, who taught seventh-grade math. He was from the North End and came from a family of boxers. A bunch of us would stay after class to fight with him. I was thirteen and he was twenty-four at the time. A good-sized guy, he didn't try to hurt us, and we all had fun fighting him. He also ran a boxing program three times a week, which I joined. He finished his career as a vice principal at the Grover Cleveland Middle School in Dorchester and today we are still friends.

I went to Boston College High for the ninth grade, but left at the end of that year to go to South Boston High, where I graduated on June 12, 1974. It was a great place to go to school. Until busing entered the picture in September 1974, South Boston High was all white. Billy and Johnny both attended Boston Latin High and English High before getting full academic scholarships to Harvard. Johnny actually got a perfect 800 on his math SATs.

Maybe things would have been different for me if I had followed in their footsteps and stayed at Boston College High. Not that staying there was my choice. With less than two weeks left in my freshman year there, I ran into a little problem. After parents' night at the school, McDevitt, a kid from Dorchester, said, "Hey, I saw your mother, Peg Leg," referring to the fact that my mother had a brace on her leg. I cracked him and he went down. When I jumped on top of him, the seminarian who taught the class turned the ring on his finger around and cuffed me on the back of the head with the ring. I couldn't see who had hit me, but figured it was another kid. I swung around and punched the teacher in the face. He went down against a desk, and the next thing I knew it had become a big thing. The faculty had a meeting to consider the fact that I had hit a seminarian.

Mr. Swain, my guidance teacher, came to my aid. "The kid is from South Boston," he said. "He turned around to protect himself." But I had to leave school for the last week and never went back. My parents told me I was thrown out.

Twenty-five years later, when my older son, Kevin Barry, got accepted into BC High, I went over to tell my mother the news. "Oh, you could have graduated from there," she told me.

"Ma, I got thrown out," I reminded her.

"Oh, that's not exactly right," she said. "We never told you the truth. We decided you should go to Southie and save the eight hundred dollars tuition." Maybe that $800 was the crossroads or turning point in my life. Or maybe nothing would have been any different. But Kevin Barry graduated from BC High four years after I told my mother about his acceptance, and I had no trouble paying the $6,500-a-year tuition. And he turned out great.

When I was in high school, I never pushed myself and coasted by easily with B's. Some of my friends went off to college and became professionals, like lawyers, while others went into construction or became policemen or firemen. By the time I was in high school, my brothers were long gone from the house. They lived at Harvard while they were students there. When Billy had gotten an appointment to Annapolis, my father had wanted him to go there, but Billy decided to go to Harvard instead. My father was so mad he didn't speak to Billy for a year. In 1972, during the Vietnam War, Johnny's student deferment ended at the end of his freshman year at Harvard. He got drafted and spent two years as an MP guarding a nuclear facility in Sandy Hook, New Jersey, which has since closed. After that, he went back and graduated from Harvard.

On June 10, 1974, just before my graduation from South Boston High, I met a beautiful dark-haired girl named Pam Cavaleri, who was a junior in high school. That day, she was standing across the street from the L Street Bathhouse with her friends when I walked by with a friend of mine who was dating her girlfriend. Right away, I noticed Pam's long dark hair, which fell down below her waist, and her beautiful brown eyes, great smile, and terrific laugh. She was about five-six and had an unbelievable figure. I started talking to her and invited her to the graduation party that my friends and I were having on June 12 at the three-decker house four of us guys were living in for the summer. She came, as did about 300 other kids, and it wasn't long before Pam and I were boyfriend and girlfriend. We married six years later. She was, and still is, the love of my life.

After I graduated from South Boston High, I got a couple of jobs. During the summer, I drove a day care bus. I always liked kids and enjoyed driving them to the D Street day camp and from the park to the beach. I was out of the house then, living in the apartment in Southie with my friends.

I started working at South Boston High as a security aide in September 1974, which coincided with the start of busing. I liked the job, being with my friends and in the place where I had always been comfortable. But thanks to Judge Arthur Garrity, whose legal decision ordered 17,000 Boston schoolchildren to be bused to integrate the Boston schools, South

Boston High became a far different place from the one I had just graduated from.

Because the quality of education in the black schools in Boston was deemed inferior to what the white kids received in their schools, the decision was made to integrate the schools. Rather than simply take whatever steps were necessary to improve the black schools with better-quality teachers and enhanced classrooms, students from South Boston and black students from other parts of Boston would now ride buses to the other side of the city to attend elementary, junior high, and high school at least forty-five minutes away from their neighborhood schools. Judge Garrity, who lived out in Wellesley, a wealthy suburb of Boston, came up with this program. But the program didn't integrate anything. Instead, the city became a battlefield. Busing tore Boston apart, pitting parents against administrators and students against students. The media loved to portray the situation as racial: whites from South Boston against blacks from the rest of the city. But it wasn't that way at all. It was about ripping kids out of their neighborhoods and sending them halfway across the city, when their schools were only two blocks away from their houses. But Judge Garrity knew what was best for South Boston from his Wellesley home. All the women of Southie, especially Boston City Council member Louise Day Hicks, stood their ground, forming an anti-busing group called ROAR, Restore Our Alienated Rights. Every politician in Southie was against busing.

The saddest part is that there is a generation of Boston kids walking around today who basically have no high school education, who were condemned to not even mediocre jobs because of one man's decision. These kids couldn't get a decent education because Arthur Garrity took that opportunity away from them. A grand experiment, at the expense of the children of Boston, ultimately failed.

But not before blood was shed at South Boston High. We now had black students in the school who were often twenty-one or twenty-two, older than the typical eighteen-year-old South Boston senior. You could feel the hatred in the corridors. Just a year earlier, there had been a great atmosphere in those same classrooms, where learning was taking place. Students looked forward to going to school, to their classes, to sports, and to just being around one another. But one year later, it was like Beirut. You were just waiting for the next fight to erupt. Kids from South Boston weren't running scared, though. South Boston High was their home, and no one was going to come in and take their home from them.

It was horrible for the black kids, but just as horrible for the poor white kids, too. Both groups of kids had to walk the corridors, which were now lined with the Tactical Patrol Force in full riot gear. These guys were a goon squad, seeming more like vicious rejects from the Boston police force. They acted unprofessionally, attacking both blacks and whites, whacking everyone with their fists and their clubs. They seemed to forget that these kids were still minors, and added to the chaos, antagonizing all the students and the teachers rather than making anybody feel safe.

A year later, when the TPF was disbanded, the state police came in and were more professional. They would break up the fights and separate everybody. Some fights would start in the cafeteria, where the kids all sat in their own groups. They would begin as food fights and the next thing you knew there were fistfights everywhere, despite the high concentration of police there. Most fights, however, began on the second floor, at a crisscrossing point outside the auditorium.

One fight involved Mikey Faith, a good friend of mine. In December 1974, he was walking out the door of the school library when a black kid used a buck knife with a black handle to stab him in the stomach. They must have had words before or else the black kid had the wrong person. But while Mikey held his stomach and went down outside the library, his assailant ran toward the stairway between the second and third floors. I heard the screaming and came running up. When I saw the kid with the knife running, I ran after him. A cop and I grabbed him at the same time and I sucker-punched the kid. Mikey recovered, but he was in the hospital for a week or so. His attacker got probation or some bullshit thing.

That afternoon, things got pretty rough. A mob of angry parents formed outside so the black kids couldn't leave the building and go to their buses. It was more of a safety issue and a fear of retaliation that made the police keep the black students inside the building until the mob dissolved. During the melee, a bunch of kids overturned a police car. In the newspaper the next day, there was a picture of the overturned car, with me standing next to it. That was typical of the media, to grab a picture of the Southie kids wreaking havoc. As bad as things really were, the *Globe* and the *Boston Herald American* (in 1973, the *Record American/Herald Traveler* became known as the *Boston Herald American*; in 1982, the name was changed to the *Boston Herald*) were portraying it as a black-and-white issue. But that was not the way it was at all. All the people in South Boston wanted was for their kids to go to their neighborhood schools.

Another fight I got involved in began when a bunch of black girls went into the girls' lavatory on the second floor and held the door shut. Then they jumped the two white girls who were already in there. One of those two girls was my Pam. When Ricky Calnan—a friend of mine who grew up in the Mary Ellen McCormack projects and was working as an aide with me—and I heard the yelling, we came charging into the bathroom and found a fight going on. When I went to break it up, this black girl named Gracie Richards, a little stocky thing, scratched my face bad. I gave her a right hand and knocked her out. Pam and the other white girl, Ronnie Barrett, were okay. The scratches on my face were pretty deep from where Gracie's fingernails had gone in and I needed a tetanus shot. We carried Gracie down to the nurse's office, where she came to.

Another fight took place outside the office of the principal, Dr. Reid. I jumped in to break it up and ended up wrestling with a black kid who was swinging and punching. When Dr. Reid opened the door to try and get the kid into his office, I ended up throwing the kid through the window next to the door. The window smashed, sending glass everywhere. The kid wasn't badly hurt. And all I was doing was defending myself.

One black kid, whose name was actually Sigfried Goldstein, would walk around with a Communist flag on his jacket. Older and bigger than the rest of the kids, around six-three and 265 pounds, he was always picking fights. Unlike most of the kids, who had no other place to go and who were trying to get an education—which was nearly impossible in that atmosphere—this kid wasn't there for education.

Finally, one day, Billy Allen, whose family was friends with mine, decided he'd had enough of Sigfried beating up on the smaller white kids. A fairly quiet, strong kid who never bothered anyone, Billy was pretty big himself, about six-five and 280 pounds. Billy came up to me on the second floor where I happened to be stationed and told me, "I'm going to get Sigfried when he comes to his locker."

"Do whatever you have to do," I told him.

That afternoon when Sigfried went to his locker, Billy was waiting for him. He walked up to him and asked, "Why don't you pick on me?"

Goldstein looked at him and said, "You ain't shit."

At that, Billy Allen knocked him out. When a few of the black students tried to jump on Billy, I jumped on them and a big brawl broke out. When it had been broken up and everything had cleared, the authorities asked me what happened. "Sigfried suckered Billy," I told them, and they put Sigfried in a holding room, where you went when you got into a fight. Nothing happened to Billy, but Sigfried got real quiet after that and stayed away from Billy and the smaller kids. A few years later, I heard that he got pinched for murder. Didn't surprise me.

One time a lady from the neighborhood came to me and told me that a black aide who was working there was giving her son a hard time. When she asked me to take care of the problem, I said, "Sure."

The aide was stationed in the stairwell in back of the auditorium, the spot where a lot of fights took place. Since I knew what time he went to lunch, one day I walked down the back of the auditorium as he was coming up the stairs and told him to leave the kid alone and quit bothering him.

"Fuck you," he told me. "You're bothering all the black kids." With that I suckered him and he fell down the stairs. When he went down, I started banging him. Then I turned around and walked back up the stairs and out. The aide, who ended up with a cut over his eye and all lumped up, went to the office and reported me. No one saw the incident, so I had my friends, who were also working there as aides, say I was with them, and nothing ever came of it. The aide was a good-sized guy, eight or nine years older than me, but I was boxing at the time and in great shape. After that day, he was scared of me and wanted no problem with me or any of the kids.

That first year, lots of teachers transferred. Joe Foley was a phys ed teacher who I knew from the Boys Club. He used to call me the Avenger, because I always got everybody back who did anything to me. But he was a great guy and a terrific teacher. He ended up getting transferred during busing, which was a real shame because he loved South Boston High and South Boston. Some other teachers left because they wanted to, some because they spoke out. The mess finally ended more than twenty years later when busing was declared a failure. But even then, Judge Garrity would not admit that. The day he died was one of the best days in South Boston history.

Even today, I get upset when I think of what one person did to a community such as South Boston. The judge's grand experiment failed, and who was left to pay the price? You could not understand what it was like unless you lived there and saw a proud town condemned by busing. If I have strong feelings on certain issues, I have a right to. I was there and lived through those times. I have seen the results of forced busing and more recently, forced housing. Where did they want to start these programs? With the poor people, of course, forcing the poor people to move out and let the minorities move in. The neighborhood went downhill and nobody got along anymore. The people of South Boston had the will of others forced upon them. Because of the actions of others, they were the ones who had to leave their schools and their houses. A true South Bostonian is someone whose family has been there for two, three, or four generations; anyone else is an interloper. Today, sadly, South Boston is just a shell of its former self. And that is all a result of busing, the grand experiment that destroyed a once grand community.

Things were rough all over Southie during those years. In 1974, a cop got beat up at the Rabbit Inn in South Boston and the TPF determined the patrons in the Inn had done it. TPF went into the bar in full riot gear, with their badges covered, and proceeded to use their sap gloves to whale on everyone there. When they started to whale on Eddie Crow, a regular at the Rabbit Inn who had braces on both legs, Flash Flaherty, another regular at the bar, dove on top of Eddie to protect him and ended up getting whaled on mercilessly. That was what was going on in South Boston, not just in the schools, but in the bars and on the streets.

Even though there was never a day at the high school without at least one fight, it wasn't a tough job for me. I could handle the fights and liked being around my friends. And besides, I could watch out for Pam. After the incident with Mikey Faith, they put metal detectors at the front door. But the black kids would take one or two teeth out of their Afro picks, put the picks between their fingers, and use them to punch kids. Unlike the black kids, the white kids weren't using weapons. They just used their hands. They would walk up to a black kid and crack him and start fighting. But the black kids were scared for their lives, and doing what they could to protect themselves.

It was a tough year for all the kids. You had white kids who were mad because no education was going on and their school and college plans were being destroyed. Attendance was way down every day. Kids were boycotting the teams, so all sports were canceled for the year. The parents who could afford it sent their kids to private schools, while some kids just quit and hung out, doing nothing during the day. Even though senior year was ruined for most kids, somehow they did manage to have a graduation. No more than twelve black kids came to graduation, but when one black kid went up to get his diploma, a white kid took off his mortarboard cap and whipped it at his head like a Frisbee.

During that year, my brother Johnny kept speaking to John Marquandt, the dean of admissions at Harvard, about my attending Harvard. I guess the folks at Harvard thought it would be special if three brothers from the projects went there, so the dean arranged it so I would spend a year at prep school. If my grades were good enough, I'd get a full scholarship to Harvard in September 1976. I got a scholarship to the Commonwealth School, an academically demanding private school for grades 9 to 12 in Boston, and left my job at South Boston High to start at the prep school in September 1975. I moved out of the apartment with my friends and back to Pilsudski Way.

But things didn't work out so great for me at the coed prep school. First of all, I was nineteen then, and the kids in my classes were sixteen or seventeen, and had been there since the ninth grade. Nearly all of them were from the suburbs, and even though it wasn't a religious school, most of the kids were Jewish. They even had this mandatory retreat for Yom Kippur. They were smart, nice kids, but I was an Irish kid from Southie and all I wanted was to be with my girlfriend. It was culture shock to be with these kids. I was a complete outsider and felt lost there.

The school was in a Victorian house with small classrooms, no more than twelve to fifteen kids in a class. I liked the classes, but I didn't fit in at all. Things came to a head for me in the dining room. Each kid was supposed to set the table and serve the food for a week. I had no desire to dish out anybody's food, and I never liked anyone telling me what to do. "Hey, you're big boys," I told a couple of kids who put their plates in front of me. "Here's a spoon. Help yourself."

When one kid said, "You have to serve me," I did. I threw a plate of food in his face. I finished the week out and never went back. I had lasted two months there. But I felt great; no regrets. Johnny was a little upset and felt like I'd thrown away my chance to go to Harvard, but my parents were okay with it. Besides, they were older and more tired by then. As I had gotten older, they had less and less control over me. My father had his first heart attack in 1974 and wasn't doing great. My mother's arthritis was as bad as ever, and she was even more exhausted than he was.

I have no idea why I was the only one in the family to become a criminal. No one else in my family rebelled against my father, and all my sisters and brothers became hard-working, law-abiding professionals. Today, all of us are close. My brothers would do anything for me, short of killing someone. The only difference is that if necessary, I would take it one step further. Yet in some strange way, my father lived through me and the life I chose. Here he had these two great sons, both of whom graduated from Harvard and went on to lead successful, respectable lives, and he was the most proud of the son who became a criminal. It's hard to understand. And sad.

But back in the fall of 1975, I was eager to get my job back at South Boston High, and help out my parents. I had been back working at the high school for just a few months when I ran into a problem. A new principal, Jerome Winegar, had been brought in from Minnesota to replace Dr. Reid, who was forced out. Winegar seemed to think he was intellectually superior to everyone around him. He had thin hair and a pockmarked face, and looked like a tall version of the comedian Professor Irwin Corey. I only wish I could have used the cord attached to the glasses that hung around his neck to strangle him. It was something that they brought in a guy from Minnesota to show the city of Boston how to achieve integration in a high school. Winegar came for the money, not because he believed in the concept. Every time I saw him involved in a situation, he was cajoling the black students or favoring the minority teachers. He was there for six or seven years and the problems from busing certainly didn't get any better under his leadership.

One day, a few months after I'd returned to my job at the high school, a group of us aides, including Richie Turpin and my best friend, Billy Connell, were on the second floor of the auditorium, taking a break. A black kid walked by and said something smart to Richie, who said something smart right back to him. The kid went home and told his father, and a couple of days later, we had this big meeting at the school. Winegar set up this long table for the major from the state police who was in charge of the troops at the school, the vice principal, the black student and his father, and Richie, Billy, and me. Richie, Billy, and I were sitting on one side and the black kid, his father, Winegar, and the police major were on the other side. We were all going back and forth over who said what to who. The father, who was wearing a black T-shirt covered with the words SUGAR SHACK in glittering letters, turned around and said to his son, "I don't care about who said what. Just show me the boy who hit you."

None of us had hit him, but the kid pointed at me of all people and said, "It was him, Daddy. It was Weeks." I'd never had a word with the kid, but the father jumped up like he was coming over the table at me. I jumped out of my seat and suckered him over the table. When Billy and Richie jumped over the table, the state police major jumped in and broke it up.

Jerome Winegar backed the kid's story, and it looked like I was going to be brought up on charges. The state police major wrote up his report, gave it to Jerome Winegar, and told him, "You should read it."

Winegar said, "I think we all saw the same thing." But he read the report and was dumbfounded. The state police major told me he'd written that the black man was coming after me and I was defending myself. Winegar insisted that he saw it the other way.

The state police major said, "I've been a trooper for over twenty-five years. In my experience, he was defending himself."

A week later, Jerome fired me, not Richie or Billy. And I got brought up on charges of assault and battery. This was my first time as a defendant, but the case got thrown out at a probable cause hearing in Southie. At that hearing, I met Billy O'Neil, one of the owners of Triple O's, a popular bar in Southie, who had been brought up on charges of beating up a black cabdriver. It was Billy who offered me a job bouncing at Triple O's and the chance to get to know James "Whitey" Bulger.

I had no idea then exactly what I was getting involved in. But I believed then, as I do now, that every time something negative happens in my life, something good will occur. It was time to begin a new chapter in my life. I never look back on anything that has happened to me and dwell on it. Not then, not now. It happened. It's over. I have no regrets about any parts of my life, except for two mistakes: losing Pam and not being a better father to my two sons.

But in the winter of 1976, as I left South Boston High for the last time and traveled one mile to the doors of Triple O's, I wasn't entering a completely unfamiliar world. In the summer of 1974, I'd been bouncing at Flix, a nightclub in the Somerset Hotel on Commonwealth Avenue in Boston. The club handled a rough crowd, and the owner had asked if eight of us would come in and clean up the place, which we did. There were lots of fights, and my friends and I were busy every night taking care of them. One night, after the bar had closed, someone rode by on the expressway and shot out the club's windows. I have no idea if they were involved in the shooting, but a half-hour later, Jimmy came walking in with Stevie Flemmi. It was the first time I'd ever seen Stevie, although I certainly knew he was a member of the Winter Hill mob, and had been involved in the gang wars of the 1960s and 1970s. My friend gave the two of them a hard time at the door and told them the club was closed when the owner recognized Jimmy and Stevie and immediately let them in.

But that was not the first time I'd seen Jimmy. Six years earlier, when I was thirteen and sitting next to my brother Billy, who was driving my father's car down Burke Street in the Old Colony projects, I had seen Jimmy walk out of the back of a building. It was summertime and he was by himself, wearing a short-sleeved, blue-and-white-striped shirt. He looked like he was in great shape.

"Stop staring at him," Billy had told me. "He's Whitey Bulger."

"I know who he is," I said.

TWO
MARRIAGE AND THE TRIPLE O'S
1978–1982

On Christmas Day 1978, at her parents' house on East Fourth Street in South Boston, I gave Pam a ring. It was a nice ring and cost me around $3,000. I had no problem paying for the ring, since I was making some money by then. I put the ring in a box and tried to surprise her with it, but like most women she probably knew exactly when and what she was going to get. A year and a half later, on April 26, 1980, we got married at the Gate of Heaven Church in South Boston. Pam planned the big wedding, with eighteen people in the wedding party, and I just agreed with everything she said. She looked absolutely stunning. It took her longer to walk down the aisle of the church than for us to say the vows. As soon as the priest finished, everyone clapped loudly and I kissed the beautiful bride.

I'd always liked Pam's terrific family, which includes her six sisters: three older sisters, Paula, Sue, and Karen; and three younger sisters, Marie, Michelle, and Christine. But you had to pity her poor father, Rocky, with seven daughters and only one bathroom. Rocky was a great guy, one of the gentlest men I ever met, and a loving father who was proud of all his daughters. But three years before we got married, Pam's mother, Marie, died at age forty-seven from lung cancer. Marie was a beautiful woman who looked like Veronica Lake. When Marie got sick, Pam quit her job and took amazing care of her, never leaving her mother's side while she was dying. But that's the kind of person Pam has always been: loyal and loving. The whole Cavaleri family has always been a warm, emotional, and outgoing family, very different from mine. While my brothers and sisters are loyal to one another, we're not demonstrative like Pam's family. We all have sick senses of humor, sort of a black humor that makes us laugh at things most people would not find funny. Like if one of us fell down the stairs, an ordinary family might run to help him, but my brothers and sisters would fall over each other laughing hysterically. Same thing if one of us got a hand caught in the door. Another person might say, "Oh, my god! Are you all right?" and race over to help. Not our group. We'd be convulsed in laughter. It doesn't mean we're cold-hearted or unloving. It's just this weird way of looking at things we all share. And it's completely different from the way Pam's family would respond to the same event. Even today, though Pam is sadly no longer my wife, I still keep in touch with her family and have always been grateful for how supportive they are of our boys.

At the wedding, Billy Connell was my best man. Billy and I had known each other since we were kids growing up in the Old Colony projects and had lived together on West Third Street before Pam and I got married. We'd had some fun times decorating that apartment. One night, around 4:00 A.M., Billy, Pam, and I walked into an all-night Howard Johnson's restaurant in Andrew Square, picked up a seventy-five-pound plant, and walked out with it. When a waitress asked us what we were doing, I told her in a serious, no-nonsense tone that we were tree surgeons. She nodded just as seriously as we carefully set the plant in the back of Pam's father's Suburban and drove off. My first parlor set came from the hotel part of the same restaurant a few weeks later. That time, around two in the afternoon, another friend and I picked up a couch and love seat like we knew what we were doing and threw them in the back of the Suburban. No one paid any attention to us. I learned a good lesson decorating that apartment: Nobody will think anything is wrong if you do it calmly. It's too obvious to be a crime. That particular lesson turned out to be useful.

The guest list for the wedding included the older guys I was now spending more time with. Jimmy Bulger and Stevie Flemmi sat at a table with Kevin O'Neil, another owner of Triple O's; Freddie Weichel, a friend of mine; and Johnny Pretzie, a friend who trained me late in my boxing career. I made sure the wedding photographer understood that there would be no pictures taken of that table. Everybody acted like gentlemen and had a great time. Pam's and my song was "Always and Forever" by Heatwave, and our disc jockey was Joey Cunningham. It was a beautiful April afternoon and a perfectly happy occasion. My new wife and I left two days later for a week in Disney World where we stayed at the Contemporary Hotel.

But from the time Pam and I got engaged, I had been spending more hours at Triple O's, the rowdy, popular South Boston watering hole on West Broadway, named for and owned by the three O'Neil brothers, Jackie, Kevin, and Billy. I'd left Flix and gone to work there, along with some of my friends, bringing up ice and beer, keeping the ice stocked. I was also working for the Massachusetts Bay Transit Authority from 7:00 A.M. to 4:00 P.M., at a job my brother Jack got me, laying track. It was simple but hard work and I enjoyed the physical labor. Even though I wasn't making great money there, I was getting all the benefits.

But on Thursday, Friday, Saturday, and Sunday nights, I was working at Triple O's, a dimly lit, smoke-filled place with booths for eating, as well as a long bar with stools. Local South Boston artists covered the walls with colorful cartoon drawings of Disney scenes and the Seven

Dwarfs and some caricatures of Triple O's regulars. Bartenders poured shots and waitresses served hamburgers and steak tips, along with cold sandwiches like ham and cheese. A small dance floor with a jukebox occupied a section of the bar. On weekends, a DJ or sometimes a live band came in. The place could hold over 150 people and was always busy, especially so on my nights. As soon as Gillette switched shifts at 4:30 in the afternoon, the place got packed. The corporate headquarters and factory for all the Gillette personal grooming products was right behind Triple O's. At 9:00 P.M., the Gillette people would filter out to go home and the locals would come in. There were all kinds of women there, from ages eighteen to sixty, looking to meet guys or spend the night with a date or just have a good time with friends. Southie girls always dressed up and looked great, pretty much staying in their own group, not mingling much with girls from other neighborhoods, such as Dorchester.

Kevin O'Neil was about eight years older than me, and a businessman, good at making money. He was a large guy, around six-four and 320 pounds, with big hands and salt-and-pepper hair. An outgoing guy, he liked to laugh, and was a good friend of Jimmy's. In 1981, when Kevin got married, I stood up for him at the wedding. His brother Billy, who I'd met at the South Boston Court House when we'd each been brought up on charges of assaulting a black person, was two years younger and a lot smaller than Kevin, at five-nine, 156 pounds, and ripped. It was Billy who had suggested I come to work at Triple O's. The two of us got along great and often worked the door together.

But despite the clusters of girls looking to meet guys and the Gillette workers, Triple O's was a rough place, where the neighborhood guys hung out, drank, and settled scores. The drinking age was eighteen then, so I knew most of the younger crowd there. Fights broke out almost every night, especially on the nights I worked. Lots of these fights were the breeding grounds for grudges that later resulted in killings, perpetrated by patients with Irish Alzheimer's, a disease where everything is forgotten except a grudge. Most often it was a fistfight that spun out of control, but other times, people would use baseball bats, knives, or serious weapons.

My rapport with Jimmy began to form soon after I started working there. Hired, along with a bunch of my friends, to help out on St. Patrick's Day, the rowdiest night of the year at Triple O's, I was bringing in the beer and ice from downstairs when a fight broke out. There were eight guys working the door that night, seven of whom were my friends, and within seconds it was a full-blown free-for-all. All my friends were busy inside and outside, trying to take care of things. As soon as I got back upstairs, I jumped over the bar to help my friends and knocked out a couple of the worst troublemakers. Jimmy and Kevin O'Neil were standing there watching the whole scene. A week later, Kevin asked if I would work the door for $25 a night plus 10 percent of the tips of the waitresses and bartenders. I accepted.

Jimmy came in a night or two over the weekends, always quiet, reserved, and polite, dressed neatly, usually in dungarees, cowboy boots, and a leather jacket. Most nights he spent talking with Kevin O'Neil, but sometimes he came in with Stevie Flemmi, the partner he'd teamed up with in the early 1970s. Often they were in suits, having just gone out on a date for dinner with the girls they brought into Triple O's. Jimmy would always say, "Hi, how you doing?" when he passed by me at the door. He never sat at the bar, but stood in his customary spot at the end of the bar, his back against the wall, not anxious to attract attention. Over time, he engaged me more and more in conversation and got to know me better. He was aware of all the fights I was in, of the people who got hurt bad and had to go to the hospital. But when the two of us talked, it was never about crime. Rather, he would tell me to read, to work hard, and to stay out of trouble and away from alcohol. Avoiding alcohol was never a problem for me, since I wasn't a big drinker. I think he liked the fact that I didn't have any major bad habits. He also liked that I kept in good shape, still running nearly every day, working out regularly at the gym and in my house, and occasionally boxing.

Some nights Jimmy, who was around forty-five then, would show up with good-looking women or young girls, anywhere from ages eighteen to forty. He never came in with the two women he shared two different homes with, Theresa Stanley, who was about ten years younger than him, or Cathy Greig, who was twenty years younger. He wasn't much of a drinker and would spend the night nursing a vodka tonic or the same beer that sat in front of him all evening. For the most part, people kept a respectful distance and would walk by, nod, and keep on going, rarely if ever invited over. Plenty of guys had no idea who he was, which was how he preferred it. The last thing Jimmy wanted was for everyone to recognize his face.

Over a period of three years, from 1975 to 1978, I could see that he was watching how I conducted myself in fights and how I handled the door. There was no doubt I had a temper and was quick to react when someone bothered me, but for the most part, I remained pretty easygoing. My objective at the door, however, was simple: Stop trouble before it came in. It was important to quickly recognize people who would become belligerent. Maybe I'd had problems with them before, in which case I wouldn't let them in again. Even though they might be mad when I turned them away, eventually they would leave. I wasn't nasty, but I would explain calmly that they couldn't come in if they were drunk or had been barred. I also kept them out if they had phony IDs, or if I just didn't like their demeanor and could sense they were going to be trouble.

I made sure I was never a bully and never hit people just to hit them. But sometimes, when people deserved it, I hit them and I enjoyed it. Still, the only time I hit anyone was if they hit me first or hit or bothered someone else. Often strangers or out-of-towners who I'd never seen before would come in and start something. Then I had no choice but to get into the middle of the fight to stop it. I didn't think about it; I just did my job. Even though some nights I was able to talk to people and calm them down, most often, I ended up physically throwing out the trouble-maker. I tried to side with the regular customers, since they were the ones spending money, and toss out the person who had come in for the first time.

One night I was at the door with another bouncer when a couple of brothers started a fight with us, just a drunken barroom thing. We had taken the fight outside when a third guy jumped out of a car and came running at us with a hatchet. Furious, I grabbed an aluminum baseball bat back inside behind the door and, defending myself, slugged him with it. As he went down, he dropped the hatchet and I picked it up, deter-mined to give it back to him, but in my own special way. A minute later, he took off and I ran after him with the hatchet in my hands, catching up with him at Cardinal Cushing High School. Still angry at his attacking me, I planted his weapon in his shoulder blade and watched as his shirt turned red with blood. He ran away, the handle of the hatchet flopping up and down in the wind. I'd never seen the guy before and never saw him again, but I was certain he ended up in an emergency room, trying to explain the huge wound in his back.

Some nights, I bartended and bounced. Before we were married, I brought in Pam, who started out as a waitress and then filled in at the bar. She made a terrific bartender, but because she was so beautiful, guys were always trying to hit on her. Knowing my temper, Pam never wanted me to get into fights, so she wouldn't tell me if someone grabbed her. But still, whenever I saw anything, I ended up knocking the guys out, break-ing their jaws and teeth or splitting their faces open. It wasn't good for business to have her behind the bar and me at the door! Once she got pregnant with our first son, she stopped working.

Working on the T—Boston's subway system—and still bouncing, I wasn't making a lot of money, but I could see that Jimmy was getting more comfortable with me and was bringing me around to his world slowly and cautiously, having me meet the people in his circle, all the people he dealt with. I understood from the beginning that he wasn't the kind of person who took a shine to someone overnight, that he would never just jump into something. If he was going to work with someone, he wanted to know exactly what he was getting before he moved even a small step forward.

But as he'd talk to me a bit more each night, he was taking pains to get to know me better. One afternoon, in 1978, right after he told Nicky Femia, one of his associates who was doing coke and getting out of hand, to go his own way, he asked me to get in the car with him and drive around. From then on, the two of us rode around more and more, often in his blue Chevy Malibu or Ford sedan, often for a couple of hours after I got off work at the T and before I started at Triple O's. His cars were always fast cars, never registered to him, and had police scanners and toggle switches for the lights so the interior light wouldn't go on, but they were nondescript and never stood out. Police scanners were pretty much standard operating procedure for most cars, but Jimmy didn't listen to the Boston police. Mostly he listened to the FBI, the DEA, and the State Police signals.

One night when I wasn't working at Triple O's, Jimmy suggested I take a drive with him and another guy. Immediately I got a little nervous and began to wonder if I had done something wrong. The three of us had been driving around for a half-hour or so when Jimmy pulled over to pick up a kid in his early twenties at a bar on East Broadway. When the kid got into the back seat with me, I still didn't know what was going on. I knew I'd been in a lot of fights. Maybe I'd hit the wrong person.

Then Jimmy started yelling at the kid for supposedly smacking his niece and pulled over to the park at M and Third streets. Then I understood what was happening. And it had nothing to do with me. Right away I saw that the kid had a buck knife in a sheath, which he tried to cover up. But Jimmy turned around, saw the knife, grabbed it off him, and slashed him across the throat with it, using the blunt side. Jimmy looked at me, and I got into it, punching the kid, busting his nose, and knocking out his teeth. Blood poured out of his nose and mouth. Then Jimmy reached into the kid's back pocket and pulled out a police-type leather sap. As he beat the kid with the sap, he managed to hit me as much as he was hitting the kid. My hand swelled right up, but I didn't notice it till afterward.

The kid ended up crouched in a fetal position on the floor of the back seat. Jimmy then drove back to the bar on East Broadway and dumped him out in front of the bar so everyone could see what had happened to him. After the kid stumbled into the bar, his friends came storming out, shouting, "Who did this?"

Jimmy and I were standing there, and I knocked out the first one who ran out. "Anyone else want to bother my niece?" Jimmy asked, and they all went back into the bar. Quickly.

"I thought you cut his throat with that knife," I told Jimmy.

"I meant to," he said. "The truth is he was just lucky I held it wrong."

We found out later on that it had been another girl, not Jimmy's niece, who had been slapped, but I didn't feel bad about it. I had shown Jimmy that I would do whatever he asked me to do. And besides, the kid still deserved to be beaten up for beating up a girl.

A couple of days later, in the car, Jimmy gave me a thousand dollars. "It's for you," he said as he handed me the cash. That was pretty big money for a young kid. It was all pretty amazing. Here was Jim Bulger giving me money. It felt good getting all this cash. Real good. From then on, I spent more time with him. I knew, of course, that my life had changed. But I could handle it. I never felt the need to talk to anyone about what I was doing. I certainly never talked to Pam, or any woman, about anything that would involve criminal activity. As the years went on, Pam might have surmised what I was doing, but I would never put a loved one in jeopardy by discussing these matters.

I had learned early that once a crime was committed, you never talked about it. There was never any reason to. If someone ever got in the car with us or came over to talk to us at a bar about something we had done, we would immediately suspect that he was wired and trying to get us to talk about a crime.

But back then, I was getting busier with my own family. Our first son, Kevin Barry, was born at St. Margaret's Hospital on December 12, 1982. Three and a half years after that, Brian Michael was born on May 2, 1986. After growing up with six sisters, it was something for Pam to get used to handling boys. But she did a fantastic job and raised two terrific sons. I was excited with each birth and cut the umbilical cord both times, so grateful to have two beautiful sons. Girls, I was certain, would have given me more to worry about. But by the time the boys were born, I was working for Jimmy full-time and it was often hard to find time for my kids. I wish I had found more.

But there were some real funny times during those years. When Kevin Barry was born, I asked Kevin O'Neil if he would be the godfather. He agreed, but when Jimmy said he wanted the honor, I said, "No problem," and told Kevin he'd have to wait till the next kid. The baptism was held at St. Augustine's in South Boston when Kevin was a couple of months old. Pam and I were up at the altar with her sister Sue, who was the baby's godmother, while Jimmy held Kevin. The priest asked Jimmy, "Will you watch out for this child's spiritual well-being?"

Jimmy kind of smiled and said, "Yes, I will." There were other families there that day whose kids were being baptized and they all knew who Jimmy was, so everyone in the church started laughing. Except for the priest, who had no idea who Jimmy was or what was going on. Pam and I were living in a first-floor apartment at 178 L Street at the time, and our family and close friends came back to our place for a celebration after the ceremony.

In 1983, I bought a nice one-family house in the suburbs. With the help of some friends in construction, I fixed it up and put in a Jacuzzi, a sauna, and a weight room. When Kevin was maybe six years old, he fell down while he was outside playing. His whole face got scraped up, his nose, his lip, his forehead. When he came in the house, Pam began to clean him up. She stopped for a minute and looked up at me and saw that my eyes had teared up and she shook her head. But I couldn't help it. It really bothered me to see him like that. All I wanted was to take the pain for him. For both my boys. Whenever they got sick, it was devastating. I had so many scars all over my face, all over my body, but my kids were different. Sure, I was a criminal and I fought all the time, but my kids were young and I wanted to protect them from any pain. I also knew that I didn't want them to be any part of the criminal life.

As the boys grew up, I made it to as many of their baseball, basketball, and football games as I could. Most nights I got home for dinner, and then, after the boys were asleep, I headed back out after nine to spend the rest of the night driving around, doing business with Jimmy. I brought in good money then and made sure the three of them had pretty much everything they needed.

I did take my boys to Disney World when they were nine and six, and we had a great time. We should have taken more trips like that. My brother Jack and I had a place in North Conway, New Hampshire, where we would all go skiing. Pam's family always had big get-togethers, at her father's or one of her sister's houses. As a result, the boys were closer with their cousins on Pam's side. To this day, neither of my boys has ever gotten into trouble. They're great kids. That's because of how Pam raised them, as well as the environment. It also shows that they have chosen a better life than I did.

Jimmy was generous to both my boys, giving them $1,000 savings bonds and cash for their birthdays and Christmas. But he had his own philosophy about children: If you're going to be a criminal, don't get married and have kids, because everything you do affects them. If you have no responsibility and you get pinched, you just have to worry about yourself. But if you're the main support for your kids, it affects you and them, emotionally as well as financially. He was right, and I experienced exactly what he said. But still, I never regretted having my boys. I couldn't be prouder of each of them.

As I continued to spend more time with Jimmy than with my own family, he had his worries about me and my fights, always telling me I was one punch away from jail. His biggest fear was that I would hit someone and kill them. That was never my intent, but once I got into a fight, I wanted to get it over with as quickly as possible, to hit my opponent hard and not end up rolling around in the street with him. There were a lot of tough kids out there, and I often had my hands full, trying to leave no doubt as to what would happen to anyone who fought me.

But not every fight I got into enhanced my reputation. Or involved tough guys. One night, in the late 1970s, a bunch of my friends and I went into the Saints, a bar near Faneuil Hall. When we walked into the bar, nothing stood out to us as unusual or different. But the bartender, a woman, greeted us with, "Gentlemen, I can't refuse to serve you, but I want to tell you that this is an establishment where women prefer the company of other women. I suggest you have a drink and move on."

My friends and I looked around and, for the first time, noticed that the bar was filled with just women, lots of them in leather jackets, holding each other, dancing with each other. I ordered a Michelob or a Miller and so did most of my friends. But one guy, who obviously did it on purpose to screw the bartender, ordered a screwdriver. "I'm sorry, but we don't serve orange juice," she told him. "Because of Anita Bryant."

My friend understood that she was referring to Bryant, a 1959 Miss America runner-up and spokesperson for the Florida orange growers, and her antigay crusade. "Hey, what are you anyhow?" he yelled. "A bunch of lesbians?"

He had barely spoken the words when they were on us, at least 125 hard-fighting women on eight guys. Suddenly it was a full-blown brawl, and we weren't winning. The women were going after us with chairs and beer bottles, glasses, everything. We were hitting them like they were guys, but they weren't backing down. They really wanted to hurt us. We ended up fighting our way out of there, laughing once we got outside, but feeling lucky that they hadn't killed us.

But Yogi Cummings pretty nearly made Jimmy's fears that I was one punch away from jail come true. Yogi, who came from Andrew Square, was one of the tougher guys at Triple O's. Around five-ten, stockily built, and strong as an ox, he was about four years older than me. One October night, Kevin O'Neil wouldn't let Yogi in the bar and the two of them had words. Outside the bar, as they continued their shouting match, Kevin punched Yogi in the mouth with a right hand. Yogi fell back a step or two before going after Kevin. Immediately I went after Yogi, and before we knew what was happening, the two of us were having an old-fashioned fistfight in the street in front of the bar. It was a weekend night and Triple O's was packed, as were the other two bars within twenty yards of Triple O's. It didn't take long for all three bars to empty, and a crowd of over 150 people had gathered to watch the two of us.

As Yogi and I squared off, I was getting the better of him. But he hit me some hard shots and staggered me a few times, keeping it a fair fight. As the fight went on, I kept knocking Yogi down and he kept on getting up. At one point, I had hit him so much that he was bleeding from his nose and his mouth and had cuts over both eyes. Every time I hit him, blood would fly from someplace on his face and splatter over the people watching us. But Yogi would not stop and kept coming straight at me. Once, he caught me one shot in the throat and I found myself unable to swallow for a few seconds. The guy could hit. Finally, when I knocked him down for the fourth time, I figured that was it. I couldn't believe it a few seconds later when he got back up and said, "Is that all you got?" That infuriated me so much that I started hitting him mercilessly.

Again he went down and I said, "Fuck this," and got ready to end it for good and kick him in the face. I'd had enough of this crap. Suddenly, out of the crowd, a voice shouted, "No!" I turned around and it was Jimmy. "Fight him fair," he told me. "He deserves it."

When I let Yogi up, people were yelling at me to stop it because he was bleeding so much. Still the bastard wouldn't quit and went right after me. Finally, I hurt him bad, he went down, and that was the end of it. Or so I thought. A minute later, Yogi was back up and, totally exasperated, I went after him. Just before I hit him, Jimmy said, "That's enough," and stopped me. "You're going to kill him."

"Get out of here while you can still walk," he told Yogi.

As Yogi walked away, he turned around to look at Jimmy and said, "Fuck you." Jimmy didn't hesitate. He grabbed a beer bottle and smashed it over Yogi's already battered head. This time, Yogi didn't say a word. He just slowly and painfully staggered away.

I looked at Jimmy and said, "You told me not to kick him."

"This was different," he said. "He made it personal."

As I walked back into the bar, all I could think of was the old saying, "Do as I say, not as I do." Everybody else, except for Yogi and his friends, walked back into the bar. I cleaned up a bit, changed my shirt, and went back to work at the door.

The next day, it was all over town that the Triple O's gang had beat up Yogi. He looked so bad that no one could believe one person could have done all that to him. A girl who worked as a waitress at Triple O's was at her bowling league when Yogi's friends started telling everyone that the bouncers at Triple O's had jumped Yogi. "It was a fair fight," the waitress told them all. "Just him and Kevin Weeks." When a couple of people from Andrew Square who had been there also told the truth about what happened the night before, Yogi's friends shut up.

There was no doubt Yogi was a tough guy who wouldn't quit, and I knew if we fought again I'd have to pack a lunch, 'cause I'd be there for a while. A week later, Jimmy and I were at Lechmere's in Cambridge look-ing at TVs when we spotted Yogi. "Here we go again," I said to Jimmy, but Yogi walked up to me and stuck out his hand. His face was still swollen and discolored, and he had a child with him. When I shook his hand, he said, "Fair fight," and that was the end.

The fight turned out to be one more thing to enhance my reputation at the door. But I was glad that Jimmy had stopped me from booting Yogi. If he hadn't screamed at me to stop, I would have hurt Yogi bad and probably been pinched for using a shod foot.

But that was far from the last time that Jimmy tried to tone down my punches. One summer night, Jimmy and I were driving from Castle Is-land on East Broadway past the South Boston Vietnam Memorial. As Jimmy took a right onto M Street, we found a car double-parked in the middle of the street. Jimmy stopped and the two of us were waiting while the kid in the double-parked car talked to someone leaning into his window. Jimmy strongly dislikes beeping horns because they draw the at-tention he shuns, but he gave his horn a light toot, which was a big deal for him. When the kid waved to him, Jimmy said, "Pull over."

"Go around me," the kid in the car said.

"I can't," Jimmy said. "You've got the street blocked."

When the kid ignored him, Jimmy touched the horn again, a little bit heavier than before. "Go around me," the kid repeated.

"I'll go through you," Jimmy said.

The kid gave him the finger and said, "Go fuck yourself."

Jimmy got out of the car and, naturally, I got out, too. He went over to the driver's side of the car and started arguing with the kid to move his car. The kid gave him another finger, opened his door, and started com-ing toward Jimmy, swearing all the while. He was maybe five-ten, regular-sized, and probably in his early twenties. And pretty damn stupid. Jimmy looked at me and said, "Kevin, hit him."

I hit him a left jab in the mouth, and when the kid went down, I tossed him into the back seat of his car. His friend took one look at the kid and one look at me, and quickly moved the car out of the way and all the way down the street. I didn't think it had been a hard jab, but the kid had gone down quickly. The next thing we knew, a bunch of his friends came running over from the park on M Street. When Jimmy and I turned around and started going after them, they all came to an abrupt stop and took off in the opposite direction.

An hour later, Jimmy and I pulled up to Triple O's and found Kevin O'Neil outside. He told us that a motorcycle cop named Luongo had been down there looking for Whitey and Kevin. Kevin kidded him, insisting he must be looking for Whitey McGrail, a South Boston guy who owned a bar. The cop smiled at the joke but told him they'd just received word that Whitey and Kevin had hit this kid and knocked his teeth out. "I just want to let them know," the cop had told Kevin.

It turned out that the father of the kid, whose name was Frank Bolstad and who came from City Point, the more affluent section of South Boston from G Street down, was a Capitol cop who guarded the State House, and his mother was a crossing guard. His folks were all upset and knew it was Jimmy and me who had done this to their kid. Someone reached out to Jimmy, and he ended up paying $1,600 for the kid's dental work, which included a bridge for his missing front teeth.

Later, Jimmy said to me, "Why did you hit him so hard?"

"You told me to hit him," I said.

"Yeah, well, I didn't tell you to hit him that hard," he answered.

When I looked at him and said, "Now, we're gonna have degrees of hitting?" he just started laughing. I still can't figure it out. It was just a jab, not a powerful punch. Maybe the teeth were loose to begin with.

But there were fights when I didn't use my fists, like the one involving Chucka Devins's brother Franny. Chucka, who was a little older than me, around six feet tall and heavyset at 280 pounds with brown hair, was always easygoing, laughing and enjoying himself. He worked at the door at Triple O's with me. One night when I was standing at the door, he got a phone call. "Is he all right?" I kept hearing him yell into the phone. "Is he all right?"

When he came walking over to me, I could see he was visibly shaken. "Chucka, what's the matter?" I asked him.

"They just stabbed my brother Franny," he told me, his eyes filling up.

"Who stabbed your brother?" I asked.

"These guys in Dorchester," he said. "I know where they are and I'm going over."

"I'll go with you," I said. The two of us went outside and I hopped into his car with him. Larry Bavis, a regular down at the bar who played on the Triple O's softball team, jumped in the back on his own accord, and the three of us drove over to Dorchester, which was about three miles from Triple O's. When we got to the park where the kids were, the three of us got out of the car and walked over to the bunch of Franny's friends who were still there. As soon as they saw us, three other guys in their mid-twenties started walking away. We didn't pay any attention to those guys until one of Franny's friends said, "Chucka, those were the guys who went after Franny."

As we approached them, they turned around with their backs against the fence. When I put my hands up to fight one kid, he broke the beer bottle he was holding against the fence. All he had at that point was the neck of the bottle, which was of no use to him. I looked at him and laughed. "Come on, motherfucker," I said, and with that, he whipped out a knife with a five- or six-inch-long blade.

He looked at me and said, "Now fuck you. You come on."

I started backing away and had my hands up. "Hey, take it easy," I told him. When I had backed up about four or five feet away from him, I reached inside my jacket, pulled out a pistol from my belt, and shot him in the leg. All of a sudden, all hell broke loose, and everyone started yelling. The kid I'd shot was on the ground, people were yelling, and I was in the middle of the street as this car came flying around the corner, heading straight at me. I dove over the hood of the car, but it sideswiped two other cars trying to hit me. Then I turned on the car and shot out its back window. The car kept on going, and the kid I shot in the leg went limping down the street.

Chucka, who had no idea who was shooting, jumped down behind a car. I pulled him up, went to his car, pushed him in, and got into the driver's seat as Larry headed into the back. With the lights off so no one could get the plate number, I backed the car up and took off. We drove along Carson Beach to L Street onto First Street and headed to Triple O's. When we got there, I parked the car and we went inside. As it turned out, Franny had gotten slashed with a straight razor, not with a knife, and had gone over to the hospital to get stitches. A week later, the kid I'd shot got out of the hospital and went down to the Devins family's house and apologized. He said he and his friends didn't want any more trouble. The next night, I saw Chucka down the bar, and he was telling me how no one wanted any more trouble with the Devins brothers. The kid must have thought I was one of Franny's brothers.

That wasn't my first time shooting a gun. I'd had guns since I was eighteen. My license to carry a weapon for protection of life and property was issued from Boston police headquarters in 1978. I lost it nine years later, in 1987. It wasn't hard to get the permit itself. I went down to the range to qualify and ended up getting a 298 out of 300. I had great eyesight, 20/10 vision, and was a good shot. I got it because at the time I was carrying receipts and money when I closed up Triple O's. Also, I was around Jimmy, so it was advantageous for me and for him that I had a permit to carry a firearm. Since he was a convicted felon, he couldn't legally carry a gun.

Most of the time I'd carry two .45s or two .38s, in shoulder holsters underneath my jacket or on my waist. It was never difficult to buy guns. I'd get them from gun stores or private people. I didn't like being around people, so I didn't shoot at ranges. Instead, once or twice a month, I would go down to Carver, where a lady I knew owned a cranberry bog, and shoot on her property. There were sand pits there and we would put down cantaloupes and targets and shoot at them. Jimmy went down to the bogs a few times with me and we shot a variety of weapons, from assault weapons all the way down to pistols.

When I shot that kid, I didn't feel anything. It just happened. He was trying to stab me, so I shot him. It was simple.

But there was rarely a night at Triple O's when I wouldn't break up a fight or two at the bar. One fight turned out to be particularly important. And it wasn't even one I fought. On St. Patrick's Day in 1976, during a big fight outside, someone stabbed a biker and handed me the knife. When I walked into the bar to get rid of the knife, Kevin O'Neil logically assumed I was the one who had just stabbed the biker. Afraid he would lose his license, he came down on me, riding me for hurting the bar with that kind of violence. Not that there wasn't plenty of violence every night in that bar, but stabbings didn't usually happen more than twice a year and were worse than the usual stuff.

For weeks afterward, Kevin would ride me about the incident, still angry about my jeopardizing the bar with the stabbing. "That's my license you were fooling around with," he kept telling me. "You should have thought about losing my license for that stabbing." I never responded much, just shrugged and went about my business.

One night when Jimmy was there and Kevin was going at me yet again about the fight, Billy O'Neil went up to his brother and said, "Hey, he didn't do it. I did it. So lay off him."

Jimmy turned to Kevin and said, "He kept his mouth shut and didn't tell on your brother. What do you think of that?"

Kevin looked confused. "Why didn't you tell me?" he finally asked me.

"I wasn't going to tell you your brother did it," I told him. Kevin just walked away, shaking his head. From then on, however, I could see that

Jimmy was taking a bigger interest in me, talking more to me and watching me more intently, noticing everything I did or said the nights he was there.

A few years later, in 1979, Billy O'Neil, who was twenty-nine at the time, locked himself out of his apartment and climbed up on a drainpipe to get inside. When the drainpipe broke away from the wall, he turned to jump and ended up hitting the back of his head on the fender of a car beneath him. I visited him every day at the New England Medical Center, but was told there was no hope of recovery. Six days after the accident, he died. A good person and a loyal friend, Billy had worked the door with me many nights, and I took his death hard.

Kevin naturally took it much worse, spending less time at the bar. As a result, I ended up managing the bar, along with a cook named Mike Whitmarsh, settling the bar's cash registers at the end of the night. Working nearly every night, often from seven till the place closed, and still laying track full-time for the MBTA, my schedule was pretty full then. In addition, I was spending time with Jimmy before I went to Triple O's. Since I knew everybody there and liked being around the wiseguys and the music, I never felt like I was working that hard.

The fact that I was always sober and didn't drink on the job made things easier for me, because you never knew what was going to happen when you worked the door there. Or who was going to come walking through it. About a month after Billy died, when Kevin was still having a real tough time dealing with the loss, Ray Flynn, a Massachusetts state legislator and Boston city councillor, who later became a three-term mayor of Boston and U.S. ambassador to the Vatican, came into Triple O's around midnight and immediately called Kevin "Billy." I could see that Flynn had already been drinking that night, but he wasn't drunk. I corrected him right away, but he kept on calling Kevin by his dead brother's name. Naturally, Kevin was getting aggravated, so I told Flynn, "Come on. What are you doing? You used to go drinking with Billy. You knew him well."

"Yeah, you're right," he said to me. Then he turned around and did it again. That night he was talking to anyone who would listen about Ireland and all the things he'd done for the Irish people. He'd come in alone and had settled himself at the same end of the bar near the door where Kevin and I were standing, along with a few of the regulars.

Sure enough, while he was talking, he kept calling Kevin "Billy." "Billy is dead," I said after I'd corrected him three more times. "Don't be an asshole."

And then he started on me. "Fuck you," he said. I didn't ask him to repeat that three more times. I knocked him out with one punch. He fell right out of the door, down the three stairs in front of the bar, and landed on the sidewalk.

Kevin came out the door and told him, "You're barred from here for life. And if you're reincarnated, you're still barred."

How many people can say they knocked out the mayor of Boston and the ambassador to the Vatican?

A few nights later while I was working the door, two fellows in their mid-twenties and dressed in suits pulled up in a Mercedes and walked into the bar. Guys from Gillette's corporate headquarters often came in dressed in suits, so that wasn't that unusual. The two fellows went halfway down the bar and sat down at a table. A few minutes later, a waitress came up to me and said, "Kevin, you better go down and take a look at those two guys."

I walked down and saw they had a bag of cocaine out on their table. "Fellows, you can't do that here," I told them. "You have to put it away."

"No problem," they told me, and I walked back to the front of the bar.

No more than ten minutes went by before the waitress came back and said, "Kevin, they're putting the stuff back on the table."

I headed back to them and said, "Fellows, I already told you that you can't do that here. Go out and do it in your car. You can't do it in the bar."

Two minutes later, I looked back at them and there they were, making lines on the table with a credit card. I walked back down and, wiping the coke off the table with my hands, said, "I already fucking told you twice. Now get the fuck out of here."

"Hey, what's your problem?" one of them yelled.

"Get out of here. Screw," I repeated.

When the three of us got to the door, they started arguing with me. "You don't know who the fuck I am," one of them said.

"Yeah, yeah," I said. "Just screw. Get out of here." With that, one of the guys threw a punch at me. I stepped to the side and hit him a right hand and he went down, falling over backward and hitting his head on the ground. I turned and hit his friend a left hook to the jaw and he went down, too. Thinking that was the end of it, I walked back into Triple O's.

A week later, I overheard two waitresses in the bar, Vicki and Pat, talking. Vicki, who was about four years older than me, well built, with short blonde hair and a great personality, was telling Pat, "You have to tell him."

But Pat was saying, "No, I'm not getting involved. I'm staying out of it."

Finally, Vicki came up to me and Kevin O'Neil and told us that Pat's mother checked coats in the Beef and Ale restaurant on Washington Street in town. She'd heard the owner, whose last name was Spelios, telling people he was going to spend money, even if he had to sell his place, to have me killed for fracturing his son's skull and was reaching out to Jack Ashley, an ex-Boston cop. Ashley, who was around six-five and 250 pounds, was now a loan shark with a reputation of being a capable guy who could handle himself. "I couldn't not tell you," Vicki said, "because if anything ever happened to you, I'd feel terrible."

Kevin assured me he knew Jack Ashley personally and would reach out to him and let him know I was with him and Jimmy. He also told me that Ashley always carried a .22 derringer under his hat.

The following weekend, Kevin and I were in the bar when Jack Ashley walked in. Kevin talked to him for a few minutes and then called me over. The three of us were walking into an alcove beneath the stairs leading to the function room when Jack made the mistake of reaching to take his hat off. Assuming he was going for a gun, I immediately pulled out a .38 pistol and stuck it in his chest.

"Whoa, hold on," Kevin said.

"Hey, I don't know anything about anything that's been going on here," Jack said, putting his right hand up in the air. "I've been out of town for a week and all I know is that Kevin wants to talk to me." I put my pistol away and let Kevin explain everything about the coke and the guys in the bar. Later that night, when Kevin and I were standing at the bar with Jack, Stevie and Jimmy walked in, and we told them about the fight and Spelios's plan to have me killed. The next day, the two of them went to see Spelios and explained I was with them and that his kid was wrong. "Yeah, well, my son ended up with a fractured skull and the other kid got a broken jaw," Spelios began to tell Jimmy and Stevie.

"Listen," Jimmy interrupted him, "you're reaching out to have this guy killed. Well, we're going to let him go after your son. How's that?" It didn't take long for the father to decide to let the whole thing go, but Jimmy and Stevie ended up making him pay a fine, basically for wanting to hit me when I was with Jimmy. His kid never came back into Triple O's, and I didn't spend any time at the Beef and Ale.

After Billy died, there seemed to be more fights, and as always, Jimmy was taking notice of how I handled them. It helped that, like Jimmy, I had grown up in the neighborhood, and knew and dealt with the younger people. When I rode around and did some occasional business with him, I was also learning that he was a pretty fair person and that although he had a penchant for violence and most people were afraid of him, he used violence only as a last resort, when all else failed.

Finally, a few years after Billy died, in 1982, one especially busy night at Triple O's, Jimmy said to Kevin O'Neil, "Kevin's fighting. He's watching out for your interest at the bar. And he's not making any money. You should make it worth his while. Why don't you give him twenty-five percent of the place?"

But Kevin wasn't interested in doing that, and I can't blame him for not wanting to give up 25 percent of his place to me. When he said no, Jimmy said, "I'm taking him with me."

Like Stevie Flemmi later said, "Jimmy captured Kevin at an early age." He might have been right. But no one ever put a gun to my head. I went willingly.

THREE

BREAKING IN

THE HALLORAN MURDER

Brian Halloran had been lucky two times earlier when he'd escaped the bullets aimed for his balloon-shaped head. But Jimmy Flynn and Jimmy Mantville, not Jimmy Bulger, had been shooting then. Once Jimmy Bulger decided to take him out, Halloran never stood a chance.

It was just luck—I'm not sure if it was good or bad luck—that made me a crucial part of Halloran's unlucky day. Since I was the only one Jimmy trusted who happened to be around on the afternoon of May 11, 1982, I got the call. And once I answered it, there would be no turning back. It turned out to be a day that ended Halloran's life and permanently changed mine.

Brian Halloran was a forty-two-year-old Winter Hill hanger-on. The Winter Hill gang had gotten its name from a neighborhood in Somerville, Massachusetts where some well-known criminals had teamed up. They had played a central role in the Boston gang wars of the 1960s. Back in the late 1960s and early 1970s, Jimmy had joined forces with Winter Hill and Stevie Flemmi, who was already involved with them. The gang had members of various ethnic backgrounds, including the Italian, Irish, and Polish. They were all independent, well-known, violent criminals who had joined forces. In 1979, twenty-one members and associates, including one of its leaders, Howie Winter, had been indicted by federal prosecutors for racetrack fixing. Jimmy and Stevie basically took over the Winter Hill rackets, and though some of the members, like Joe MacDonald and Johnny Martorano, were on the run, the gang continued on.

But Halloran was also a bully who'd ended a life himself. To be specific, he had taken out George Pappas, a reputed drug dealer, in a Chinatown restaurant, the Golden Dragon, a year earlier. I'm not quite sure what that murder was about, probably drugs, most likely cocaine. As it turned out, Halloran had one of his first strokes of good luck here. Jackie Salemme got nabbed for that murder, and after he served a few years, the case was overturned. Salemme walked and the case remained unsolved. So in 1982, Halloran was trying to trade info to get off on any future case against Pappas involving him and headed to the FBI with stories about Jimmy. Only one group of FBI agents believed his shit; the other camp didn't believe his story because he made his worth to the Winter Hill gang more than it was. A lot of them knew Jimmy didn't like Halloran and wouldn't use him for any jobs. But the info that Halloran was talking came straight through to Jimmy from sources he had at the FBI, so it didn't make any difference what any FBI guys thought. Of course, at the time I knew nothing about Jimmy's "other" relationship with the FBI and merely knew that he paid money to his sources at the agency for information about the law and his crimes.

Halloran's first story was that Jimmy and Stevie had asked him to murder Tulsa millionaire Roger Wheeler. Wheeler had bought World Jai Alai, a sports betting enterprise with headquarters in Florida and Connecticut, in 1978, and was beginning to figure out that Jimmy and Stevie were skimming money, extorting $1 million a year from the company's Connecticut operation. Jimmy and Stevie had gotten involved with the operation through former FBI agent Paul Rico, who was now head of se-

curity at Jai Alai. Actually, it was Winter Hill mob hit man Johnny Martorano who ended up taking care of Wheeler at his Tulsa, Oklahoma golf
course, shooting him between his eyes as he got into his Cadillac after a
round of golf. When Halloran refused to take a lie detector test about his
role in the murder plan, that turned out to be fuel for the camp that
thought he was a liar. Which he was. The idea of Jimmy offering Halloran a contract was bullshit.

The second piece of info Halloran was feeding the FBI was closer to
the truth. It had to do with the murder of Louie Litif, one of Jimmy's
bookmakers, in April 1980. I remember the date well because Louie was
invited to my wedding later that month and Pam and I were having a
hard time with the seating arrangement. We couldn't figure out where to
put Louie because he was a loud, abrasive guy and certain people didn't
like him. I had no trouble with Jimmy's table, where we sat Stevie,
Johnny Pretzie, Freddie Weichel, Kevin O'Neil, and others, but Louie
was harder. When I told Jimmy I didn't know where to put Louie at the
wedding, he told me, "Don't worry about it. He probably won't show."

And he was right. A bookmaker in his late forties, Louie had made
things hard for himself when he suddenly decided he wanted to be a bad
guy and started killing people. The first person Louie shot was a guy in
his early thirties named Lip Mongelio. Louie and Lip were involved in a
card game at Hap's Lounge in South Boston, a bar Louie owned with his
partner, Jimmy Matera. Lip accused Louie of cheating, which he was.
When an argument ensued, Louie shot Lip four or five times, but Lip
survived.

The next day, Jimmy told me all about it. It seems that right after he
shot Lip, Louie had been walking down Broadway when Jimmy drove
by. Jimmy pulled over to the sidewalk and asked Louie, "What are you
doing?"

Louie said, "I just shot Lip and I'm going to turn myself in to the police." Obviously, it was Louie's first time shooting anyone and he'd pan-

icked. He was a bookmaker, not a violent criminal, so there he was, heading for the District Six police station near D and West Broadway.

"What are you, crazy?" Jimmy asked him. "Get in here." Jimmy put him in the car, calmed Louie down, and dropped him off at his house. Then Jimmy sent Alan Thistle, a fucking piece of shit in the street who later became an informant for the FBI, to talk to Lip in the hospital. Thistle persuaded Lip not to testify against Louie, and everything was dropped. After all, Louie was also a good moneymaker. No reason to send a profitable bookmaker away for attempted murder.

A few days later, however, Louie decided he wanted to kill Alan Thistle, for no reason other than he just didn't like him. But Jimmy told him he couldn't. "He just talked the kid out of pressing charges against you and now you want to kill him?" Jimmy said. "He did you a favor." And that was the end of that.

But a month or so later, Louie made things more complicated again when he got into an argument during another card game, this time with his partner, Jimmy Matera. Matera caught Louie cheating and slapped him in the face during the game. About a week later, they were having problems at the bar with an outrageous water bill, and Louie convinced Matera there must be something wrong with the water meter. When the two of them went down into the cellar, Louie told Jimmy to take a look at the water meter, which he said was broken. While Matera was staring at the meter, Louie shot him in the head for slapping him.

Unfortunately for Louie, there was a witness, Bobby Conrad, the bartender who was working that night. Conrad, around fifty, was a nervous wreck over what he'd seen, so Louie wined and dined him in Las Vegas. Then he took him to a little place he had up in Nova Scotia, where he promised to hide him till everything blew over, assuring him everything would be fine and he had nothing to worry about. He killed him there, took him out of the back of the house in a wheelbarrow, and buried him. He ended up hiding him so well that thanks to the laws in Canada limiting their access to search for bodies, the DEA and State Police couldn't find him.

After that murder, Louie came back to Boston, convinced now that he was a killer. It didn't take long for him to have another falling-out with a partner, this time with Joe the Barber, a barber by trade and his partner in the bookmaking operation.

One night, around eleven, Louie strolled into Triple O's, dressed in his usual stylish manner, perfectly groomed, his fingernails manicured, a flat scally or newsboy cap covering the balding top of his dark hair, anxious for people to notice him. Louie's clothes were always color-coordinated, like if he wore a red jacket or shirt, he put on red shoes. He had green shoes to go with his green jacket. And so on. That night, he was decked out in black flared-leg pants, a black silk shirt open at the neck, a short black leather jacket, black shiny shoes, gold chains, and rings. That was Louie.

He wasn't a big guy, maybe five-seven and 185 pounds. Of Arab descent, he had a mustache like Saddam Hussein. He also had a wife and couple of kids, and a three-decker townhouse on East Broadway and G. I was friendly with his daughter Louanne, who was a few years younger than me. That night, as always, he was talking in his obnoxious loud voice. Even when there were 400 people in the bar, you always knew Louie was there.

Jimmy was standing by the front door, at his usual place at the edge of the L-shaped bar. I was by the door, bouncing, maybe six or seven feet away. Louie came in with his loud, "Hey, Jimmy. How you doing?" and ordered a round of drinks for Jimmy and Kevin O'Neil and whoever else was there. There was a lot of small talk at the beginning, but then Louie brought up Joe the Barber and accused him of stealing money from the business. Jimmy knew the truth was just the opposite, that Louie had recently begun stealing money and selling drugs without paying Jimmy. He told Louie that Joe was a good guy and that he trusted him completely. The conversation, I could see, was getting Jimmy mad.

"You've stepped over the line," he told Louie. "Now you're a killer and people are going to treat you differently. If there's a problem, no one's going to just talk to you about it. They'll know you're capable of killing someone, so when they have a problem with you, they're going to want to kill you. You're no longer just a bookmaker."

Jimmy's voice was getting deeper and more pronounced, quieter and lower in tone, with stronger emphasis on each word he spoke. I knew right away that was a dangerous sign. I also noticed that the corner of his mouth was curling up and his eyes were turning bloodshot. Since I was bouncing, I wasn't drinking and I observed everything clearly.

I could always tell when Jimmy was getting mad. He has these crystal-clear blue eyes, and when he gets angry, they turn from blue to bloodshot. It's like a Dracula movie when Christopher Lee is about to bite his victim and you can see the red veins in his eyes. It was the same thing with Jimmy.

I could see that Jimmy's blood was boiling and his blood pressure was rising, but Louie had a couple of beers in him and he didn't pick up the danger signs. "I got nothing to worry about," Louie told Jimmy. "I got you as a friend."

"We're not friends anymore, Louie," Jimmy said coldly. But Louie just laughed and tried to shake it off like Jimmy was joking or this was a mere scolding. But I knew Jimmy was dead serious. And I also knew Louie had a problem. He was acting like a fool, talking about killing Joe the Barber, thinking he was on equal footing with Jimmy, that he was a killer now and Jimmy would respect him for that. He couldn't have been more wrong.

Personally, I liked Louie. Every Sunday night, he'd come down to Triple O's and we'd play cards or pinball, twenty bucks a game. He was loud but funny, and had always been a good moneymaker for Jimmy. He should have just stayed a bookie and not tried to jump from the minor leagues to the majors. And now he wanted to kill a friend of Jimmy's. There was no way that would be allowed.

Shortly after that, a week or so before my wedding, Louie was found stuffed into a garbage bag in the trunk of his car, which had been dumped in the South End. He'd been stabbed with an ice pick and shot. "He was color-coordinated," Jimmy told me. "He was wearing green underwear and was in a green garbage bag."

At the wedding, when I went around to greet his table, Jimmy pointed to the empty chair beside him and said, "Say hi to Louie."

Stevie picked up a napkin and made like he was wiping his face. "He keeps on drinking and it keeps on leaking out of him," he said, reminding us that Louie had been shot in the head and any drink he might have put to his mouth would pour right out of his face. And they all broke out laughing.

Louie's family wouldn't have thought that was funny. The day after Jimmy took care of Louie, his nephew went to the South End to pick up his uncle's car. When he got back to Southie, he opened the trunk to get his golf clubs and found his uncle. No one was ever tried for Louie's murder, but now Halloran was putting himself at the scene.

Halloran told the FBI he had driven down to Triple O's with Louie and that Jimmy and someone else were there when he dropped Louie off. He said Jimmy and that other person had killed Louie and carried him out the back door. Strangely enough, Jimmy told me, "Louie's last words to me were a lie." Apparently Louie had insisted that he'd come by himself and that no one had driven him over. It was hard to figure out why Louie lied to Jimmy that night. If he'd told Jimmy that someone had driven him, he might have gotten a pass. But it wouldn't have lasted long, since Jimmy had no intentions of letting Louie run wild.

Now Halloran was playing just as dangerous a game as Louie. And making fatal errors. The worst mistakes were coming back to Boston and trusting the FBI. Of course, FBI agent John Connolly was feeding Jimmy all the info about Halloran. Jimmy and Stevie talked about it in front of me, saying Halloran was lying, at least about the Wheeler case.

Figuring it was just a matter of time until Halloran was taken off the streets and put in Witness Protection, Jimmy went looking for him. I assumed we were just going to brace him, read him the riot act, but let him go. After all, if the FBI didn't believe him, why should we have to take him out? But I was new to the game and didn't understand all the ways in which Jimmy's mind moved. Nor did I know all the goings-on with the Wheeler murder. Twenty-six years old then, I was still holding onto my job at the MBTA, working from seven to four, laying track. I'd also been working for Jimmy for five years, and after work I would head over to the Broadway Appliance and Furniture store on F and West Broadway that I now owned with Kevin O'Neil to meet Jimmy and ride around with him for a few hours, collecting envelopes and beating up people. Even though Jimmy and I had opened a bar on F and West Second called Court's Inn, I was still bouncing some nights and weekends at Triple O's, from nine to two. I had more than a few jobs, but I needed the dough. At that time I was a married man and planning on starting a family.

And I had other responsibilities, too. Every Thursday, from the time I'd graduated South Boston High and begun to work full-time, I'd go over to the house in the Old Colony projects at 8 Pilsudski Way, apartment 554, second floor, to give my mother an envelope. That was the right thing to do. I gave her cash, usually a couple hundred each week, most of it money made working illegally from Jimmy. She was still suffering from her severe arthritis and other health problems. My father had a bad heart and couldn't work much. Ma was grateful for the money and always said, "Thank you."

My mother had heard things about me, but she chose not to believe them. Once I was involved in a fight with a kid who pulled a gun on me, then jumped in his car and took off. I hopped into my car and followed him, each of us shooting at the other through the windows. He drove through the Old Colony projects, right by 8 Pilsudski Way, and I was still shooting at him out of my car window. My mother looked out the window and started yelling to my sister Patty to call the police. When Patty told her, "Ma, that's Kevin," Ma said, "Oh, my God!" and moved away from the window.

Anyhow, the day Jimmy went looking for Halloran, I'd just gotten off work at the T, and was still dressed in my work clothes—dungarees and work boots. I was talking with Jimmy down at the Broadway Appliance store when John, a capable fellow from Charlestown and an old Winter Hill associate of Jimmy's, stopped by to shoot the shit. Casually, he mentioned that he'd just spotted Brian Halloran on a pay phone outside the Pier restaurant on the South Boston waterfront. John knew from conversation around certain criminal circles that Halloran was cooperating, and that Jimmy had been looking for him for over a month. Jimmy also knew that the window of opportunity for taking out that piece of crap was closing. He wouldn't be left unprotected on the streets for long.

Jimmy, John, and I got into our separate cars and headed to the Mullins Club at O and Third. Even though it was officially called the CPAA, or City Point Athletic Association, most people knew it as the Mullins Club, which was also the place where the Mullins gang hung. Jimmy was driving his green Olds Delta 88 and I was in my green Thunderbird. Jimmy walked into the Mullins Club to see if anyone else was around to help him. When he didn't find anyone, he told me to leave my car there and drive him over to Theresa Stanley's house on Silver Street in South Boston. When I dropped him off, he said I should head back to the Mullins Club. By then it was about four-thirty in the afternoon. I had no idea exactly what was going to happen, but I could tell that there was an urgency to whatever it was. I drove back down to the club where, fifteen minutes later, Jimmy pulled up, wearing a light brown wig, floppy mustache, and dark clothes, driving the Tow Truck.

The Tow Truck was basically a hit car, a modified high-performance blue 1975 Malibu. We had nicknamed it the Tow Truck so if anyone ever picked us up talking about it on the radio, they would think we were talking about some tow truck. When Jimmy had bought it a year or so earlier, it was a two-toned blue, but he had it painted a dark green. Jimmy had a master mechanic work on it according to his own specifications, and garaged it on K Street. It was a beauty, its engine all souped up, with over 900 horsepower. Jimmy's mechanic had gone over it from head to toe: shocks, springs, the transmission, the whole suspension system, the motor, the driveshaft, the rear end. Every part of the car was high-performance. From the motor to the rear suspension, everything had been replaced because with so much power, the weakest link would break under full acceleration. You could turn each light on or off with the flick of a switch. If you got in a chase, all the lights but the headlights could go off so it would be hard for anyone to follow you. Jimmy had a smoke-screen put in it where enough thick fog would come out the tailpipe to shut down an entire street. The mechanic had added an extra oil well that was filled with Marvel Mystery Oil, which fed into the exhaust manifold. The heat from the exhaust manifold produced smoke that seeped out of the tailpipes and created a heavy fog. You hit a button and oil would be pumped into the exhaust manifold and the red-hot pipes would steam up. We tested it late one night and watched as it fogged out all of First Street.

There were also little nozzles on a pipe underneath the rear bumper that were pressurized so oil would shoot out of them. If you were getting chased, as you went into a turn, you'd lay down an oil slick. You could make the turn, but the cars behind you would be spinning out of control. It was like James Bond's Aston Martin, without the ejector seat. You couldn't look at that car and not hear the roar of the engine. It literally growled. When you'd step on the accelerator, the car would stand up on its four wheels. The driveshaft, the whole engine would try to twist inside the car. I'd never seen such a phenomenal car. It looked like an ordinary Chevy Malibu, but only until you stepped on the gas. It was a beast.

I had my own set of keys and would take it out at night once a week and make sure everything worked. I'd be out on the Southeast Expressway or the Mass Turnpike, going 90 mph, and I'd step on the gas and the car would leave rubber. If a cop ever went after me for speeding, I wasn't stopping. One night, when I had the car out on the Turnpike, a Porsche Targa 911 and a Corvette blew by me, so I stepped on the gas. The car took off like a rocket and I shot by the two of them. The needle on the speedometer was buried at 160 and the car was still accelerating. Jimmy hardly ever drove it, but he would have been bullshit if he ever saw me racing down the Turnpike that night.

The Tow Truck was just another example of how far ahead Jimmy thought. There wasn't one tiny detail that wasn't perfect on that car as an escape vehicle. It showed how 98 percent of his life was business, with maybe 2 percent pleasure. While other guys might be out drinking, he'd be thinking. While other people would be going to sleep at night, he'd be up planning. He was disciplined and lived and breathed the life of crime, which explains why he is still out there today, rather than in a jail cell.

Even though we'd tested the Tow Truck's different features together and I'd taken it out many times, seeing Jimmy pull up with the wig and mustache was the first time I'd ever seen him use it for real. And in broad daylight.

But the minute I saw him, I thought, *This ain't good*. Actually, he looked just like Jimmy Flynn, an old-time Winter Hill associate. Flynn and Jimmy Mantville, who had been part of the original Mullins gang on the other side from Jimmy when the gang wars broke out in Southie in the late 1960s and early 1970s, had allegedly made two prior attempts on Halloran. The story that was circulating was that both Flynn and Mantville had attempted to get Halloran because he was talking on them about a bank or armored car robbery they were allegedly involved in. One attempt had been at Halloran's house, and the second at a teachers' union hall parking lot. Both times he got shot at, but they missed and he'd escaped uninjured.

This time, I was sitting in my car, staring at Jimmy in the Tow Truck, thinking there would be no escape for Halloran. I wasn't upset or nervous or scared. It was a whole different feeling, with all my senses heightened and the adrenaline starting to flow big-time. I'd only seen Halloran twice in my life, both times at the Black Rose in Faneuil Hall, but I knew time was running out for him. And I knew I was a part of that fact. But, as I had learned earlier in life, the human mind can justify anything, and I was having no problem justifying my role here. After all, once Jimmy made his mind up that Halloran had to go, it was gonna happen. With or without me. Jimmy was tapping me for the job, and there would be no way I could walk away.

Not that I'd want to. I was working for the top gangster in the city, a cold-blooded murderer, and I'd always known that if he asked me to kill someone, I would do it. It didn't bother me to live like this. I knew a lot of people couldn't handle what was about to happen. They'd become nervous wrecks, but it didn't faze me in the least. I had come to accept the fact that someday, sooner or later, I'd be involved in a murder. We were, I understood, brutal people. We hurt a lot of people. I wasn't hanging around with Boy Scouts.

The truth was that I genuinely liked Jimmy; to me, he was a great guy. We shared a lot of laughs and I always saw the good side of him. Sure, I'd seen his temper, but it had never been directed at me. The two of us worked well together. I had a reputation for fighting with my hands, so moving from boxing to bouncing to working for Jimmy was a natural progression for me. And it carried a lot of prestige. My father was pleased with my working for the top gangster in the city, someone most people in Southie respected for helping people in need, and used to say to me, "Listen and learn." He would talk about me at family gatherings, telling more stories about me than any of his other five kids. It was as if I was doing what he wanted to do in life. When you consider the odds, it makes some sort of sense that out of his six kids one would turn out to be a criminal. It was the same thing in Jimmy's family. He'd been a criminal since he was a kid, the only one like that in the Bulger family. His brother Billy was president of the Massachusetts State Senate for sixteen years and later became president of the University of Massachusetts, while another brother, Jackie, was a clerk magistrate in the Boston Juvenile Court. His sisters were all housewives and professionals of one type or another.

Until I got married and moved out of the house, when I came home at night and my clothes were bloody, from stabbing or fights or bouncing, my father wouldn't ask me what happened. All he'd say was, "You all right?" and when I'd answer, "Yeah," he'd say, "Give me your clothes," and he'd throw them in the washing machine. He'd give them back to me when they were done and nothing else was said.

I still kept all kinds of weapons in my parents' house—pistols, silencers, machine guns with silencers, assault rifles, hand grenades. Over the years, Jimmy had acquired a lot of weaponry, and I had also picked up a lot from the streets. People who had stolen guns were always looking to sell them. Jimmy also traveled to New York to buy some. My weapons were locked in the foot locker in my bedroom. When I told my father I'd move them out of the house, he shook his head. "If the cops come here looking for them, I'll say they belong to me," he said. "What are they going to do to me? Put me in jail?"

But seven years before that, there I was, sitting behind the wheel of Jimmy's Delta 88 at the Mullins Club, staring at Jimmy in his Tow Truck and wig and mustache. This time, he told me to meet him down at Jimmy's Harborside restaurant, and to be sure to back the car into the parking lot. I'd been at the Harborside no more than fifteen minutes when Jimmy pulled the Tow Truck in nose-first so our driver's sides were facing, and handed me a walkie-talkie and binoculars. The Olds already had a police scanner. He told me that Halloran was sitting in the window of the Pier restaurant, about 400 yards away from where I was parked, so I'd need to get a little closer. When I was settled, I was to keep an eye on the restaurant and let him know when Balloonhead got up from his seat.

There was no doubt Halloran fit his code name perfectly, with his round, melon-shaped head that looked like it had been filled with a blast of helium. At six-four, he was powerfully built and barrel-chested, a big guy. If you ever see the movie *The Brink's Job* with Peter Falk, made in the late 1970s, you might see Brian Halloran. I have no idea how Halloran got the role. Maybe from the Teamsters' local? When Specs O'Keefe is in a jail scene, Halloran plays the prison guard who hits him from behind; the perfect role for this bully.

Before Jimmy took off, I noticed a man in the back seat of the Tow Truck, his face hidden behind a dark blue ski mask. He raised himself up and waved at me. I waved back with no idea who he was. Then I drove a short distance to Anthony's Pier Four parking lot and backed in so I could see the whole front of the Pier restaurant across the street. By then it was five or five-thirty.

I sat in the car, the windows open, trying to look inconspicuous as I moved the binoculars from my lap to my eyes and stared into the window of the restaurant. I kept an earplug in my ear so I could listen to the police scanner without anyone hearing the chatter of the scanner through my open window. I kept wishing I had a hat to change my appearance so no one would be able to recognize me. Unfortunately, there were no hats in Jimmy's Olds. From that day on, no matter what car I was driving, I made sure that I had a few hats available to put on at a moment's notice.

That early in the evening, there was nothing particularly interesting coming through the scanner, just the typical domestic violence stuff and a few minor incidents. It's funny, but an ordinary person might not pay much attention to a guy sitting in his car, staring at a restaurant through a set of binoculars. But a criminal would. I'd want to get his plate and find out who he was and why he was staked out there. But that spring evening, none of the people walking up and down the waterfront seemed interested in me or what I was doing. And I was grateful that I didn't see anybody I knew.

So I kept sitting there, staring straight ahead, through the binoculars at the 100 feet separating me from Balloonhead. As I looked at Halloran at a table of four having a few beers, I was glad it was him and not me having his last beers. Even though I was carrying a gun at my waist, I was pretty sure I wouldn't be using it. My role was basically the lookout, to call the hit in. Not that it made a difference who pulled the trigger. Everyone played a part to make it happen, and I was playing mine. Jimmy had often used the analogy of a finely oiled machine or a watch when discussing jobs. Everyone had to do his part for everything to go smoothly. All the little cogs in the watch had to move perfectly. If one wheel stopped or broke, then the watch would stop working. More important than committing the crime was getting away with it. And in order for that to happen, everything had to go just right. It didn't matter who pulled the trigger. The person who called in the hit or drove the crash car or listened to the scanner was equally as important. There were times when we would stop before the crime was committed, like with a shakedown, because one of us didn't think everything would work perfectly. That afternoon, if I wasn't there to call in the hit, Halloran would have gotten away. My role, I understood from the beginning, was no different than Jimmy's. Just like him, I was committing the murder.

I wasn't there more than ten minutes when Halloran got up, and the other three guys he was with followed suit. I figured they were all leaving, so I called out on the walkie-talkie, "The balloon is rising." A minute later, Halloran came walking out the front door of the Pier with one other guy in front of him. That guy, who I didn't recognize, was six feet tall and heavyset. When he got into a car in the parking lot, I realized that Halloran had probably come with him. For a minute I wondered if this might mean Jimmy would call off the hit. If Halloran had been with a small child, the hit wouldn't have happened, since Jimmy would never have taken the risk of hitting a kid. But I was pretty certain he wouldn't let this one detail of another guy in the car stand in his way of getting the job done.

This time I gave Jimmy the message, "The balloon is in the air," knowing he'd understand that meant Halloran was now outside. A minute later, a four-door blue Datsun pulled up, Halloran got into the passenger seat, and I repeated two or three more times, "The balloon is in the air." I knew from the minute I spoke those words that my life, along with Halloran's, had forever changed.

And faster than either of us could ever imagine. Halloran was barely seated in the car when, suddenly, across the street, Jimmy whipped the Tow Truck next to the Datsun. Halloran was in the passenger seat, facing out to the streets, and the Tow Truck was facing the opposite direction, the two cars passenger window to passenger window. It was a beautiful Tuesday night in May and all kinds of people were still walking around the waterfront, dressed in business suits and casual wear, looking to enjoy the night.

Jimmy had the passenger window of the Tow Truck down, and he slid over and yelled, "Brian!" Halloran turned his giant head and the shooting began.

"Shit," I said to myself, "here it comes." Through the binoculars, I had a clear look at Jimmy's face, and when he opened his mouth to yell Brian's name, I could see that he was gritting his teeth. Hard. I also knew that he was using a .30-caliber carbine with a selector switch so it could fire fully or semiautomatic. As it turned out, although Jimmy thought it was on full, he had forgotten to switch the selector, so he was actually on semiautomatic. Later on, he said it was better that way because he could place his shots easier. The shooter in the Tow Truck's back seat popped up and started firing, too, using a fully automatic Mac-10 with a silencer. Jimmy had no silencer. The autopsy report would say Halloran was hit twenty-one times, his driver, multiple times. All that made sense, since Jimmy emptied a thirty-round clip that afternoon.

Once the shooting started, Halloran's car began drifting across the street and I could tell the driver, whoever he had been, was gone. The area was still filled with people, lots of them standing in front of another lobster place across from the Pier, most of them panicking, screaming, running, and ducking behind cars. A few, I noticed, seemed paralyzed by the shooting and just stood there, transfixed by the scene around them, staring and not moving, maybe not even realizing that bullets were flying around their heads.

Jimmy then made a U-turn out of the parking lot, pulled up near Halloran's car, which was in the middle of the street now, and shot out the open driver's window. I couldn't believe it when Halloran stumbled out of his car, walking, stunned and dazed, toward the rear of his car, straight into the path of the shots coming at him. He'd been hit everywhere except his head, which later turned out to be a stroke of good luck for Jimmy.

At that point, a van drove up and blocked my view, so I pulled out onto the edge of the parking lot into the street to see what was going on. Halloran didn't look good. There was a lot of blood coming out of his body. He'd taken a hell of a lot of punishment and staggered for yet another few seconds before he finally went down. I could see the shots still going into him while his body bounced on the ground, twitching every time he got hit. Some of the bystanders were crying, probably not about the body, but about being in the line of fire, while others looked terrified as they realized what had just gone down.

As a kid, I'd seen people being stabbed in bars, lots of fighting, and more than one violent death. But what I was witnessing now was a scene from a Sam Peckinpah movie, only in slow motion. It was surreal, and I felt the adrenaline moving through my veins. I glanced at my watch and was surprised to see that the whole thing had taken maybe ninety seconds.

People were still ducking every which way, yelling, screaming, and hiding behind cars. Jimmy tore away and a police wagon pulled up thirty seconds later. The driver of the Datsun, who we later learned was Michael Donahue, never got out of the car. Later people would say he was an innocent bystander, just some poor jerk who was offering Halloran a ride home. That's bullshit. Donahue was an unintended, but not innocent, bystander. He was a player who had been involved in the Pappas murder at the Golden Dragon in Chinatown. That night, Halloran had shot Pappas in the head and Donahue had driven him away from the murder. People had a misconception that Donahue, a cop's son, was a legitimate guy. He wasn't. But he died instantly that night, with a bullet to his head. When you think about it, Jimmy was a good shot because not one innocent person died that night.

As I drove away, I began to hear the calls coming in on the police scanner about shots being fired on Atlantic Avenue. While I was listening to that and thinking about where I was supposed to go next, I wasn't sweating or nervous. Even though it always takes a lot to rattle me, I was still surprised at how calm I felt. I had no worries that we might get caught. Rather, I was just glad it was over and was anxious to get back to some kind of normalcy. After all, this Halloran thing had been going on for about six weeks. Not that I ever thought I'd be as involved as I was that day.

I pulled away from the scene, remembering that Jimmy had told me if anything happened I should meet him at Capital Market on Morrissey Boulevard. So I drove over there and waited twenty minutes, but he didn't show up. I called him on his beeper and punched in the number of a nearby telephone booth that took incoming calls. He called me back and said, "What are you doing?"

"I'm at Capital Market," I said.

"I'm at Theresa's, eating," he told me. "Grab something to eat and I'll speak to you later."

So I headed over to my in-laws' to eat. When I got there, I put on the news at six o'clock and watched it with my wife's family. It was all over the news. Gangland slaying at the waterfront. Nobody around me was treating it like a big thing, and no one in my wife's family would ever suspect I had anything to do with it. I was hungry, watching the news, and thinking, *Hey, we got away with it.* I didn't drink that night, not even a beer. But that wasn't unusual for me, since I always like to be in control, especially so that night.

Around nine, Jimmy beeped me and told me to bring his car to Theresa's and pick him up. When I pulled up, he got into the driver's side and I moved over to the passenger side. As always, we didn't talk in the car, assuming it was wired. Jimmy was back to his usual self, wearing his regular clothes, no mustache or wig. He drove us to the scene of the crime to look for a hubcap that had fallen off the Tow Truck, taking a right up the viaduct ramp that led to the old World Trade Center and driving right back down to where they had all the police lights set up in the crime scene. We saw the hubcap just where he thought it had landed, right at the corner by the curb, less than a quarter of a mile from where the police had set up the crime scene. Jimmy had to take a series of rights to get on the viaduct but when he got to the spot, I jumped out, grabbed the hubcap, and threw it in the back seat of the Olds. If the police had found it, they could have linked the model of the car and maybe found a print on it. Not that I was worried about that. You just didn't get worried around Jimmy, maybe because he had plenty of nerve. Too much nerve. Everybody around him absorbed his energy. Since he was fearless, you assumed you were going to get away with it. And we did.

From there, we drove to Stevie Flemmi's mother's house, a two-story at 832 East Third Street. Stevie had the whole house done over for his parents and put in a modern kitchen with all up-to-date equipment. It was a good-sized room with a glass-topped kitchen table that seated four people. There was also a parlor with a couch and a TV across from the kitchen, along with a formal dining room and a bedroom with a bathroom on the first floor. On the second floor were two bedrooms and a bathroom. Mary Flemmi, a short, plump lady, probably in her seventies, her black hair in a bun, wearing a simple housedress, was busy moving around the kitchen making dinner. Her husband, John, was already in bed, but she was delighted to feed the three of us. She spoke good English, with a slight Italian accent, a friendly little lady who liked everybody and loved to cook up a big meal. I'd eaten over there before, as had Jimmy. That night Jimmy spoke to Mary for a few minutes, as usual, polite and warm to her.

Stevie and Jimmy stayed in the kitchen, talking about the day's events, but I went into the parlor, which was right next to the kitchen, to catch the latest news and see what they were saying about the murder. While Jimmy was explaining to Stevie what had happened, I could see Stevie, wearing dungarees and a shirt, punching his hands together. He was bullshit that he hadn't been there. I didn't know him that well then, but as I got to know him I understood that Stevie enjoyed a good murder.

In that way, Stevie was just like Jimmy, who killed people every which way there was—stabbing, strangling, shooting, beating them with bats, changing up all the time, with no rhyme or reason, using whatever method he thought was the best way to kill that particular person. To my knowledge, Jimmy killed at least forty people. But that night, I could feel that things were different between the two of us. Jimmy knew it, too. He'd always said that once a murder was committed, we were all hostages to one another. From then on, I was as tied to him as he was to me.

When I went back into the kitchen to eat, Mary was still busy taking stuff off the stove and putting it on the glass table in bowls, making sure we all ate everything. Jimmy kept telling her how delicious the food was and what an excellent cook she was. Not that every visitor to this house on East Third Street got to spend such a pleasant evening at Mary's house. Certainly not her son's beautiful, blue-eyed, blonde, twenty-six-year-old girlfriend Debra Davis. Debra had been brought to the house a year earlier because Stevie was worried that she was trying to leave him for some guy she met on a vacation to Mexico. It's open to debate exactly who strangled Debra that night in Mary's basement. Stevie said Jimmy did it, but Jimmy told me Stevie kissed her on the forehead and told her she was going to a better place. Where she went was to a grave on the Quincy side of the Neponset Bridge where the train goes over the bridge and where the two of them buried her at low tide.

I never met Debra, but it's public knowledge that she was knock-dead gorgeous. And seventeen when she started to date the forty-plus Stevie. I blame her mother for Debra's death. What kind of a mother lets her teenage daughter date a man that age? Especially a man like Stevie. If I had a teenage daughter and a forty-year-old guy showed up at my door, he'd have a problem. He'd be going in the hole.

After Debra got killed, Stevie convinced Jimmy to go on a vacation to Mexico with him. Jimmy told me he didn't realize till he got there that it wasn't a vacation. It was a pilgrimage. Stevie only wanted to trace Debra's footsteps during her trip so he could find the guy she planned to dump him for. And kill him. Jimmy was grateful they never found the guy. I should have been grateful that Jimmy hadn't involved me in that murder. Guess he felt killing a beautiful girl wasn't the best way to initiate me into murder. But Halloran's killing was.

That May night at Stevie's parents' house, Jimmy and Stevie were still discussing Halloran's murder. Stevie was occasionally laughing, and Jimmy was maybe a little more excited than usual, but he was still pretty much his typical calm self. Never mentioning the guy in the back seat of the Tow Truck, Jimmy told Stevie how the gun had stayed on semiautomatic. How much better it was to place the shots that way. How he made the U-turn and fired into the back of the head of the driver. How he didn't realize who the driver was. How the guy's head fucking exploded when he shot through the back window. How we had to go back and get the hubcap. All the while we were chowing down spaghetti with eggplant and veal parmesan.

Around ten, the three of us drove over to Castle Island and walked around. It was a beautiful night, but the two of them couldn't stop talking about the murder. A little before midnight, Jimmy dropped off Stevie and took me back to my car, which was back on Third Street at the Mullins Club, and I drove home.

My wife and I watched some late news, which was the same recap about a gangland slaying. Pam had no idea that I was involved in that murder. She knew I was involved with Jim Bulger, but she knew no particulars about exactly what I did with him. I had no fear of being caught, but I was tired and knew I had to get up to work in the morning. I slept okay and got up early the next morning and went down to a breakfast place on K and Broadway. I got the newspaper, sat down in a booth, and ordered eggs, sunny-side-up, an English muffin to dunk in the yolk, orange juice, and coffee. I was reading the paper and eating when Jimmy Mantville came over to my table. Mantville, who was in his forties, five-nine, around 160 pounds, with curly brown hair and in great shape, sat down, looked me straight in the eye, and said, "We finally got him."

I just looked at him and smiled, thinking, *I know I was there, but I don't remember seeing you. Unless you were the one in the ski mask.* He kept talking about Halloran and what a piece of shit he was. How he was a bully who threw his weight around, intimidating people, just taking stuff and never paying for it, pounding on people for no reason. And I listened and continued eating my breakfast.

That night, I was waiting for Jimmy to tell me to get the Tow Truck out of the garage and bring it down to the mechanic so he could fix the odometer. But since I hadn't heard from Jimmy about the car, I left it there. It came out that evening that Halloran had given a dying declaration that Jimmy Flynn had killed him. It turned out to be lucky for Jimmy that he hadn't shot Halloran in the head and that he hadn't died instantly, like Donahue had. "When I think about it, I did look like him," Jimmy said. But he hadn't done it on purpose. A few months later, Flynn was in a restaurant when the cops came to arrest him for the murder. He tried to run out but they chased him and took him away. He went to trial but was found not guilty. No surprise there.

On Friday night after the murder, around midnight, Jimmy beeped me and asked, "Did you take care of it?" Of course, he would never have mentioned the word "car." We never talked about anything specific on the phone.

But I knew what he was talking about and said, "No. I hadn't heard from you."

"Come on over," he said. I drove over to Quincy and he met me outside his condo in Louisburg Square. When he asked me if I moved the car, I said no. "Thank God for Beck's beer," he told me. It seems that FBI agent John Morris, who was an incompetent wimp, had dropped by and all Jimmy had in the house to drink was Beck's. When Morris had a few in him, he blurted out that the hit car was a bore job, meaning the engine was bored out, souped up, worked up. Apparently an FBI agent who had been assigned to Halloran had been down the street at the time of the murder and had watched the whole thing and gotten the plate, which was legally registered but in a fictitious name. As it turned out, that particular agent died of cancer six months later. But now they were just waiting for the car he had seen to surface. And it would have been me driving the car when it did.

So we left the car where it was until Jimmy had it moved and chopped it up without anyone ever seeing it. Within two weeks of the murder, it was gone. But it had fulfilled its mission and gotten Jimmy away from the scene. There was never any reason for Jimmy to create another car like that. After that murder, he changed his MO, sucking people in, meeting in houses and making them come to him. He didn't need a hit car for that. That was Jimmy's brilliance, always finding better ways to do the job.

One afternoon, Jimmy and Stevie and I drove over to the tow lot on Dorchester Avenue to take a look at the Datsun. As always when the three of us went anywhere together, Jimmy drove, Stevie sat in the passenger seat, and I was in the back seat. That was fine with me. I wouldn't have wanted Stevie sitting in back of me. Jimmy walked right up to the driver's side of the Datsun, opened the door, and hit the back of the headrest with his hand. As he did that, a piece of scalp with some hair attached to it fell off, a little piece of Donahue that the police had missed. You could see the holes where the bullets had ripped through the doors and the windows. It was a mess with blood all over the place, on the seats, on the roof, on the floor. The car was shredded like Swiss cheese, with gaping holes everywhere.

As we looked at the car, I was thinking about how much punishment the human body could take. Donahue might have gotten hit in the head and died instantly, but Halloran had taken twenty-one bullets. As Jimmy commented again about how he had placed the shots through the rear window into Donahue's head, Stevie walked around looking at the car, shaking his head, still pissed he'd missed out on that murder. Finally Jimmy said, "Let's get out of here," and we took off.

A few months later, I stopped working for the T. From that point on, I worked for Jimmy full time.

FOUR
LEARNING THE BUSINESS
LOAN-SHARKING, EXTORTION, AND MURDER

Once I started working with Jimmy full-time in 1982, the year I left the T, I had a much closer view of his criminal activities. He would confide about them more openly and dealt more frequently with people in his circle in front of me. Although I rarely dealt personally with any of these bookmakers, as all those business deals had been established before I came on board, Jimmy included me in most of these meetings. For instance, I was now included in sitdowns with bookmakers who were arguing about money owed or paid out or complaining about certain customers not paying or complaining about their own payments to Jimmy and Stevie. I was also present at meetings with other loan sharks or those who owed debts. While most of these sitdowns or meetings took place in Triple O's or later at the variety store or liquor store that Jimmy owned, some were inside clubs, restaurants, or bars.

Although there were some people to whom I was introduced, often I wasn't introduced at all, and just stood there and listened. If the people had no idea who I was, they'd just glance nervously at me, most likely wondering what I was about. Inevitably, it would create a chilling effect as I watched and listened and didn't say a word.

The first and only time I met Chico Krantz, who ran a bookmaking operation, was at an afternoon meeting in Triple O's. Chico was in his late forties or early fifties, kind of a big guy, with a mustache and bald head with hair on each side, always covered with a Stetson hat with a wide brim. At this meeting, there seemed to be a problem concerning the amount of money Chico was receiving and what he was paying to Jimmy and Stevie. There were about twenty people in the bar, none of whom noticed the three of them sitting quietly at a table. Jimmy and Stevie did all the talking and I stood off to the side. It took no more than fifteen minutes before Chico agreed to pay them around $90,000 more. The meeting never got heated and all three of them remained calm. After the meeting was over, Chico stood up, they all shook hands, and he left.

When I first went to work at Triple O's, I had begun my own loan-sharking business. It was a simple business. I'd taken whatever money I made and turned it over, increasing it little by little by lending it to people who paid it back at a certain rate, between two and five points a week. It wasn't rocket science. I simply decided my own rates and loaned to people, mostly my age or a little bit older, who I had known over the years. It was a quick loan for people who couldn't go or didn't want to go to a bank; people who had jobs or who I knew could come up with the money they'd owe me.

Someone would come up and say, "Kev, I need five hundred bucks," and I'd give it to them and say, "Here you go. You pay me twenty-five a week on interest for the five hundred." That was the juice that didn't come off the principal. When I began, I had from twenty to twenty-five customers and I lent from $100 up to $25,000, with interest from two and half points to five points. If someone borrowed $25,000 at two and a half points, they'd have to pay me $625 a week interest, which I collected weekly. Sure, they paid more interest than at a bank, where they paid a maximum of 21 percent a year on a credit card. With me, it was up to 260 percent a year or five points a week, while a bank could only do 21 percent a year or a point and a half a month. But my customers needed cash quickly with no questions asked, and that was exactly what I provided, albeit at exorbitant rates.

Since I knew everybody I dealt with, there was no need for me to keep detailed records on every loan I made. I'd keep the smaller ones in my head and just write the larger ones down for my records. Now that I was with Jimmy, I was loan-sharking at the variety store and the liquor store, as well as at Triple O's and the L Street Tavern, and my reputation grew even stronger. When I told Jimmy I was going to continue to do it, he had no problem. "Fine. Just be careful," he told me.

As my business expanded, I had $150,000 to $200,000 on the street, still not a large business, but a comfortable one. My base continued to grow as customers would introduce me to other people who needed money. I rarely said no to the criminals who I knew would make money. There was no violence involved in my loan-sharking business because most people paid it back. If they didn't pay it back on time, they'd tell me a story and I'd say, "Don't worry about it. You'll pay me back when you get on your feet."

The only loan-sharking customer I ever had a problem with was Jimmy Santry, and it didn't involve the money I had loaned him. One night, in front of people in a bar, he told me to go fuck myself, so I knocked him out. That has always been a good reason for me to fight. Always has been. Always will be.

Spending more time with Jimmy Bulger, however, I got to see that his personal habits were pretty simple. Unlike me, he didn't care for sports. He considered professional sports prolonged adolescence and felt they prevented people from moving forward with their lives. All sports, not just professionally played sports, were not only a waste of time, but were dangerous. For instance, if you were playing a pickup basketball game, you might get injured and miss work. You were better off, he'd tell me, reading a book than playing a game of ball. Working out and keeping yourself in shape was different. That you did for yourself and there were less chances of getting hurt.

And he certainly didn't approve of the paintball games I enjoyed or the tournaments I went to four or five times a year. Nor did he support my interest in karate. I was in my mid-thirties when I started taking karate lessons with Pat Nee, a friend of mine, at the Boston Athletic Club. Pat and I had only been taking the classes for two weeks when we heard about an upcoming tournament for the New England championships. As it turned out, none of the black or brown belts who had been taking lessons for years at the karate school wanted to enter the tournament and represent the school. So Pat and I went to the instructor, Clarence Wilder, and told him we would fight in the tournament. Clarence, who was a fifth-degree black belt, felt that we were too inexperienced and that it wasn't a good idea for us to go. But after Pat and I assured him we could take care of ourselves, Pat, Clarence, and I headed to the tournament at the Walter Brown Arena at Boston University.

Students from karate schools all over New England were there, with nine rings set up for fights scheduled in every ring. In my first tournament fight, when the signal was given to start, my opponent suckered me with a right hand. They stopped the fight and gave him a warning for illegal contact. I went back to the corner and told Pat and Clarence no one was suckering me and that I was going to knock this kid out. Pat called over a couple of black belts he knew and told them, "Kevin's mad. You better watch this fight."

When the fight resumed and they gave the signal to start, I hit the kid a left hook and knocked him out with one shot. But because he had hit me illegally first and then I had hit him illegally, he could no longer continue. As a result, I was allowed to go on to the next round of fights.

Pat won his first fight, too, though legally. In my second fight, because of all my years of boxing, I had the advantage with my hands. So when my opponent threw a roundhouse kick, I stepped inside and hit him a right hand to the ribs, breaking his ribs. When he couldn't continue, I went on to the next round. In Pat's second fight, he won a close decision, so the two of us continued on to the third round.

In my third fight, in the quarterfinals, I hit my opponent in the chest and knocked the wind out of him. He went right down. When he couldn't continue in the time allotted, they stopped the fight and I got a warning, but was allowed to go on to the next round. Pat won his third fight easily.

In the semifinals, my opponent jumped up in the air to deliver a kick to the head. I stepped inside to hit him a body shot underneath his heart, but when he came down, he landed on his feet and went down lower than I expected. I caught him square in the jaw, knocking him out, and was disqualified from the tournament. They said I was being malicious, intentionally trying to cause bodily harm. In all four of my fights, my opponents had gotten hurt. It wasn't that I was trying to hurt them. I just knew I couldn't compete with them with their feet and that they couldn't compete with me with my hands. So when I hit them, I tried to hurt them. Pat got outpointed in his fourth fight, so we were both out of the tournament. But since we had only been taking karate for two weeks and had made it to the semifinals, we felt we'd made a good showing.

The fellow I'd fought in my last fight went on to win the division and was given a six-foot trophy. When the tournament was over, I told him, "You know that's my trophy." He didn't say anything to me, but just walked away.

A month later, Pat and I fought in a tournament at UMass Boston, where we took first and second place. In a third tournament on the South Shore, we did equally well. We were throwing some kicks in the fights, but mostly we were using our hands. We continued taking classes at the BAC for about a year. They also had an open night of sparring every

Thursday night, so we would go down to spar. It was something different for us and I enjoyed the exercise and the workout. But a lot of Boston police were coming down to the BAC to work out and were getting a good look at us. Jimmy didn't like the fact that I was down there with the cops, so finally I stopped going. He always used to say to me, "You know what beats a black belt? A gun belt."

Jimmy couldn't tell you a thing about baseball or football, but once the daughter of Theresa Stanley, his longtime girlfriend, married Montreal Canadiens hockey player Chris Nilan, he took an interest in the Montreal games. Even though he's wearing a Red Sox cap in the only photograph of us together, he had no special feeling for the team. In the summertime when the sun was out, he'd put a hat on but couldn't care less what emblem was stuck on it.

The only sports he ever watched were the fights, and I got a kick out of seeing him come up to my folks' house to watch them with my father. He usually came over when there was a title fight. Jimmy looked far younger than my father, who was only seven years older than him, but my dad had a bad heart and poor health and always looked older than he was. Even though Jimmy avoided funerals and wakes, when my father died of a heart attack at the age of sixty-six on June 17, 1989, he paid for the funeral.

While Jimmy avoided big crowds and never tried to draw attention to himself, he was acutely aware of what was going on around us, both in Boston and in the world. He didn't watch much TV, but did catch the news or a good movie and liked the History Channel. Every night at midnight, the two of us would drive over to Store 24 on West Broadway and grab the first editions of the next day's two Boston newspapers. Then we'd pull into the parking lot next to Southie Savings Bank to read them, passing them back and forth. First Jimmy would read the Metro section of the *Globe* and then the crime section of the *Herald,* commenting aloud on anything referring to our business or associates. Most often he would pick out an inaccuracy in one of the articles, saying the reporter or the law enforcement official quoted didn't know what he was talking about. "The Boston press is not known for its accuracy," he would tell me. "And they never let the truth get in the way of a good story." But he felt that it was a good thing for us that none of these people knew what they were talking about, since that meant they had no idea what they were looking for in their investigations. It's like reading fairy tales, he would say, instead of solid newspaper reporting.

But mostly he read books. When he had been in prison, he'd read a lot of history and psychology books. Although he rarely talked about prison, he did discuss the LSD program he'd been part of in Atlanta, blaming his frequent insomnia and nightmares on that useless, torturous experiment he'd taken part in during the late 1950s and early 1960s to lessen his prison sentence. He'd been one of eighteen inmates in the MKULTRA program under Dr. Carl Pfeiffer, a program that the public knew little about at the time. Funded by Coca-Cola, the program had supposedly been created to find a cure for schizophrenia, but in actuality it was run by the CIA, which was looking for a truth serum.

Jimmy told me that for eighteen months he was either injected with the LSD or given it as a liquid. He said it made him crazy and unable to stand the thought of a needle ever again piercing his skin. It was also the reason he never got a good night's sleep and still woke up screaming in the middle of the night and frequently suffered hallucinations. He had no idea exactly what the LSD had done to his brain, but its aftereffects stayed with him long after his last shot. He'd been sent to jail in 1956 with a twenty-year sentence and ended up doing nine, rather than the twelve that he most likely would have served without his participation in that experiment. Not sure it was worth it.

I'm also not sure if Dr. Pfeiffer ever cured one schizophrenic or if the CIA got its truth serum, but I do know that out of the eighteen prisoners who took part in the experiment in Atlanta in the hope of shaving a few years off their sentences, some went stark raving mad and some even committed suicide. Jimmy had been a pretty violent guy when he'd gone into prison at age twenty-six, so it would be hard to determine just how much more vicious he became as a result of the LSD.

Besides the nightmares and insomnia and hallucinations and maybe a shade more violence in his system, Jimmy left prison with an insatiable hunger for knowledge. He rarely passed a bookstore without going in to check out the latest books, usually buying at least one each time. He especially liked true crime, World War II, and history books on the Vietnam War. Some of his favorites were *The Tunnels of Cu Chi*, about the Vietnam War, and *Murder Machine, A True Story of Murder, Madness and Mayhem,* an interesting book about Roy Demeo, a New Jersey/New York criminal. He'd read the true crime books carefully, often at night when he couldn't sleep, looking to find some insight into police operations, anything that would give him an edge in his constant attempt to keep one up on the law. He'd make special note of the techniques of bugging operations, as well as the specific equipment criminals might use. In the past, he'd been in touch with other high-powered criminals such as Mickey Spillane and Tommy Devaney from the Westies, from New York's Hell's Kitchen, who'd come up to Boston to help him out years earlier during the South Boston gang wars. He'd often hand a book over to me, telling me what he'd found worthwhile in it, or insist on buying me a copy at the bookstore. An avid reader myself, some I liked and some didn't hold my interest.

Our discussions about current affairs were never one-dimensional. We'd talk about politics, particularly the Kennedys, all of whom he despised because of their busing stance. Since his brother Billy was such an influential politician and president of the Massachusetts State Senate, Jimmy stayed away from politics, anxious not to shed light on any connection between the two of them. Jimmy and I often discussed history, education, and business, even legitimate business, like our investments in the stock market. We both made some money when someone told us RYKA, a Massachusetts women's sneaker company that was later absorbed by another company, would be a good investment. We often talked about how much time and effort we put into being criminals, as well as into not getting caught. We discussed how, if we had legitimate jobs, we would have made more money with the same amount of time and effort. And we would have enjoyed the money so much more. We even talked about the possibility of getting into a legitimate business, but it was too late in our lives for that. We were too well known by law enforcement to make such a change.

It's important to understand that our relationship was not just focused on crime. Yeah, it took up most of our time, but there were lots of stretches when we weren't doing stuff and were simply sitting around. Some of those times, we sat around and laughed and joked and had a good time. But many of these days were just downright boring. We'd go for a walk around town, for some exercise, but also to let our presence be known. We always had to look formidable, never meek. We worked out and kept in shape. We'd let certain people have a look at Jimmy and know that he was around. Many times, the only thing we'd do during an entire day and night would be to pick up some envelopes containing rent and stuff, keeping ourselves busy for no more than an hour. The rest of the time, we'd just keep our eyes on what was happening around us and our ears tuned into what people were saying and who was doing what. But then when something happened, it was adrenaline time—and a relief not to be bored any longer.

But there was always plenty of time to talk about the many topics that interested Jimmy and how they affected legitimate people, like unemployment. Jimmy was concerned with social injustice, especially with what busing was doing to the people of South Boston. Nothing got him more aggravated.

Even though I was twenty-four and he was fifty-one when we began to work closely together, our relationship never seemed like father–son, boss–employee. From the earliest years, I felt we were associates. We would exchange ideas and more times than not thought alike. He was surprisingly open-minded, listening to people for four to five hours at a time, considering it well worth his time if he gleaned one bit of information or one piece of knowledge from that conversation, usually filing it away or learning more about it. It wouldn't necessarily be information having to do with crime. We could be sitting on a bench and he would turn to a person sitting nearby and strike up a conversation, curious as to where the guy came from and what he did, genuinely interested in him. And not just so he could relieve the guy of his money.

This made him different from most criminals, who were one-dimensional, thinking about nothing but crime. Sure, he was all the things people said he was: a killer, fierce, forceful, dangerous. But he was also fair, respectful to people and their opinions, treating most of them courteously. If someone was right or had a valid point or opinion, he gave them credit for their attitude. Sometimes he did things that I didn't understand, but I knew he had his reasons, and I would never question them. I never tried to figure out why he didn't like certain people or question his opinions. Again, I figured he had his reasons. I also knew he'd never ask me to do anything that he wouldn't do himself, and I was never afraid to do anything he asked, no matter what it was. I learned early on how things could change rapidly with Jimmy, how a person could say the wrong thing and his whole standing would change. I was surprised also to learn that, unlike Stevie, Jimmy considered violence the last step. But once he made up his mind to use it, that was it. If you put him to that point, there would be no talking. Someone was going to be badly hurt or murdered.

One of the first things Jimmy taught me was to consider the long-range ramifications of whatever we did. The idea of committing a crime was to get away with it. He wasn't interested about the next six months, but rather with how things would work out years down the road. There were lots of scores we would pass on because the percentages weren't there. Sure, we could take the person down, but Jimmy always thought about what that action would mean later on. What might this person do in a few years? What kind of life did he lead? If he got pinched and needed an out, would he give us up? Every extortion, every dealing, every action, large or small, was carefully thought out far beyond the present moment.

One of the scores we passed on was a home invasion involving a vault with thirty million dollars in it. It was brought to us by another fellow who I had little doubt would be looking to give us up if anything went wrong. I was also worried that there would be a lot of heat and we would be the fall guys. Jimmy and I talked about it for a week or so and finally scrapped the plans. No one else took the job, and neither of us ever regretted our decision.

Most times we worked with a regular schedule, but the hours could be long. Because of his nightmares and insomnia, Jimmy was not an early riser and rarely came in before 3:30 P.M. Then we'd take care of business: loan-sharking, shakedowns of drug dealers, accepting money that was dropped off, collecting other money owed, all the illegal activities, plus running the stores and bar we were involved with. In addition to the furniture/appliance store that I owned with Kevin O'Neil and the Court's Inn bar that Jimmy and I bought, Jimmy, Stevie Flemmi, and I bought a liquor store in South Boston in 1983 and the Rotary Variety Store and the building that housed it at 309 Old Colony Avenue a year later. At the beginning, I would come down to one of the stores at eight in the morning to take care of what needed to be done. Later, I started coming in around noon and stayed till five. After his rounds, Jimmy would usually go to Theresa's for dinner. Then, around nine, he'd call me and tell me where to meet him. He had code names for each of the stores, which was usually where I would meet him, hop into his car, and drive somewhere, staying out till midnight or later. Sometimes we worked on Sundays, too, but mostly it was a six-day-a-week job, so that he could spend Sunday with Theresa and her family and the evening with Cathy. And I could spend some time with Pam and the kids.

Jimmy always tuned into the weather reports, making sure we used the bad weather to commit certain crimes. Since most people stay in when the weather is bad, the only people out usually have their heads down or are carrying umbrellas and not paying attention. All they want to do is get where they're going quickly. If we had to do some criminal activity, like moving guns, hurting someone, or meeting someone without being followed, Jimmy would check the weather forecast and plan accordingly, since these plans always worked better when it was raining or snowing.

Many nights, after midnight, when bars were closed and only crooks or cops were out, we'd pack it in and go home, rather than draw attention to ourselves at that hour. During a typical day, we'd put in around six hours, but if something was going on, it would be longer. But I was more than well paid for the time I spent working with Jimmy. Working at Triple O's and the MBTA, I had been making around $800 a week clear. Once I had been working with Jimmy for a year or two, I was making thousands a week, and that didn't include scores from shakedowns and extortions that would bring in additional lump sums. As the years went on, I figured I made between five and seven million, while Jimmy pulled in least thirty to fifty million.

With a lot more money to be enjoyed, I had no trouble finding ways to spend that money. Like buying new cars. In 1979, I was driving a blue Audi Fox, but I got rid of that and bought a 1980 Thunderbird. After that, every year I bought a new car, a Lincoln, a Cadillac, or a Pontiac, whatever I wanted. Even though I spent my money on clothes and jewelry, I didn't do much traveling, preferring to take a vacation to play paintball. Jimmy was never happy when I went to tournaments all over the country or to the Caribbean. He worried that I was not thinking about the business or could get hurt. But I won many of these tournaments and found them relaxing, exciting, and competitive, as well as a chance to meet interesting people and get a good workout.

Jimmy and Stevie took vacations together, traveling to Europe or to Florida with different girls. I never traveled with them, but it was a vacation for me when Jimmy was away. Then I could take care of what had to be done and wouldn't have to head out every night. It was a chance to relax and not be on twenty-four-hour alert for business concerns.

Jimmy's health was pretty good, but he did have an occasional attack of arrhythmia. When I went with him to see his doctor at Massachusetts General, Dr. Pakau said it was nothing to worry about, that he was just experiencing a little stress. His advice to Jimmy was to simplify his life, so Jimmy cut down from four major women in his life to just two, Theresa and Cathy. We both agreed that the most stress in a man's life came from women, who create more stress than complicated and danger-filled business deals. All the stuff and rumors that questioned Jimmy's sexuality were lies spread by the media. He had more women than Hugh Hefner. Guys like Donald Trump weren't even in his league. Whenever we went out to bars and clubs, women of all ages were after him. "Variety is the spice of life," he'd say as he enjoyed all of them.

But nothing was more important to Jimmy than business, and he never ceased to ponder all aspects of it. He spent a lot of time teaching me how to deal with the people in our business, stressing the importance of never leaving them with a bad feeling and never socializing with them. He'd tell me to always remember that we were not dealing with regular people, that we couldn't be nice to the people we did business with. They were criminals. When you're dealing with regular people, you're nice to them, they're nice to you. While there were some criminals who might be regular, normal people who happened to be involved in criminal activity, you had to remember that they, too, were criminals. "No one is happy about paying you," he told me. "Don't ever think you're their friend. Some of these people don't understand anything. You can't reason with them. Then you have no choice but to use violence to make them understand."

He had his own unique way of dealing with people when things went wrong. It was fascinating to watch how he could come down on someone, reduce him to the ground verbally, putting him in his place and degrading him completely. But then he would slowly bring the guy back up, so ultimately the guy left with a good feeling, understanding exactly what he had to do to improve himself, how he had to work hard, save money, and stay away from drugs and gambling.

But there were some people Jimmy simply didn't like at all, and these people were rightfully afraid of him. As a criminal, he made a point of only preying upon criminals, as opposed to legitimate people. And when things couldn't be worked out to his satisfaction with these people, after all the other options had been explored, he wouldn't hesitate to use violence. Certainly, if he thought there was a chance of this person coming back to cause some harm, there was no sense in bothering to give him a beating. He might as well fucking kill him. And he did.

Tommy King, in 1975, was one example. Although I was nineteen at the time and not yet working for Jimmy, he told me the whole story. Tommy's problem began when he and Jimmy had words at Triple O's. Tommy, who was a Mullins, made a fist. And Jimmy saw it. The next day, Tommy went to the Old Harbor projects where Jimmy was living with his mother and tried to make amends. He said he had been drunk and hadn't meant anything he had said the night before. Jimmy told him, "Don't worry about it. Forget it." A week later, Tommy was dead.

Tommy's second, and last, mistake had been getting into the car with Jimmy, Stevie, and Johnny Martorano. That night, Jimmy put Tommy in the passenger seat with Stevie and Johnny in the back seat, and told him that they were looking for someone to kill. That someone, of course, was

Tommy. As they were driving around, Tommy banged on his supposedly bulletproof flak jacket and joked, "If we don't find him, we can try this out." The minute he finished that joke, Johnny shot him in the head from the back seat. The bullet went right through his head, splattering blood and brains all over the place, but Jimmy just reached over, propped Tommy up, and put a baseball cap on his bloodied head.

A minute later, Johnny said he had to make a phone call and asked Jimmy to pull over by the Dunkin' Donuts in Quincy. He was gone a few minutes, supposedly to make a bet, then got back in the car and the four of them drove off. Jimmy drove around for a few more minutes and then found a spot at the Neponset River where they buried Tommy. Later that same night, Jimmy killed Buddy Leonard and left him in Tommy's car right on Pilsudski Way in the Old Colony projects to confuse the authorities.

Tommy, a raw-boned, six-four rough guy, had been a perfect example of a loose cannon. Jimmy knew that Tommy was someone who couldn't be controlled, so he might as well kill him and get it over with. Although Jimmy always said, "Act in haste, repent at leisure," once his mind was made up, that was it. There was no sense in trying to get him to change his mind.

As it turned out, the night King and Leonard were killed there was supposed to be a third victim, Billy Gallant, but he didn't show up. I'm not sure exactly why Jimmy intended to kill Gallant. I think he just didn't like him. A few years after that night, Jimmy and I were driving up Dorchester Avenue when we saw Billy walking alone. It was raining out, so Jimmy pulled over and said, "Billy, come in. I'll give you a ride."

I hopped into the back, but Billy just leaned into the passenger door and said, "Whitey, no offense, but people get in that car and they never get out. Thanks anyhow, but I'd rather walk."

Jimmy nodded, I jumped back into the front seat, and we drove away. Jimmy started laughing, looked at me, and said, "Smart guy."

There was no doubt he would have killed Billy that night. As it turned out, Billy died of pneumonia a few years later. Maybe he got a cold that rainy night.

It didn't take me long to learn how to grasp Jimmy's reaction to people by his facial expressions. Even though he wore sunglasses a lot, when I could see his eyes, I read them perfectly. And who was going to stop him then? Nobody. I certainly wasn't going to put myself between him and some asshole who deserved what he was going to get. It was rarely necessary for Jimmy to tell me to hit someone who was bothering him. I could just see that he was getting madder. Then someone would say something smart and I would just crack him.

There were times, of course, when Jimmy would get mad at me. Sometimes he'd yell. Or be cold. Those times, I'd give him his time and when he was ready, usually a few hours later, he'd come looking for me and we'd talk about what had gotten him upset. One thing that did bother him was if I was out drinking, which I didn't do very often. He always worried that when we drank in local bars, I might get into a fight there, and if I did, the outcome would never be good. "You're not being fair," he always told me. "If someone has a fight with you and you beat him up, you could do serious damage, even kill the person. Yet if by some chance he beats you, he thinks it's over, but it's not the end of it. You're not through. You're going to want go back and kill him."

And he was right. When I was younger, it had been different. I could have survived losing a fight. But as I got older, I couldn't live with the idea of someone walking the streets saying they beat me. I'd just have to kill him. At the very least, I'd have to hurt them badly to make an example. I could never afford to let them win. I was never the toughest guy out there, but I was of a different mind-set than other guys. I couldn't handle not beating them. I certainly wasn't worried about someone coming after me after I beat him. I knew I could handle myself no matter what came my way. But if someone beat me, I would bide my time.

Whether it took six months or a year, I would wait for the talk to die down and the person to think he didn't have a problem, and then I would go after him.

And Jimmy was just like me. He, too, couldn't live with being beat. If someone ever did anything to him, we'd be out every day and every night hunting him down. Neither one of us could afford to be beaten. We made a living being feared. If one person beat us, then he would have made it easier for the next person to come after us. So we'd take care of the person any way we could.

I did have guys shoot at me, but I always carried a pistol, for which I had a permit, and quickly shot back. And the time when Chucka Devins's brother Franny got hurt and some kid pulled a knife on me—to be truthful, I hadn't been thinking about trying not to kill that kid. I hadn't cared one way or the other. To me, it was just a fight.

There was no doubt I hurt a lot of people. But when you're hurting people that often, it doesn't affect you. You don't enjoy it. You just get immune to it. I figure I must have had over 500 fights in my lifetime. Just working at Triple O's four nights a week with at least one fight a night, over a period of a year, I'd easily have 200 fights. I had too many fights, but with each one, I always wanted to hit hard and get it over with as soon as possible. The last thing I wanted was to end up wrestling in the street and looking bad.

Still, I always believed that when it came to a street or bar fight, there was no such thing as a winner. We were all losers. Even if someone wins the fight and is a winner in the eyes of others, he still pays a price, both physically as well as mentally. In nine out of ten of my fights, the person I fought was hurt badly. And when it was over, I was always mad at him, thinking, *You made me do this to you.* In professional sports, like with boxing, the fighters aren't mad at one another. It's a professional fight. But in street fights, even when you win, a little bit of you is hurt. And chances are you've made an enemy as well.

Despite Jimmy's concern about how hard I hit, we went to whatever clubs we wanted. We never expected a problem. We never looked for a problem, but we never walked away from a problem. And if it wasn't handled that night, it would be handled later, but on our terms. The outcome was never good for the other person. Neither Jimmy nor I drank much, but there were times when I might drink a bit more than he thought safe. And even if he wasn't with me when that happened, somehow he managed to keep tabs on me. One afternoon, I was with a friend, Brian Lee, having a good time in a Faneuil Hall bar owned by Sean Driscoll. Around nine that night, Sean came over to tell me that I had a phone call and I could take it in his office.

It was Jimmy on the phone. "What are you doing?" he asked me. I could tell he was upset.

"Having a few beers," I told him.

"Meet me in fifteen minutes," he told me, and that was the end of my drinking. I left right away and drove over to South Boston, grateful that I wasn't drunk. I have no idea how he found out where I was. Maybe one of the owners wanted to get me out of the place before anything happened.

One thing Jimmy did not tolerate was drug use among his associates. It made them too unpredictable. Nicky Femia, who was hooked on cocaine, was an example of what happened when that rule was ignored. After Jimmy pushed Femia out of the business, Femia got killed trying to shake down a kid, robbing him of his coke.

After I'd been with him a year or so, Jimmy told me that I was the smartest guy he'd ever met. I think he meant that I considered everything carefully, thinking over all aspects of a situation before I acted. Not that he had any fools around him, but what he did have around him were a lot of tough guys. But he wasn't interested in just tough guys; he wanted smart tough guys. Over and over, he explained to me how we were all hostage to one another, how everything one of us did reflected on everyone else. I understood exactly what he was saying. And I knew that whatever he asked me to do, I would do. If we killed somebody and the police came upon us, we were prepared to handle the situation. We would have shot it out with them. I wouldn't say that we were armed to the teeth, but we always had arms available—assault rifles, hand grenades, whatever we might possibly need, more arms that we could possibly use in a lifetime. Some we'd bought in New York and some Jimmy had that went back to the 1960s.

Unlike me, most of the people around Jimmy went back years and years. But like me, most of these men were extremely violent men. I thought of the people surrounding Jimmy as being in three tiers. In the inner core were Jimmy, Stevie, myself, and two other people who were out on the streets at the time, both of whom will remain unnamed, who went back to the 1960s with Jimmy. The second group was composed of men, also violent, close friends of ours and involved with us, but not around us all the time. And the third tier included men who were not violent but were moneymakers who worked for us, like the bookmakers, drug dealers, and people involved in illegal activities, like card games or Vegas nights. Jimmy paid special attention to this important third group. If any of them were out drinking and had a problem that night, it quickly became our problem; to be specific, a problem in our pockets. The fact that these guys were paying us money, monthly or weekly, meant that we would have to go out collectively and straighten out their problem—another reason why Jimmy never liked people with bad habits to work for him.

But Jimmy also kept an eye on what was going around in the neighborhood, even on people who had nothing to do with us. One summer night, while the two of us were driving on East Eighth Street and Covington, by the old German Club, we saw two Southie brothers, Frankie and Kevin MacDonald, fighting, really going at it. Jimmy got out of the car and told Frankie's three friends who were watching the fistfight—Ricky Marinick, Paul Moore, and another guy named Kevin MacDonald who we called "Andre the Giant"—to break it up. "Don't let them fight," he told the guys. "They're brothers."

After Frankie's friends grabbed the two guys and broke up the fight, Jimmy ordered Kevin into the car while Frankie took off with his three friends. Kevin, seven years younger than me, was a nice kid I'd known for a long time, while Frankie, who was a few years older than Kevin, was a talented boxer and a tough kid. His body was like that of a Greek god, in tremendous shape from always working out hard.

Jimmy and I drove around with Kevin for a while. "He's your brother," Jimmy said to Kevin as we drove off. "It doesn't look good for people to see you like that." But Kevin told us Frankie was going on a score the next day and he didn't want him to go, that he had a bad feeling about the score.

We dropped Kevin off at his house and sure enough, the next day Frankie got shot during a Wells Fargo armored car robbery in Medford. The bullet went under his arm where there was no cover from the bullet-proof vest he was wearing, traveling through his lungs and ripping his aorta. Because he was in such tremendous shape, Frankie was able to run to the getaway car with a bag of money before collapsing in the back seat. Afterward, some people accused his friends of leaving him on the score, but the truth was he bled to death in a matter of minutes. Even if they had gotten him to the hospital, there was no way they could have stopped the bleeding. Frankie died on July 17, 1984, at age twenty-five. It was a terrible shame.

I went to the wake, which was painfully sad. Jimmy didn't believe in wakes and didn't attend. His feeling was that if a person died, that was it and there was no reason to have a wake or a funeral. When Jimmy's mother died on January 1, 1980, Jimmy didn't go to the funeral, knowing it would bring a lot of publicity to the family, especially to Billy. But he did go to the funeral home after it had closed so he could see her when no one was there.

But riding around with Jimmy at night, I never knew what could happen from one moment to the next. One particular night, Jimmy and I were in his Ford LTD when another car began to jockey for position with us on Morrissey Boulevard. It went on for a few minutes until we stopped at a set of lights. The other car pulled up beside us and the two guys in the car gave Jimmy and me the finger and began swearing at us. Jimmy started to get out of the car, but I jumped out first, went to the passenger window where the guy was still giving me the finger, and put my fist through the window. After I hit the guy in the face, I got back in our car and Jimmy drove off.

My hand was bleeding, and when I went to wipe off the blood, I noticed that a little piece of the three-carat diamond ring I wore on my pinky finger had sheared off. I wasn't sure if the diamond had a flaw or what, but one of the corners of the ring was gone. Jimmy took a look at it when we pulled up to Theresa's house, and then I drove the car back to my house. A couple of hours later, after dinner, when I came back to Theresa's to pick up Jimmy for the evening, he handed me a new ring. "Here you go," he said as he gave me a solitaire five-carat diamond pinky ring.

"Thanks," I said and removed the old ring and put the new one on. It was the only time he had ever given me jewelry, and it was a beautiful ring, worth, I was certain, over $100,000.

I knew that Jimmy bought most of his jewelry from a particular jeweler in the Jewelers Building on Washington Street in Boston, and that he also bought hot stuff. On his own hand, he wore a five-carat solitaire pinky ring. Around his neck, he wore a gold Christ's head medallion on a chain, and on his wrist was a gold Patek Phillippe watch given to him by the guys at Winter Hill. In addition, on his left pinky he wore a four-carat Irish claddagh ring, with two hands holding a heart, a ring he'd had made after he'd seen my three-carat claddagh ring.

Jimmy had great taste in jewelry and was generous with gifts to the women in his life, buying diamond earrings and diamond cocktail rings and watches for Theresa and Cathy, and expensive pieces of jewelry for the other girls he dated, as well as cars and condos for many of them.

He never worried about the price of the clothing he bought for himself. One day when we were shopping on Newbury Street, we went into the El Paso shoe store, where they sold custom-made cowboy boots. He ended up paying $2,500 for black alligator-skin boots, made specifically for his feet. These boots were made by Foley, who made only fifty pairs a year. He also bought a couple of other pairs of boots, somewhere around $1,000 a pair. Another time, we went into that same store, and I bought some beautiful ostrich-skin custom-made cowboy boots, which cost $1,700 and looked nice with a pair of dungarees. The salespeople at El Paso knew who James Bulger was and were unfailingly polite and helpful to him. Why not? He was courteous to all of them and paid cash for everything he bought. The two of us shopped in the finest men's clothing stores on Newbury Street, like Daniel Rene and Louis, where we each bought custom-tailored suits. I ended up with dozens of Louis suits in my closet, but I hardly wore any of them.

But no matter how much money we made, we were always looking for new ways to make more. So I was pleased one night when the opportunity to make money for myself simply presented itself in front of my eyes. I was in the variety store, standing behind the counter, watching the place for Mark, the guy who owned the ticket concession in the store that sold tickets for concerts and sporting events, when a heavyset customer came in and asked for him. When I said Mark would be back in a while, the customer told me he had to hurry up, because he had to go see some bookmakers. "If you need to place a bet," he told me slyly, "come see me."

"You got a lot of guys working for you?" I asked him.

"All over Charlestown, Southie, Dorchester."

"Really?"

"Yeah."

"What's your name?"

"Kevin Hayes. What's your name?"

"Kevin Weeks."

"Oh, shit."

"You never know who you're talking to. Nice meeting you," I said, and left it at that. But now I had him on my radar. A short time later, I had a friend who knew Hayes arrange a meeting at the house of another friend, who happened to be in prison. I had Hayes come down to the cellar, where I had stretched out a plastic tarp on the floor. As soon as Hayes walked in, I took out a pistol. "You're going to pay me one hundred thousand dollars for your football action or I'm going to kill you," I told him.

He started talking, real crazy stuff that I could hardly understand. All of a sudden he yelled, "Do you think I'm wired?" and pulled off his shorts. The 400-pound gorilla stood there with no underwear, his little dick looking like he had a piece of bubble gum stuck to his bush. The last thing I had thought was that he would be wired, so I had no idea what he was doing.

After some more of his crazy talk, he agreed to pay us $25,000 a few days later and then $5,000 a month till he had paid the whole amount. We had the lunatic get dressed and the person who had brought him drove him away. After a couple of years, he had only paid us $50,000, but he went out of business and got indicted for something he did while working for the Boston Election Commission. In 1999, he gave me up as part of my indictment. Another great standup guy.

But my extortions could never match Jimmy's, who was Machiavellian in the way that he was able to outthink other people. Eventually everyone he extorted understood that we would either take them down or take their money. In every case, these guys made the decision to part with their money rather than their lives. No one, it seemed, was willing to make an enemy out of us. Sometimes all you had to do was threaten people with a physical beating and they would pay you. But, as with everything Jimmy did, violence was the last resort. Yet no matter what it took, we always managed to get what we wanted.

Still, some people made things difficult for themselves, like this one fellow who owed us fifteen grand. We got him into the car and sat him in the back seat next to me, while Jimmy and Stevie were in the front seat. The guy was complaining, giving Jimmy a tale of woe about how he didn't have the money to pay, how he had put bets in and lost, how his daughter was getting married and he had no money for the wedding. At first Jimmy and Stevie were talking nice, but when it became obvious the guy thought it was all a game, Jimmy let him know it was for real. "Give me the money or I'll kill you," he told him.

Still playing around like we were suckers, the guy said, "You'll be doing me a favor if you'd kill me."

With that, I grabbed the guy and put his arms behind his back. Jimmy took out a pistol, leaned over the seat, and put it to his head. Now the guy started screaming, "I'll get you the money!"

Jimmy said, "When?"

"Let me get into the house," he said. We were parked in front of his house, so he went in and came out with the fifteen grand in twenty minutes.

When it came to extortion, Jimmy was anything but ordinary, often creating the problem and then solving it. Now, if a guy actually had a legitimate problem, such as someone trying to kill him, we would put ourselves between the two of them and make his problem our problem. Of course, the person in danger would have to pay us to do this.

But many times the problem was not only not legitimate, it wasn't real. In those cases, we searched out someone we knew had money, created a problem for him, and solved the "problem" for a large sum of money. For example, we would corner the guy coming out of work and inform him that someone had been paid to kill him. We would take turns speaking, but it didn't matter if it was Jimmy and me or Jimmy, Stevie, and me. The reaction was always the same. The person would be scared to death. But we'd calm him down quickly by telling him that if he paid us somewhere between $50,000 and $500,000, we would back the killer off. Ten out of ten times, the person would pay, always coming to the conclusion that while he could make more money, he couldn't make another life. And this life was his most valuable commodity. If it was a large payment, we would put him on a payment plan with a certain amount of time to pay. And if we liked him, at the end, we might even tell him to forget about the final payments. But if we didn't like him, we'd make it clear that this wasn't a bank where you have lots of different payment plans. Here there was only one payment plan: We wanted our money now.

One night Jimmy and I went to the home of a drug dealer, rang his bell, and shook him down, telling him we had been paid to kill him. "You sold drugs to a guy's grandchild," we said. "And this guy offered us fifty thousand dollars to kill you. Now, you have the chance to pay us the same amount and we'll back this person off so he won't bother you." That dealer ended up paying us $25,000 right away and then paid us the balance monthly. And ended up working for us from then on.

There were, of course, times when some people really did offer us money to kill someone. Then we would go to the potential victim and tell him we were being offered money to kill him. Every time that person paid us. Who wouldn't?

Another example of creating a problem and charging to solve it involved a man who owned a bar in Dorchester. We heard he was having trouble with a guy around thirty who kept coming into his bar. One night, Jimmy, Stevie, and I drove by the owner's house with a couple of other guys and shot it up while he was standing by the window. We didn't try to kill him. We just wanted to scare him. In a few minutes, we blew out all the windows and the doors. The next day, when the owner of the bar reached out to us, Jimmy and Stevie told him that the guy who was giving him trouble in the bar had tried to kill him, but we would straighten it out. Without hesitation, the bar owner handed us $25,000 to make the problem go away. In this case, the problem was us, not some customer at the bar, but the bar owner never saw that.

Ray Slinger's extortion turned out to be a perfect example of the media publicizing a story that was totally different than the event I personally witnessed. Ray was a real estate and insurance agent in South Boston who had done business with Kevin O'Neil. One day around noon in 1986, Jimmy and I were upstairs in Triple O's, eating the egg sandwiches and frappes we had just gotten from the deli next door. Fitzie, the bartender, called up to tell Kevin that Ray Slinger was downstairs. Even though Ray was in a legitimate business, he didn't have a sterling business reputation. Unbeknownst to me, Stevie and Jimmy had already talked to Ray and told him they wanted to talk to him. When Jimmy heard Fitzie's message, he looked at Kevin O'Neil and said, "What's up with him?"

"I want to talk to him about an insurance bill," Kevin said. "I gave him the money but he kept it and didn't pay the bill."

Jimmy said, "Tell him to come up." When Fitzie then reported that Ray was with a woman, Jimmy told him to tell Ray to come up by himself.

A few minutes later, Ray, who was in his fifties, heavyset, around six-one and with thin silver hair, walked into our room, wearing a long tan trench coat, white shirt, black dress pants, and dark shoes. When he saw the three of us sitting at a table, he began to shake visibly. As he stood off to the side, his coat separated and I noticed a pistol tucked into his pants. Without a word, I jumped up over our table and, knocking him over, grabbed the pistol out of his pants.

"Whoa, slow down," Jimmy said, but when I pulled out the pistol, he got mad. "You dirty motherfucker!" he shouted at Ray. "You bring a pistol around me? Where did you get it?"

"I borrowed it off a friend," he told Jimmy. "For protection."

With the gun now in his hand, Jimmy told Ray to sit down. After that, despite the lies printed by the media, no one beat up Ray or punched him. All I had done was thrown him off his feet, making him bang off the wall. But the guy was hyperventilating as Jimmy put the gun to the top of his head, saying, "I could shoot you on the top of your head and there would be no blood." Ray started shaking uncontrollably, tears coming down his face, as Jimmy continued. "Listen," he told Ray, "I've been offered fifty thousand dollars to kill you."

"By who?" Slinger got out.

"It doesn't matter," Jimmy answered him. "Unless you give me the money, I'll kill you."

When Slinger said, "I can give you two thousand dollars," Jimmy kicked him in the shin with his cowboy boot.

"My boots cost more than that," Jimmy said, and Slinger looked like he was going to have a heart attack. "Hey, calm down," Jimmy told him and then told me to go downstairs and get him a beer.

I had started to head down the stairs when Slinger said, "No, I want a mixed drink." I went downstairs and got him a gin and tonic. He drank half of it down in one gulp.

Then Jimmy said, "I'm going to talk to Ray," and Kevin and I went downstairs. Fifteen minutes later, he called the two of us back upstairs and told Kevin, "You're going to meet Ray on Friday and he'll give you an envelope. And then, every other Friday, he'll meet you with an envelope until everything is straightened out." At this point, Ray was sweating and pale. As it turned out, Ray Slinger paid us $25,000 of the $50,000 we charged him for not killing him. No one had offered money to kill Ray, but Jimmy was shaking him down because he didn't like the way Ray treated people in town.

After that scene in Triple O's, Ray went to a local politician to try and get us to back off and stuff, but to no avail. Then he started talking around town and telling people what had happened at Triple O's. That story got back to the FBI and subsequently got back to us, and Jimmy told Kevin O'Neil to tell Ray to forget about the rest of the money. When Ray was first approached by the FBI to tell them what had happened to him, he was hesitant. But then he gave them a story in which Jimmy had told me to get a body bag, not a beer. I know he heard exactly what Jimmy had said to me, because he had asked for a mixed drink instead of a beer. And I never heard of any bar in South Boston that has a body bag behind a bar, not even Triple O's back in those days. But after that conversation with the FBI in which he had thrown in that body bag detail to make his story more dramatic, Ray understood that he could never come around us, that we would never talk to him again. Whatever he said would be his word against ours. He had no proof of what we had said. If he ever got wired up, we would have known and would have answered his questions with, "What are you, crazy? Are you on drugs?" As it turned out, Jimmy got what he wanted that afternoon, and Ray Slinger got his mixed drink, not a body bag.

One extortion concerned me personally. It was a case where I literally had the guy over the fence. After I bought a house in a Boston suburb, the bank came out to survey my property for insurance purposes and discovered that my neighbor's thirty-foot-long fence was six inches on my side of the property line. When I told my neighbor it had to be moved, he went to a friend of his, a developer named Richie Bucchieri. The guy who sold me my house told me that Bucchieri wanted him to backdate a bill of sale for the land the fence was on. The next thing I knew I had Richie Bucchieri meeting Jimmy and Stevie at Stevie's mother's house, where he was fined $200,000 for—for lack of a better term—interfering. Since I ended up sitting outside in the car during the meeting, I got $50,000 for basically doing nothing. Nothing happened to the neighbor, but the developer had to pay $200,000 for six inches of fence.

Another extortion involved Michael Solimondo, who turned out to be a standup guy. In 1982, after John Callahan, the accountant who was cooperating with the FBI in the Roger Wheeler World Jai Alai murder, was killed, we extorted Solimondo, who had been Callahan's partner in the construction business. We had him come down to Triple O's, where Jimmy, Stevie, and I were waiting for him upstairs in the function hall. Here we sat him on a stool in the little bar, where Jimmy was holding a machine gun with a silencer under a towel on his lap, and I had a pistol tucked into my waistband, which he might or might not have seen. Jimmy started to talk to him about Callahan's offshore account in Switzerland, telling Solimondo he wanted his money.

"I know nothing about that," said Solimondo, who was a bodybuilder. Jimmy went on and on about wanting "his fucking money."

Finally Jimmy ripped the towel off his lap and stuck the machine gun into Solimondo's massive chest. "Your muscles aren't going to do you any good now," he told him. "Give me your fucking money or I'm going to kill you." Solimondo gave in right away and within a day or two we got $120,000. Not too long after that, we got six payments of $80,000 until we had the $600,000 Jimmy wanted.

A few years later, when Solimondo got called to a grand jury, we found out about it. Jimmy grabbed him again, and this time he and Stevie told him exactly what to say to the grand jury about the extortion. I don't know what he actually said, but that was the end of it. Nothing ever came out of his appearance.

None of these extortions were hard to put together. We did them so often, it was second nature. We'd be driving around and see someone and we'd formulate a plan. And I never felt bad about any of them. These people had something I wanted, so I took it. The only time I might have felt bad was if they didn't give me the money.

As for money laundering, that was a mundane crime, not an exciting one. Any time you take illegal money and put it to work for you, that's money laundering. Even if you take money gained illegally, deposit it in the bank, and put that interest to work for you in any business or transaction, that's money laundering. For instance, Stevie bought businesses with illegal money he saved and that was money laundering.

It was just one more thing the government can get you for, as obscure a crime as it is. While money laundering might still be considered a big crime, to my way of thinking it is just an attempt to put money back into the economy. All we were trying to do was to help the growth of our gross national product. I call it economic stimulation; the government calls it money laundering.

The truth is that this book contains some of what we did, but certainly not all. It would take another two to three books to chronicle the other 80 percent of the story. But whatever Jimmy and I and all the others did, it was always for the money. Not even for the power. Just the money.

FIVE
THREE MURDERS
BARRETT, MCINTYRE, AND HUSSEY:
1983–1985

The first body I buried was in 1983 in a house at 799 East Third Street in South Boston, diagonally across the street from Stevie's mother's house. The house belonged to the brother of a friend and the body to Arthur "Bucky" Barrett, a hoodlum from Quincy in his mid-forties who was skilled at bypassing alarms and robbing banks and safes. He was also a drug dealer who'd hooked up with Joe Murray and the Charlestown crew that was involved in Murray's drug operation. Bucky might have been a talented safecracker and successful drug dealer, but he'd made a big mistake three years earlier, neglecting to pay Jimmy from a $1.5 million heist at the Depositors Trust bank in Medford in 1980. Instead he'd reached out to Frank Salemme, Stevie's partner from the 1960s, giving him $100,000 to keep people, specifically Stevie and Jimmy, off of him and the rest of his money. Since Salemme was doing time for a crime Stevie had been involved with, Stevie had no choice but to back away when Frankie told him Bucky was with him. Bucky's going to Frankie didn't sit well with Jimmy or Stevie.

Three years later, however, a chance meeting with Jimmy drastically changed things for Bucky. That day, Bucky was heading down a flight of stairs in a building in Dorchester, having just visited his probation officer, when he ran into Jimmy and me. We were headed to a travel agent in the same building so Jimmy could plan a trip. Jimmy introduced me to Bucky and the two of us shook hands. I continued walking up the stairs and left them talking for a few more minutes. Then Bucky left the building and Jimmy and I walked into the travel agency. That little encounter was all that was needed to pique Jimmy's interest in Bucky Barrett.

A few months after that encounter, Jimmy and Stevie worked out a plan to shake down Bucky. At the time, there was no mention of killing him, so I thought all we were doing was a shakedown for that bank heist money and whatever else we could get from his drug business. Since Bucky had a penchant for diamonds and liked to collect jewelry, the plan was to have him come over to the house on East Third Street to meet with a fellow who deals in hot diamonds. My part in the plan was to be that fellow.

That August afternoon, around noon, a friend of Bucky's who knew Bucky was going to be shaken down rather than buy hot diamonds brought him into the house. While most of the houses in South Boston were triple-deckers—three-story row houses—this house was a two-story structure. It was a small house, with two rooms on the first floor, one an ordinary kitchen with the basic sink, oven, and refrigerator, and the second a parlor with a couch against the front windows looking out to the street, a couple of chairs, TV and stereo, and no carpets on the floor. There were stairs off the kitchen that led to the second floor, where there were a couple of bedrooms and a bathroom. A wrought-iron fence wrapped around the outside.

When Bucky walked into the house, I was standing in the parlor, which was connected to the kitchen, and reached out and shook his hand. Heavyset, maybe five-nine, Bucky was an average-looking guy, wearing dungarees and a long-sleeved button-down shirt with an open collar.

When I said, "How you doing? Nice to meet you," I could tell he didn't recognize me and assumed I was the diamond guy.

He didn't get a chance to say anything to me because the minute I stopped talking, Jimmy, holding a Mac-11 nine-millimeter machine gun with a silencer, stepped out from behind the refrigerator, and yelled, "Bucky Barrett, freeze."

At that moment, Bucky looked panicked. I have no idea what he was thinking, but I still thought this was just a shakedown. Pointing the gun toward Bucky, Jimmy motioned for him to sit down in a kitchen chair and told the guy who had walked him in to get out of there. Before Bucky had come into the house, Stevie had removed chains and hand-cuffs from a small black zippered carryall bag and placed them near the chair. It didn't take long for him to handcuff Bucky and put the chains around his legs and waist and manacle him to the chair.

Jimmy sat down on a chair across from Bucky, placing the machine gun on the table in front of him, while Stevie sat down in another chair facing Bucky. At that point, I wasn't doing anything besides standing there, watching. As Bucky sat there, I could see that he was nervous, but he wasn't trembling or shaking or anything. He was taking it like a man. I went to sit on the couch in the parlor while Stevie and Jimmy began to interrogate Bucky. Although I could look into the kitchen from the couch, I couldn't see the table. But I could listen to the conversation, which was going on in a nice calm manner, with no yelling or anything.

Bucky answered their questions for hours, talking about the drug business, how much pot he was selling, how much money he was mak-ing. Jimmy and Stevie were particularly interested in Joe Murray, the drug dealer Bucky was involved with who was making millions. Bucky was giving up information for the next crime, probably a shakedown on Murray. Even though Jimmy kept the machine gun on Bucky, since he was well shackled, there was no further need to threaten him.

A couple of times Jimmy came out into the parlor to tell me what was going on, what Bucky was saying about the drug business, how he'd offered to pay us $40,000 a month from now on. But Jimmy rejected that offer and decided instead to pay a visit to Bucky's house in Squantum to get some more of his money. Using a telephone with a speaker hooked up to it, Jimmy had Bucky call his house. When his wife, Elaine, answered, Jimmy made Bucky tell her he was bringing some friends over and she had to leave for a couple of hours.

After the phone call, Stevie and Jimmy led Bucky down to the cellar and then called me down there. The basement was unfinished, with a cement floor painted military gray and overhead lighting. Off that main room was a small room with hot water heaters. A little step led up to another small room, maybe 12 feet by 12 feet, with a dirt floor and a ceiling so low you couldn't stand up in it. A bulkhead opened to the backyard, with a driveway to the side. Handing me the machine gun, Jimmy told me to watch Bucky while he and Stevie went over to his house. Bucky and I were down there for about an hour, but I didn't say a word to him during that time. I didn't think it was appropriate for me to talk to him. He was sitting there, softly saying his prayers to God. That whole time, I didn't think about anything in particular. It was just business. But I did feel bad for him, for here was this guy, chained up and saying his prayers. I still thought it was just a shakedown, but I wasn't in charge and I understood that whatever happened to Bucky was not my decision.

When Jimmy and Stevie returned from Squantum with only $47,000 from a hide that Bucky had told them about in his house, they brought him back upstairs. At that point, I was sent out to pick up an Asian guy who will remain nameless to accompany me to a restaurant, Little Rascals, at Faneuil Hall. Our job was to collect the $10,000 that belonged to Bucky from his partner. When we got to the restaurant, I remained in the car while the Asian fellow went in to pick up the envelope with the money. Once he got back in the car, I took the envelope and dropped him off at another location and went back to the house on East Third Street. I ended up receiving between nine and ten thousand from the money taken from Barrett. Jimmy and Stevie got approximately the same.

An hour or so after I got back to the house, around 6:00 P.M., Jimmy told me to go grab a bite to eat, so I went home and ate. I'd only been home forty-five minutes when Jimmy beeped me to come back. Back at the house, I saw that Bucky looked pretty much the same as when I'd left. He hadn't been beaten up or tortured or anything like that. And I still assumed he was going to be shaken down and released. But when Jimmy said, "Bucky's gonna go downstairs and lay down," I understood something else was up.

Bucky turned his head and, with no begging or pleading for his life, looked at Jimmy and said in a compliant way, "Yeah, lay down." He knew the end was near and just acquiesced to it.

Still manacled, he started to walk down the stairs, very slowly, one step at a time, following Stevie, with Jimmy behind him. A few steps from the bottom, Jimmy put the gun to the back of Bucky's head and pulled the trigger, but nothing happened. Jimmy stopped, took his glasses out of his shirt pocket, and, realizing the safety was still on, flipped it off. Bucky had continued walking very slowly down the last two stairs. Jimmy descended a few more stairs and then put the gun to the back of Bucky's head a second time, this time killing him instantly, splattering blood, along with brains and skull, all over the stairs and floor.

Once Jimmy and Stevie were positive Bucky was dead, Jimmy went upstairs to take a nap. He was nice and relaxed, not the least bit excited or anything. He just lay down on the couch and went to sleep while Stevie and I set about cleaning up the mess. I noticed that Jimmy seemed to calm down after the murder, almost as if he'd just taken a Valium. Although he stayed that way for a while, eventually he turned a bit hyper. I noticed this after other murders, too. Nothing seemed to relax him or make him feel quite so good as a murder. The first thing Stevie did was to remove Bucky's teeth with a pair of channel-lock pliers in order to foil dental identification. This was before DNA was being used to identify bodies. He tossed the teeth in a bag that he would dispose of later. Stories about Barrett being terrorized while he was alive, of his feet and hands being cut off, of his teeth being removed while he screamed in pain, were pure fiction.

After I dug the hole and began to bury the body in the basement, Stevie opened the bulkhead and Phil Costa, an associate of his, came in. Phil handed me a couple of bags of lime, which we spread over the body to help speed up its decomposition. Then Stevie and I went upstairs, where he took out a blue plastic basin, sort of a tub that you would wash dishes in, filled it with cold water, and put liquid soap in it. Then Stevie grabbed a sponge and we both went back downstairs to clean up the blood and brains. We used cold water, which, unlike hot water, helps to congeal the blood and the brains. Since the basement floor was painted with gray deck paint, blood was unable to seep into it.

After the execution and burial, when I went back upstairs, I caught a glimpse of Bucky's wallet on the kitchen table. It was open to a photo of a little blonde girl, who looked to be around two or three. I had no idea, and never found out, if that was his daughter, but I had a year-old kid of my own and felt bad when I thought about a little girl maybe growing up without her father. But I had had no say. The die had been cast years earlier. As soon as Bucky had run to Frankie, the whole deal had become personal between him and Jimmy. Bucky had been killed because he had a big mouth and Jimmy couldn't trust him. He wasn't going to let Bucky run to someone like Frankie to back him off a second time. But I had to hand it to Bucky. This time he had been a man from the minute he'd been walked into the house until the very end. He never begged, he never complained, he never pleaded for his life.

After the cleanup was finished and Stevie took off to get rid of the teeth, I drove Barrett's brown Cadillac over to Savin Hill, where I parked it and made sure it was all wiped down. Jimmy had followed me, so I hopped into his car and we headed over to Castle Island, where we parked and took the garbage bag filled with Barrett's clothes out of the trunk. After we poked a couple of holes in the bag, we walked to the end of the pier and dropped the bag into the water. For a few minutes, we just stood there and watched it move out noiselessly with the tide. It was a warm summer night and a couple of guys were right there, fishing out on the pier, with their gas lanterns set up not too far from where we stood. When we had walked out with our two bags and dumped them over the side, they had barely noticed. As a matter of fact, when Jimmy and I walked back by them after we'd taken care of our business, one of the guys said, "I'll watch your stuff for you while you're gone."

"Okay," I said. "We'll be right back."

It was just another example of how when you go about your business in a normal way, no one pays any attention to what you're doing. When you're in these types of situations, you don't run, you walk. Growing up in the projects, I learned early that when someone slammed a car door, everyone looked to see what was going on. To escape attention, you close the door quietly and click it shut with your hands. That night on the pier, Jimmy and I strolled calmly off the pier as Barrett's clothes sank to the bottom of the ocean.

The second murder in that house was John McIntyre's. He was a thirty-two-year-old drug smuggler and, like many from the Irish communities of South Boston and Charlestown, had a lot of sympathy for the IRA and their cause.

In 1984, Jimmy and I had been involved with an attempt to smuggle seven tons of ammunition and weapons on board the Gloucester-based *Valhalla*. Around nine o'clock on a September night, Jimmy and I arrived in Gloucester in his Malibu to await the arrival of vans carrying the weapons and ammunition that would be loaded on the *Valhalla* and sent to the IRA in Ireland the next morning. The ship was owned by Joe Murray, who used it to run drugs out of South America for his Charlestown drug business. That night, Jimmy and I found a spot with a view of the dock, as well as the road from opposite directions. Dressed in dark clothes, we sat in the car, monitoring the police calls with the scanner.

At one point, I did get out of the car and walked to a spot a little bit higher with an even better view. Things were quiet until, about an hour after we had gotten there, we got the call on our walkie-talkies from one of the drivers of the vans. "We're on our way," the driver said, and I answered with one word, "Green," meaning, "Go. The coast is clear." Since our job was to provide security, Jimmy and I stayed in the Malibu and watched as five vans pulled up to the dock. Everybody involved in the operation had their job to do, so the drivers had plenty of help on the pier as they emptied the five vans. We remained in our spot as one van after another pulled up, and its crates and duffel bags, filled with pistols and high-powered rifles of all different calibers, bulletproof vests, and various kinds of ammunition and explosives, as well as a variety of parts of weapons and replacement pieces they needed for guns already over there, were passed from person to person. A lot of the stuff had been bought from gun stores and warehouses all over the country and sent to different addresses in Boston. It took around an hour until all the stuff was loaded onto the ship. It would take longer to stash it all away on the ship, but once the transfer was completed and the empty vans left, our job providing security was done. So Jimmy and I called it a night and drove away.

I'd actually been at the Gloucester dock a few days earlier to see how the operation was going. That day, Joe Murray happened to introduce me to McIntyre, who also worked as a mechanic on the ship. Things had seemed to be moving along on schedule, but Joe, Jimmy, and I were not the only ones involved in this operation. Much of the money for the weapons had come from different sources all over the country, from a lot of other people supporting the cause. Jimmy's and my role was to make sure all the weapons and ammunition got on the *Valhalla* without any problems.

Not that this was my first involvement with the IRA. Jimmy and I had shipped other guns in the past, but nothing as big as this load. During the past couple of years, we'd put the guns together and someone else had shipped them over. We'd also sent guns by other methods to Ireland, once inside a van with a secret hide built into it, other times in hides constructed in pieces of furniture. Jimmy and I had never done it to make money. We did it because we believed in the cause.

After the *Valhalla* had left Gloucester the day after everything had been loaded on it, we didn't know about any trouble until we heard on the news that the Royal Navy and the Royal Air Force had seized a ship off the coast of Ireland. Naturally, Jimmy and I were very upset and waited to hear exactly what had happened. It wasn't until months later that we learned how it had actually gone down. Apparently, as expected, the *Valhalla* had met the *Marita Ann* in Irish waters, and the weapons and ammunition had been successfully transferred to the second ship. However, during the transfer, as the ships sat side by side, the Royal Air Force had been buzzing around, circling both ships. As the *Marita Ann* was heading back to port in Ireland, the Royal Navy had intercepted the ship. Obviously, they had been tipped off.

We also found out that the *Marita Ann* had been in dry dock for six or seven years on the southern coast of Ireland. It hadn't been used during those years, but suddenly there had been a spurt of activity getting the ship ready to go back to sea. The IRA operates different cells to keep information separate, so not everybody knows what is going on. However, we were able to learn that Sean O'Callaghan, an Irish nationalist and an informant for the British against the IRA, had gotten involved in the cells. It was he who had given up the *Marita Ann*.

When the *Valhalla* finally came back, having sustained a lot of damage in a big storm—all its windows had been blown out—it docked in South Boston, not Gloucester. It got back to us that two fellows who had been on the boat had gone down to inspect it, and when they were coming off, they had been stopped by U.S. Customs Agents Defago and Grady. The FBI, through John Connolly, told Jimmy that someone who had been grabbed that day coming off the *Valhalla* was cooperating with the law enforcement. This person was giving us up, telling about his own involvement with the *Valhalla*, including Jimmy, Stevie, myself, and a few other people involved with that ship. A short time later, we also learned that John McIntyre, one of those two fellows stopped by the customs agents, had been grabbed for domestic violence. As a result, he had immediately started cooperating with the authorities.

All we knew at first, however, was that one of those two people who had originally been stopped by the customs agents, McIntyre or Anderson, the captain of the ship, was cooperating. It was quickly determined that it would be best for us to grab McIntyre, since Anderson was older and more old-school. Also, since McIntyre was geographically close to us, it would be easy to grab him.

In the meantime, since the *Valhalla* had come back, the *Ramsland*, an old freighter from South America also owned by Joe Murray, was presently in the Chelsea Naval Yard, scheduled to be scrapped. This ship was presently carrying thirty tons of marijuana for Murray's operation out of Charlestown, with a street value of $30 million minus expenditures. Jimmy and I each had a piece of that. In all, there were six people involved, each with equal shares that came out to about two and a half million to three million apiece after expenses. Although we'd used the *Valhalla* to send guns to Ireland, we had never sent drugs over there. It was fine to send the drugs to the English who were oppressing the Irish, but never to our own people.

But now, all of a sudden, the *Ramsland*, which had been sitting there for a month, got raided. And the customs agents who had boarded the boat knew exactly where to go for the hide. Taking the ballasts off the secret compartment, they had easily found the thirty tons of marijuana. We knew right away that they had been tipped off, and that the same person who was cooperating about the *Valhalla* was also cooperating here. And chances were excellent that that person was McIntyre.

The plan to grab him didn't take long to arrange. Since McIntyre worked for Joe Murray, we talked to Joe about the situation, although we never needed permission from anyone. We did whatever we wanted to do. First, we discussed the possibility of sending McIntyre to South America where Murray had connections and could kill him or hide him till everything blew over. Then we considered whether we should prep him on what to say to the grand jury. But the plan we decided on was for Murray to tell McIntyre that he could invest in a drug deal with him that would pay ten times the return on his money. We would be dangling a carrot in front of him, playing on his greed. As it turned out, McIntyre went back to the customs agents, who gave him the $20,000 to invest, figuring they could set up a sting operation and nab Murray.

On November 30, 1984, McIntyre met with Murray on the South Boston waterfront, supposedly to give him the $20,000 to invest in the drug deal. On the waterfront, McIntyre got into the car with Murray and another individual. The three of them drove around and then dropped off Joe. When the other guy said he had to drop off some beer for a party on East Third Street, McIntyre went along, thinking he was doing a simple errand with him.

Around noon, the other guy walked into 799 East Third Street with a case of Miller Light and put it on a table. When he went back to the car to get another case, McIntyre, who was six feet tall, around 220 pounds, with brown hair and a light beard, came in, wearing dungarees and a light jacket, thinking he was coming to a party and carrying a case of beer himself. When he walked into the kitchen, he immediately saw me and Stevie and started to turn back. But I grabbed him by the throat and the back of his head and he went down to the floor. At the same time, Jimmy stepped out from behind the refrigerator with a machine pistol, a Mac-10 with a silencer, and said, "Let him up." When I helped him up, Stevie and Jimmy sat him in a chair where Stevie handcuffed, shackled, and chained him. Leaving the three of them alone in the kitchen, I walked into the adjacent parlor and sat on the couch. For the next five or six hours, McIntyre was never tortured, although he was obviously mentally terrorized.

It took no more than two minutes of interrogation in the kitchen for McIntyre to admit he was the informant. From the parlor, I could hear him say, "I'm sorry. I was weak."

Jimmy told him to take it easy, to calm down. "Don't worry," he told him. "We're going to send you to South America or tell you what to say in front of the grand jury. You'll be all right."

Jimmy came out a minute or so later to tell me what was going on. When Jimmy went back into the kitchen, the three of them continued to talk about Joe Murray and his operation. Jimmy wanted to find out about McIntyre's involvement in the drug business, who he was working for, how much he was making, how much he was bringing in. He was more interested in that information than in the fact that McIntyre was talking to the law about us.

It didn't take long for Jimmy to realize that the plan to send McIntyre away or to tell him what to say to the grand jury was not going to work. He understood that eventually McIntyre would talk again. I think it was already predetermined by Jimmy that he was going to kill him. But the conversation lasted a few hours, with no yelling and Jimmy talking to McIntyre in a nice calm manner, getting all the information he needed as McIntyre replied in an equally calm manner.

Around five, Jimmy told me to leave and get something to eat, so I went over to my in-laws' house and ate there. About an hour later, he beeped me and I came back to the house. McIntyre was still shackled to the chair in the kitchen. Ten minutes later, Jimmy told McIntyre, "Get up out of the chair. We're going downstairs now." Without a word, McIntyre stood up, and made it down the stairs with his chains intact, Jimmy and Stevie right behind him and me following the three of them.

In the basement, Jimmy and Stevie sat him back in a chair, but this time Jimmy placed a rope around his neck. Although Jimmy tried hard to strangle him, the rope was too thick to cut off his air supply and merely made him gag and throw up. Finally, after a few minutes of this, Jimmy took the rope off McIntyre's throat and asked, "Would you like one in the head?"

The guy sat up straight and answered, "Yes, please." You had to give McIntyre credit. Like Bucky, he had shown tremendous bravery. He knew he was going to die and somehow he came to terms with it. He wasn't begging for his life. He was just asking politely to get shot in the head. The guy went out like a man, with no pleading or crying.

So Jimmy shot him in the back of the head with a .22-caliber rifle, cut down to a pistol grip with a silencer on it, and the bullet exited underneath his chin. When McIntyre fell to the floor, Stevie went over, propped him up, put his head on McIntyre's chest, and reported he was still alive. Stevie grabbed him by his hair and shoulder and Jimmy put five or six more into his face. Then Jimmy turned to Stevie and said, "Well, he's dead now," and that was it.

When Jimmy went upstairs to take a nap on the couch in the parlor, Stevie and I cleaned everything up. Unlike with Bucky, whose brains and skull were everywhere, there hadn't been a lot of bleeding with McIntyre. But once again, we got out the basin and filled it with liquid soap and cold water and took care of the remains. After we'd cleaned up the floor, Stevie stripped McIntyre down so the decomposition would take place faster and began using the channel-lock pliers to remove his teeth. I was digging the hole for the grave when Stevie called me over and showed me a piece of McIntyre's tongue that he'd accidentally caught in the pliers. "Look at this," he told me. "He won't be using this no more." I kind of chuckled, turned away, and returned to the hole I was digging.

A few minutes later, Stevie told me he was thinking of doing an autopsy on the body. Genuinely curious about what was inside, he wanted to cut open the body and check it out. But he changed his mind and helped me put the body in the hole. When I told Jimmy about Stevie's desire to do an autopsy, he said, "Let's just get him buried and get out of here." But then he started laughing and said, "See, I told you Dr. Mengele was crazy."

As it turned out, the customs agents never got back the $20,000 they had given to McIntyre to invest in the drug deal in their hopes of setting up a sting operation. Jimmy kept the money and gave Murray and Stevie and me each $5,000. Actually, he exchanged it for another $20,000, just to be safe, before he handed money out to us. A week later, we found out the agents were upset because not only had they lost an informant, but they'd also lost $20,000.

But that November night, after Stevie and I had cleaned up the site, Stevie and Jimmy followed me while I drove McIntyre's dark-colored pickup truck with a standard shift on the column to Neponset Bridge. I parked it next to the Upstairs Downstairs Lounge, wiped it down, and got into Jimmy's car. Stevie had McIntyre's clothes and teeth and said he would get rid of them himself.

The two of them dropped me off at my house and went out for dinner. As soon as I got home, I threw my clothes in the washing machine and went into the shower. And how did I feel? Fine. Because to me it was just business. All I thought about when I was doing business was making money and staying free. There was no sense in doing a crime if you couldn't get away with it. And McIntyre had turned into an informant who was trying to make me lose my freedom. As an informant, he got what he deserved. A legitimate person would have been different. But someone who comes around and is involved with us and then is giving us up is trying to hurt us. McIntyre wasn't my partner. He was just a score, an informant who had to be taken care of. Luckily, I can compartmentalize things so they don't eat away at me. While it's happening, it's just business. When it's over, it's over. And I don't think about it ever again. To me it didn't matter if McIntyre was dead or in South America, as long as he couldn't hurt us.

The third murder that took place in the house at 799 East Third Street was Deborah Hussey, Stevie's "stepdaughter." Stevie had been complaining that Deborah was bringing blacks to the house in Milton where he lived with Marion, Debbie's mother and his common-law wife, or whatever you call her, and their other kids. Marion said that Debbie was upsetting the household, that she was stripping in town and doing drugs. Little by little, Marion was souping Stevie up, but I hadn't realized the severity of it or how mad he was getting over the situation.

I had also heard that 799 East Third Street was being sold and that eventually we were going to have to move the two bodies already in the basement. Jimmy and I had been talking about acquiring the house so we could control it and not have to bother moving the two bodies. And I knew Stevie had been talking about buying the house himself.

One day, Jimmy called me up and told me to meet him, and the two of us drove down to that house. I didn't particularly care for that house because every time I was there someone got killed, but he had called me, so I went. When I asked him what was up, he said we were meeting Stevie at the house, that he had taken Debbie shopping and was buying her a coat. I was thinking maybe that meant he wanted to buy the house for her, which would eliminate the need to move the two bodies.

There were lots of women in Stevie's life, all beautiful young women, of different nationalities and different backgrounds. It had only been a few years earlier, in 1981, that he'd killed his gorgeous longtime girlfriend, Debra Davis. She had tried to leave him, but his ego had gotten in the way, making it impossible for him to live with her leaving him for another guy. If he couldn't have her, no one could. So he had killed her, strangled her in his mother's house at 832 East Third Street. That's the type of guy he was.

But that night, four years after he killed Debra Davis, Stevie came walking into the house at 799 East Third Street, diagonally across the street from his mother's house, with Debbie Hussey, also twenty-six. At the time, Jimmy was on the first floor while I was upstairs using the bathroom. As I was heading downstairs, I heard a thud, and when I walked into the parlor, Debbie, her brown hair falling against her shoulder, was lying on the floor. I'd never seen her before and she certainly wasn't looking good. I could see that she was a rough-and-tumble kind of girl, sort of small, probably five-three and 115 pounds, and not the prissy type. I knew she'd been drugging and stripping in the Naked Eye in downtown Boston, so even if she had been pretty at one time, she wasn't any longer.

But at that moment, Jimmy was on the floor, too, with his arms wrapped around Debbie's neck, his legs wrapped around her waist and her chest, squeezing, strangling her. I could see that her lips and face were blue, that her eyes were bulging, that she was already dead. But Stevie put his head on her chest and insisted she was still alive. It was another case of him and Jimmy trying to outdo each other on who's the better killer here. To prove his point, Stevie took a clothesline type of rope, wrapped it around Debbie's neck, stuck a stick in it, and kept on twisting it and twisting it like a garrote.

She was definitely dead then, so Stevie and I took her downstairs while Jimmy just laid on the couch upstairs. The two of us basically went about the same thing we'd down twice before, with Stevie stripping her down, removing her black dungarees, blouse, and thin coat, and pulling her teeth out with the pliers while I dug the hole. Then we put her in and buried her. There was no blood with this murder, so there was little cleanup.

Stevie said he'd take care of the clothes and teeth. He was all business, going about the task of cleaning up and pulling teeth. Even though he had a long-term relationship with Debbie, this wasn't bothering him any more than it had bothered Jimmy. Stevie was actually enjoying it, the way he always enjoyed a good murder. Like a stockbroker going to work, he was just doing his job. Cold and relaxed, with no emotion or change in his demeanor, he was performing a night's work. Whether he then went out to meet another of his girlfriends or went home to Marion, I have no idea.

Later on, when I was alone with Jimmy, I asked him what that was all about. "Who knows?" he answered. "She was bringing blacks back to the house. She was doing drugs. Stevie was probably fucking her." I never asked again, but it was just kind of distasteful killing a woman. I can see killing guys. That's the life they chose, the life they're involved with, the life we all chose. But a woman is different. It wasn't a nice thing.

Years later, it came out that Stevie was in fact having sex with Debbie. And she'd been his stepdaughter since she was three years old. Who knows if she knew anything else about him? But to kill a woman because she threatened to tell that you were fucking her didn't make any sense, no more than it did to kill a girlfriend because she wanted to leave you. According to Stevie's testimony in a later trial, when it came out that he had been having sex with her daughter, Marion still continued to see him. She didn't know about the murder, but she knew about the sex. That didn't make any sense, either.

But that was the last murder in the house.

As it turned out, six months after Debbie Hussey's murder the house got sold, so we had to get the bodies out of there. On Halloween weekend in 1985, an appropriate time for such a move, Stevie and I and another fellow went down to the house to exhume the three bodies and put them in body bags. The three of us arrived around five in the morning, put gloves on our hands and little painter's masks over our noses and mouths, and got to work. Since Bucky Barrett had been there for a couple of years, McIntyre maybe for a year, and Deborah Hussey for less than that, we knew it wasn't going to be a pleasant task to dig them all up.

The first body we dug up was Bucky, who had kind of mummified rather than decomposed, because of the lime we'd put on him. Apparently Phil Costa had brought us the wrong kind of lime the night Bucky got killed. Instead of buying the lime that helps with decomposition, Phil had bought the lime that is some kind of fertilizer you use for gardening. As a result, when we pulled Bucky out of the hole, his head snapped off and broke away, but we managed to get it into the bag with the rest of the body. The other two bodies were a little fresher, so it was pretty gory with the stench of the flesh, but we got each of them into a body bag without any parts breaking off. It took us a good eight hours to dig up the bodies, put them in the bags, and clean up everything, including all the small bones and the bits and pieces.

Stevie and I waited upstairs until it got dark out and Jimmy pulled a station wagon, with its back seat down flat, into the driveway at the side of the house. The three of us carried each body into the wagon, which we called the hearse, and drove off. Master criminal that he is, Jimmy had already figured out exactly how we would dispose of the bodies. We'd spent days riding around scouting out possible locations before he finally chose a wooded spot, a gully overlooking the Southeast Expressway, across from Florian Hall on Hill Top Street in Dorchester. At the time we had the DEA all over us, but we never had any problem losing them.

The night before we took the bodies out of East Third Street, the three of us had gone to that wooded spot, predug a hole six feet wide and eight feet deep, filled ten duffel bags with dirt, stuck them back in the hole, and piled the remaining dirt on top of them. Jimmy even put a twenty-dollar bill under a rock on top of the dirt so we would know if anyone had spotted the grave. He left nothing to chance.

On Halloween night, after we arrived at the selected spot, Jimmy checked to see if his twenty-dollar bill was still there. When he saw that it was in the exact place, under the rock, where he'd left it, he put it in his pocket and we took the bodies out of the hearse before he drove it to a nearby spot. While he was gone, Stevie and I carried each body over to the little wooded area. When Jimmy got back, the three of us took turns on watch, with one of us working the police scanner and holding the grease gun, a cheaply made World War II machine gun fitted with a silencer, just in case anyone stumbled upon us while we were burying the bodies. Jimmy went on watch first while Stevie and I began to replace the duffel bags with the three body bags. As we were transferring the bodies out of the bags into the hole, Bucky's head got loose again and rolled out of the bag. This time I had to push it into the hole with my foot.

The whole time we were working, a big Halloween party was going on across the street at Florian Hall, spilling out into the parking lot. Twenty yards from us, people were parking and heading to the party. While I was lying facedown with the gun and Stevie and Jimmy were busy at the hole, a kid got out of his car maybe twenty feet from us. We had been real quiet, so I was sure he hadn't heard or seen us. All he did was relieve himself, since he'd obviously been drinking, and then got back in his car and drove away. After the kid left, Jimmy was a little upset with me for letting anyone get that close and not killing him. He would never have taken a chance and would have shot him the minute he stepped out of his car. "There's plenty of room in the hole for the kid," he told me. But there had been no reason to kill the kid. He hadn't seen anything. That kid never knew how lucky he was that it was me on the gun, not Jimmy.

Anyhow, we finished up burying the bodies right there under everybody's noses. One of the body bags ended up with a broken zipper and couldn't be used again, so we tossed it into the hole with the three bodies. When we were through, about forty-five minutes after we'd gotten there, we stuffed nine of the empty duffel bags inside the tenth bag and carried it, along with the two body bags, back to the hearse. Later, after I got into my own car, I pulled off my boots and tossed them out the window onto the Expressway. When I got home, I threw all my clothes into a garbage bag and got rid of it in a Dumpster behind the Stop & Shop in Dorchester. But for three days, I could still smell the stench from the bodies in my nostrils. It was a pretty gruesome, rough night, but I don't think much about it anymore. It had to be done. And that was just the way it was.

SIX

STEVIE FLEMMI

I first met Stevie Flemmi in 1974, the night he and Jimmy walked into Flix, a downtown bar where I was bouncing. I knew Stevie's reputation as Jimmy's close associate and supposed hit man for the Winter Hill gang. He wasn't a big guy, maybe five-eight, 156 pounds. I was pretty sure he was around forty, a few years younger than Jimmy, but it was obvious that he, too, worked out and took good care of himself. Clean-shaven, wearing jeans and a black leather jacket, Stevie had dark brown hair, neatly trimmed, and brown eyes.

The press idiotically loves to call him "The Rifleman," referring to the Roxbury native's days as a paratrooper/shooter with the 187th Airborne Regimental Combat Team in the Korean War. But even I knew that no one close to him would ever use that inane nickname. I'd also heard a bit about his two brothers, Vincent, who had his own nickname of Jimmy the Bear, and Michael, a sergeant with the Boston Police Department. His brothers gave Michael lots of business, as the Bear's capability for violence was as legendary as Stevie's.

From the first time I met Stevie, I was surprised at how likable and easygoing he was. When I started to work at Triple O's and got to know him better, he was still friendly and outgoing, a nice guy who liked to joke around. For the following twenty-five years that we worked together, I rarely had a problem with him and never incurred his wrath. I learned right away that his main goal was making money, which he accomplished exceptionally well, and that even though he was an intelligent, creative thinker, his first course of action toward anyone who went against him, who wasn't doing what they were supposed to do, who so much as talked to him in a way he didn't like, was to kill them. In fact, while Stevie was eventually charged with ten murders, the correct number is more like thirty. Like Jimmy, he had a violent temper and was extraordinarily brutal. But while Stevie was hot-blooded, Jimmy was cold-blooded. Stevie would kill someone anywhere, anytime; Jimmy was more calculating and took his time to pick the right place and the right moment. The badge Stevie had earned during the Korean War as a highly skilled shooter was all the more reason to fear his hot-blooded temper. I was never afraid of Stevie, but I knew he was explosive and I knew when to be cautious around him.

When we first met in 1974, Stevie had just come back from five years on the lam in New York and Canada with Frank Salemme. In 1968, the two of them had taken off after blowing up the car of John Fitzgerald, the lawyer who was representing Joe Barboza, a mob hit man who'd flipped and turned into a government witness. Fitzgerald, who Frankie and Stevie figured facilitated Barboza's flip, lost a leg in the car bombing, but survived the attack. As it turned out, Salemme got pinched in 1973 by John Connolly on a New York sidewalk. But Stevie played it safer and was able to wait it out another year until the heat died down, the case fell apart, and he could safely return to Boston. There was, I later learned, more to that story, but it was many years before I understood exactly who was helping Stevie stay out of prison for that crime.

When we met, Stevie was living with Marion Hussey in Milton, near Curry College, in a house that once belonged to his parents. But he was still legally married to Jeannette, the woman he'd married in the 1950s, when he was a paratrooper. He'd had a couple of girls with Jeannette, and he and Marion had two sons together. I only met Jeannette a few times, once in the early 1980s, at Stevie's mother's house. Her blonde hair done up in a bun, she was around five-four, of medium build and very pleasant. Jimmy, Stevie, and I were in the house when she came in to say hi to Stevie's mother, Mary. We chatted for a few minutes about nothing special and when the three of us left, she stayed at the house to spend some more time with her mother-in-law. I'm pretty sure that a few years later, Stevie did go to Haiti for a quick divorce, but he never married Marion.

Stevie and Jeannette were still married at the time of the wedding of their daughter Jeannette to Al Benedetti in 1983. It was an expensive wedding, done up right, with the reception at a beautiful Boston hotel, a fancy affair with an open bar, lots of hors d'oeuvres, a live band, and a big crowd. All the South Boston gang, Jimmy and Stevie's inner circle, were there, having a terrific time and a lot of laughs. We all brought our wives and I was there with Pam and Jimmy was with Theresa. Stevie looked handsome and proud as he and Jeannette walked their daughter down the aisle of the church, and he remained the perfect host all evening long.

When Theresa Stanley's daughter Karen married hockey player Chris Nilan, the wedding at the Copley Plaza was equally as lavish, and Jimmy, like Stevie, spared nothing to make it so. The ceremony took place in a church, but the reception was at the hotel. There was a large crowd, which included all of the Montreal Canadiens, as well as lots of friends and relatives and many of Jimmy's business associates. Theresa looked especially lovely that night, as did Karen, who was every bit as beautiful as her mother. Like Stevie, Jimmy provided an open bar, as well as expensive bottles of wine and Dom Perignon on every table. Karen and Chris raised their family in Hingham until they were divorced about ten years later.

Stevie loved women and was attracted to them in all shapes and sizes, so Jeannette and Marion were far from the only females in his life. A good-looking guy, he looked a little like Robert De Niro and always bought expensive clothes. He and Jimmy traveled all over Europe, Mexico, and the islands, bringing beautiful women with them. One of Stevie's favorites, of course, was Debra Davis, whom he killed when she tried to leave him. His ego could never stand the thought of any woman leaving him. Jimmy could see a relationship end and say, "See you the fuck later." He could walk away from the woman without feeling the need to kill her in order to keep his ego intact. But Stevie couldn't do that. He couldn't just say goodbye. He had to kill her. It's funny, but people don't think criminals have women problems like everyone else. Yet they do. But most criminals don't handle this stress from women the way Stevie did.

You never knew what was going on in Stevie's mind. Anyone who met him couldn't help but like him, but you never knew when that nice manner was going to transform into his violent temper, which most often ended up in someone's death. And you never knew when you were going to end up involved in his violent behavior. One morning in 1981, around 4:00 A.M., I got a phone call from Jimmy to meet him outside my apartment on L Street. I didn't need him to tell me that this was going to be a business call, so I dressed appropriately. Jimmy always said nighttime was the best camouflage. And it was free—just there, waiting to be used. Heeding his advice, "dark clothes for dark deeds," I threw on a black, long-sleeved T-shirt, black dungarees, black socks, black sneakers, and black leather gloves and waited outside for him. The blue Chevy Malibu pulled up a few minutes later, with Jimmy, of course, behind the wheel, and Stevie beside him. I hopped in the back and we drove in silence to Medford. Stevie looked pretty souped up and didn't say much. When we pulled up to the house of Loretta Finn, one of his current girlfriends, I said to myself, "Oh, shit. This ain't good," figuring we might be going to help Stevie kill her.

When Stevie got out of the car and walked into the house, I asked Jimmy what was up. "You never know with Stevie," he answered me.

"He's been fighting with Loretta. She's lucky if he doesn't kill her." My thoughts exactly.

Loretta was a tall girl, about five-nine, with long brown hair and big brown eyes. Part Japanese, she was really gorgeous. But, surprisingly, she survived the night. Less than ten minutes after he went into the house, Stevie came out, this time carrying a bunch of fur coats and bags of jewelry. Without a word, he threw them all into the back seat beside me, got into the front, and off we went. Jimmy dropped me off around five, saying, "Get you tomorrow," as I got out of the car. It was too late to try and go back to sleep, so I stayed up and got ready for a day of work on the MBTA.

But Loretta tested her luck a second time. She and Stevie were back together within a week, and one night when they were at Triple O's with Jimmy and me, she joked to us, "You know, I could eat peanuts off Stevie's head." Jimmy looked at me and rolled his eyes. I knew what he was thinking. Yeah, the girl was an inch or so taller than Stevie, but that was no joking matter. Whether she realized it or not, she was insulting the guy in front of his friends. Lucky for her, Stevie was hard of hearing in one ear and hadn't heard her. But she had to be crazy or just plain stupid to have fooled around with a guy like that. People think they're joking, and it's usually okay as long as they don't try and embarrass someone. Then it isn't funny at all. It's deadly.

Although Jimmy went out to dinner frequently with Stevie and his different women, the only place I ever ate with Stevie was at his mother's house. Since I was mostly in Southie and Stevie was all over Boston, we didn't see each other every day. Stevie would come over to talk business with Jimmy for an hour or so, at the variety or liquor stores or at Triple O's. Then he would be on his way, to do business in another part of town, or whatever he wanted. The three of us did spend a good deal of time together in Jimmy's car, heading to a meeting or an extortion or whatever. But thanks to our caution about being taped, our conversations were always minimal and never about business or anything important.

With his brilliant head for business, Stevie was easily a millionaire, investing the prodigious amounts of money he earned through illegitimate means in real estate and other legitimate businesses. To Stevie, money was god. It was important to Jimmy, but not as much as to Stevie. Stevie might have made even more money than Jimmy, since Jimmy had been in jail for nine years, while Stevie hadn't lost a day of work. But even though both of them made a lot of money, Jimmy had no problem giving someone a break. Like if someone owed him $100,000, after he'd paid a portion of the money, Jimmy might well say, "Forget about the rest." But Stevie would never do that. Stevie would have the guy pay him dollar for dollar, with no break whatsoever. Jimmy also had deep loyalty to me and to other people. Whenever possible, he would make sure not to involve any of us personally or expose us to danger. Stevie was loyal, but just to a point. His loyalty went mostly to his greed. Big-time.

Stevie was close with his two sons, Billy and Stevie Jr., with whom he helped develop Schooner's, a nightclub near Faneuil Hall. It opened in late December 1994. Stevie had done the whole place over. He knew a lot about construction and liked to build things. He enjoyed watching the projects come together and had an eye for all the little details, paying careful attention to each one and making sure everything was done perfectly. One of his investments was in a laundromat in Back Bay. While he was in the process of designing and building it, Jimmy and I met him over there a couple of times, but, unfortunately for Stevie, he got pinched before it reached its full potential.

Although there was no doubt that Stevie had a sharp mind and handled business details exceptionally well, he was not as alert to the presence of the law as Jimmy and I were. No matter how many times Jimmy would warn him to be more cautious, Stevie just wasn't as attuned to what was going on around him as Jimmy felt he should have been. This was probably because we were always in South Boston and could recognize an unfamiliar car or face easily, while Stevie was all over Boston and had too big an area to cover well. That was one of his few shortcomings, but it was a major one that eventually did him in.

In 1980, Jimmy opened up a garage with Stevie on Lancaster Street in downtown Boston, which George Kaufman ran for them. They often used the garage as a business office and had meetings and conducted business there. It was an indoor parking garage, with many permanent spaces for cars. There was also a typically inaccurate dumb story that the newspapers printed about a scene at the garage, a story that was spread as the gospel, even though it was too ridiculous to be true. But, like Jimmy always said, "Never let the truth get in the way of a good story."

According to the local newspapers, who were quoting from an equally inaccurate police report, one afternoon Nicky Femia, the 240-pound mob enforcer who spent most of his time at the garage, was eating his McDonald's lunch on the hood of Jimmy's black 1979 Chevy Caprice. The story describes how Jimmy came out of the garage, saw Femia messing up his car with the food, and proceeded to humiliate him by flinging French fries into his face and screaming at him in front of a small crowd. The story is too ridiculous to repeat, and even more ridiculous to have ever happened. In the first place, Jimmy never acted like that to any of his associates. Second of all, Nicky was a very dangerous guy and if Jimmy ever humiliated him in front of others in that manner, Femia would be looking for revenge and Jimmy would have had to kill him. Just another example of inaccurate reporting and distortions of the truth about Jimmy.

The garage was the real setting, however, for some of Stevie's best jokes. I used to call him Judd for the Defense, referring to the 1967–69 ABC television show about a flamboyant lawyer named Clinton Judd, because every time Stevie tried to stick up for me, he'd get me in more hot water with Jimmy. Even if it was a dead issue, something I had already done that had gotten Jimmy annoyed, Stevie would try to stir it up all over again. He'd get such a kick out of seeing Jimmy get on me. Like with my paintball tournaments. "So, how was that paintball convention last weekend, Kev?" he'd ask me days after Jimmy had gone at me for taking off for Texas for a tournament. "Where exactly did you say you went? I heard you did real well."

Jimmy would start at me all over again and Stevie would stand in back of him, facing me, barely able to conceal his laughter. There was nothing mean-spirited about what Stevie was doing when he brought up my paintball tournaments. He was doing it all in fun. But all I knew was that every time Judd for the Defense stuck up for me in any matter, I always ended up getting convicted. "Hey, do me a favor and quit sticking up for me," I'd tell him, but he would just smile and keep on busting my balls.

In his typical joking manner, Stevie had tried to convince me to take care of a cat, Mactavish, that he had over at the garage. I'd never seen such an ugly cat. First of all, it was the size of a dog, and it was missing an ear, which it had lost in a fight, along with large chunks of its fur. The dirty street cat was all scarred up and would attack anything that came within five feet of its broken tail. "Come on, Kev," Stevie was always going at me, laughing as he was talking, unable to keep a straight face. "This cat loves you. It would be perfect for your kids. They'd love it. Come on. Take him home for a few days. He needs a good home. Give him a try."

"Oh, yeah," I told him. "He'd be great with my boys. Just the perfect family pet. I'll come home one night and find the cat grazing on my kid's arm." But he never gave up pulling my leg about that miserable cat. Stevie never ran out of jokes, mostly off-color jokes, a lot of which he got from George Kaufman, an old Winter Hill associate of his. Stevie was a great joke-teller and got Jimmy to laugh at most of his jokes.

But he had his own passion, which wasn't for paintball competitions, but rather for parachuting. He'd joined the International Association of Airborne Veterans, and with other former paratroopers, he jumped from planes in South Africa, East Germany, Israel, Russia, and Thailand, forming friendships with other Korean War vets. He enjoyed the jumps, and was always commenting about how modern the equipment was now as compared to what he had used during the war. He would describe the different types of parachutes the Army used and how they had improved over the years. Once when he was talking about his experiences during the Korean War, he told me and Jimmy how he could look from one mountaintop to the other and see the faces of the people he was shooting at. But most of his reminiscing about those days took place at the reunions with other vets that he attended faithfully, making jumps right up until the 1990s.

Stevie was close with his parents, who had both emigrated from Italy to the United States before he was born. He took good care of them, buying them houses and cars and whatever else they needed. His father, John, was a quiet guy, old school, who spoke broken English. He had served in World War I with the Italian army and had been a bricklayer in the old country. But there was still plenty of spirit in him. When John was ninety-two, Stevie couldn't find him one day, so Jimmy and I took off looking for him. About a half-hour later, we found him outside his house. He was sitting on the roof, which had a severe slant to it, quietly watching the roofers working on the other side of his house. When Stevie looked up and saw him up there, he muttered "Jesus Christ" in amazement. The three of us watched, not saying a word, until, when he was ready, John got down by himself. A couple of years later, he told everyone he was planning to go to Italy. By himself. Sure enough, a month later, he took off for Italy and stayed there for about a month, having himself a great time until he decided it was time to come home.

Stevie's mother, Mary, was a terrific little lady, one of the world's sweetest. Her greatest joy was cooking for her sons and their friends. Stevie had bought his folks a single-family home in Milton, but later moved them to Southie, where they lived next door to Billy Bulger. It was here where Stevie murdered Debra Davis. But it was also here, in her kitchen, that Mary happily cooked so often for Jimmy and Stevie and me, serving us delicious Italian specialties from large pots simmering on her stove. Jimmy did tell me that Marion wasn't nice to Stevie's parents, and I could never understand that.

When Stevie's brother Jimmy the Bear died of a heroin overdose while serving a life sentence at MCI Norfolk for the murder of Francis Benjamin, Jimmy and I went to the wake. While we were viewing his brother lying in the casket, Stevie was standing there with his mother and father and Michael. Mary went over to Jimmy and said, crying, "Vincent was such a good boy. He never hurt anyone."

Stevie looked at her and said, "Stop, Ma. He killed everybody." Stevie was right. Jimmy the Bear was an extremely violent man, and as Barboza's partner had been involved in the Boston gang wars of the 1960s. The murder of Francis Benjamin, for which the Bear had gotten the life sentence, was a particularly ugly one. After he'd shot Benjamin in the head, using a gun that belonged to a cop, the Bear had cut off the head to avoid any ballistics evidence tracing the gun to the crime. But they fingered him anyhow.

But Stevie had his own unique streak of violence. As I started to work more with him, I'd see him explode, at people who owed him money or didn't do what they were asked to do. He'd start berating them, screaming at them, and I'd just watch. Jimmy, Stevie, and I never tried to calm one another down in a scene like that. We'd never embarrass one another by showing any divisions in public. If something had to be said about an incident like that, it was said in private when the three of us were alone. There were times when one of us would play the good guy and the other the bad guy, assuring the guy in the mess that we'd try to work things out. But the only way things could ever be worked out was for the guy to do exactly what Stevie wanted. Stevie rarely had to work hard convincing someone to do what he wanted. His reputation preceded him.

Like Jimmy, Stevie kept himself looking good by eating healthy and working out nearly every day in his own house, where he had weights and did calisthenics. He maintained vigorous exercise workouts because he felt the young guys were always sizing him up and he didn't want to appear out of shape to them. Like Jimmy, Stevie felt that if you look formidable, there is less chance that people will challenge you. Stevie had a juice machine where he made himself all sorts of weird concoctions out of fruits and vegetables. He even bought me my own juice machine, which I used for a while. When I saw how hard it was to clean out every time I used it, I stopped using it. But Stevie never gave up on his. He was also big on vitamins, which he kept at his mother's house and tried to convince me to use, too. Occasionally I would take them, but never as faithfully as Stevie. Like Jimmy, Stevie bought most of his food at the health food store, Bread & Circus, and didn't smoke, gamble, do drugs, or drink much.

All three of us were big readers and talked about the different books we read. Like Jimmy, Stevie particularly liked books about World War II or Korea or Vietnam. He was close with his kids, especially his two sons, Billy and Stevie. Although, like Jimmy, he wasn't big on professional sporting events, he made it to most of Billy's wrestling matches. Stevie Jr. ended up straight, but even though Stevie didn't want his kids involved in crime, Billy got mixed up in some criminal activities. It's sort of interesting that the Italian mob most often replicates and goes on and on with family members joining, but the Irish gangs seem to last just one generation per family.

Stevie and I certainly didn't work anywhere near as closely as Jimmy and I did. And we never ran in the same social circles. Like Jimmy and most of the guys, he didn't bring a woman to my wedding, but had a great time. He always acted respectful and friendly to Pam and the boys. Like a regular friend, he was concerned with anything that came up in my life and offered to help in any way if he could.

Jimmy trusted Stevie, but he always said that he never knew what

Stevie was thinking. The two of them had respect for each other, and even though they might have had disagreements, they were never heated. It would have been dangerous for them to have cross words with each other. On a typical day, Jimmy and I would spend an hour a day with Stevie, walking around doing business. I mean, we weren't doing crimes every day. We weren't animals, and except for the business aspect of our lives, we led boring, regular lives. But depending on what was going on, if we had an extortion or were collecting tribute from established rackets, we'd spend more time together. Stevie was exceptionally smart business-wise, paying attention to all aspects of business and always staying on top of things. I have little doubt that Stevie could have been successful at anything he tried to do. If he'd gone legit, he could have easily figured out how to let his excessive greed work for him, having people work for him and make him rich. But crime was his field and he did it brilliantly. He was a master criminal, involved in all aspects of crime, in loan-sharking, drug dealing, extortion, everything. I never realized till much later just how good he was at what he did, how adept he was at working both sides.

Like all big-time criminals, Stevie was involved in a network with other criminals in all facets of crime. Everyone he dealt with was a criminal to one degree or another. Even legitimate people who were around him were like groupies, people who wanted to be able to tell others they knew this guy or were connected to him. No matter what it cost them to be able to do that, they found it advantageous just being able to say that Stevie was a friend of theirs. That went for Jimmy, too. These wannabes thought they could ask Jimmy or Stevie for a favor at any time. They wanted to be able to say they knew wiseguys, that they had friends who would do anything. I still don't know why legitimate people feel that way about wiseguys. Maybe it's for the same reason, whatever it might be, that girls want to be around rock stars.

While Stevie and I spent most of our time together with Jimmy, the two of us did handle a few situations together. One involved the transfer of guns from the hide in George Kaufman's house in Brookline. It was a move made necessary when George, a terrific guy who became our liaison with the Jewish bookmakers, sold his house in Brookline. So we decided to move our weapons, gathered from years before, from Brookline to Stevie's mother's house in South Boston.

Before the move, Jimmy, Stevie, and I spent a lot of time checking weather reports, waiting until we heard a report about a rainy night when not too many people would be out and about. Since those who were out would be hidden under umbrellas or looking down trying to get out of the rain as quickly as possible, it would be easier for us not to draw any attention on that type of night. Once we got the weather we wanted, I took off for George's house and, around 9:00 P.M., backed my car into the garage underneath his house. After George and I walked into the basement off the garage where the hide was, George took out a putty knife and slid it down the wall between the molding to a spot where it touched two copper nails with wires attached to them that were sticking out. As soon as the putty knife hit the nails, it made a connection and I heard a motor turning. As George and I walked out of the room, I saw that the wall had been on a track. Now the other side of the house opened up and we could see the hide. The two of us spent the next hour taking all the weapons out of the hide and packing them into the five duffel bags I had brought with me.

We were always acquiring guns and had stashed others in different houses, but it was certainly time to get them out of George's house. It wouldn't have been great for the new owner to have somehow moved the wall and discovered more than 200 weapons in his new home. Weapons were our tools of the trade, and we needed easy and constant access to them. We had to be prepared for anything that might come up. Obviously, we needed different weapons for different tasks, each need depending on the setting. For instance, if we were going car-to-car, we might need an assault weapon or a carbine machine gun with a silencer. Or if we were going after someone on foot, we'd need a pistol with a silencer. This arsenal had all those weapons, plus hand grenades, AK-47's, Thompson and 9-mm submachine guns, bulletproof vests, and C-4 explosive, along with .25s, .32s, .38s, .45s, ski masks, holsters, walkie-talkies, and handcuffs. And boxes of ammunition for every caliber of gun there. More weapons than we could possibly use in a lifetime. Some we wanted to have with us if we were doing something, perhaps a hand grenade, just in case we might need it.

Jimmy, Stevie, and I, of course, knew how to use everything in this arsenal of weapons. We'd picked up a piece here or there, maybe from somebody selling one. They were often guns from robberies, stolen guns. It was never hard to get guns, since people were always wanting to sell them. And Jimmy, Stevie, and I took good care of ours, going down to our various hides once a month to clean the weapons and make sure they were functional.

Since we were criminals dealing with violent crimes, it wouldn't have done much good for one of us to have walked up to someone with a fly-swatter and said, "Give me your money." Of course, not every criminal needs a weapon to commit his crime. White-collar types like WorldCom CEO Bernard Ebbers or Andrew Fastow of Enron use a pen or a computer, not a gun, to steal someone's money. At least our weapons were easy to identify and there was nothing underhanded about our crimes. You knew when you were being robbed.

Anyhow, when George and I were through putting the duffel bags into my trunk, we went back into the house, made the connection again, and watched as the wall closed itself up. Then I drove to Stevie's mother's house in South Boston and backed the car into the driveway. In the rain, Stevie was waiting for me on the other side of the fence. I took the duffel bags out and passed them, one at a time, over the fence to Stevie, who carried each heavy bag into the screen house where he had built his own hide. The screen house was a separate building constructed in the yard with sliding glass doors that could open to let in the air while keeping out the insects. Here people could come out to relax. Ironically, it was constructed by Richie Bucchieri, the same man we shook down for $200,000 for putting a fence on my property. It had marble tiled floors, along with a bar, a kitchen, and a bathroom. The hide was in one of the walls. There were clips that attached to the interior wall, so that if you knew where to pull on the outer wall, the clips let go and the wall would open.

Around eleven, when I was through with my part of the maneuver, I said good night to Stevie and headed home. The whole deal had taken me maybe two hours from start to finish, and no one had noticed a thing.

Stevie and I also worked well together when one of us was involved in any sort of fight. For instance, one afternoon the two of us were down at the variety store when I got a call from the Fitzie—Steven Fitzpatrick, the bartender at Triple O's. Fitzie wanted to tell me that some guy named Tommy McClure was demanding I come to the bar so he could show everyone I wasn't as tough as I thought I was. He was giving the bartender a hard time, pulling money off the bar and being a complete asshole. Stevie was even more excited than I was when I told him what Fitzie had said, and he was in his car heading to Triple O's before I could get into mine. When we got to the bar, Stevie headed for the back door and I walked in the front door and stood where I usually did.

Tommy was standing in the middle of the bar, shouting to Fitzie, "I told you to get him down here." As Fitzie glanced at me, Tommy saw me. Tommy McClure was a redhead, five-eleven, maybe 190, with a medium build. I had my hands on the bar and was looking nonchalantly around the room. As Tommy turned the corner and started to approach me to say something, I lifted my hands and hit him. Tommy fell hard against the windows, where I proceeded to beat on him. In less than a minute, I had split him open and broken his ribs. This time he had showed how tough he was by hitting the floor and pissing and shitting himself as he went down.

I was still going at him when Stevie grabbed me off him. "You're going to kill him," he told me, pulling me away from the guy. That was pretty strange coming from Stevie, who would most likely have shot him in the head the minute he walked into the bar. But when Stevie let go of me, I saw the kid's face was soaked with blood, while his pants were sopping with shit and urine. Not a pretty sight any way you looked at him. But I was through with him. I saw no reason to kill him. I'd just wanted to give him a beating. And I had.

Outside the bar, a cable crew was digging up the road to lay new cable and a cop was standing near the crew. The real tough guy who had wanted so badly to fight me staggered over to the cop and tried to tell him what had happened. The cop took one look at Tommy, saw the piss and shit, figured he was drunk and, disgusted, told him to get away from him. Somehow, Tommy pulled his stinking, bloodied body away from the street.

About six hours later, I noticed that my left hand had blown up, and two red lines were moving up my left arm. I drove over to the New England Medical Center, where an emergency room doctor examined me. It only took him a few minutes to see that when I hit the tough guy a left hook, I had knocked out one of his teeth, which then pierced my finger. The doctor didn't hesitate. Explaining that I had blood poisoning from where Tommy's tooth had entered my finger, he wrapped a rubber tourniquet around my arm and rushed me into an operating room to excise and drain an abscess where the tooth had gone into the knuckle of my ring finger and infected my entire arm. I ended up staying in the hospital for three days on intravenous antibiotics. After that, I was confined to my house for another seven days with a heparin lock inserted into my hand to administer IV antibiotics three times a day. Pam took one look at me when I got home from the hospital and said, "Now, you tell me who won the fight."

Two weeks later, I walked into the liquor store to go see Bo McIntyre, a friend of mine, and immediately spotted my buddy Tommy, holding a case of beer. He handed the beer to his friend and said to me, "We have something to finish."

I nodded, hit him in the forehead with a right hand, and split him wide open. He also suffered a concussion. Bo McIntyre turned and looked at me and said, "What are these people thinking when they challenge you? Do they really think you're going to walk away? They're all nuts. What would make someone want to fight you?"

"I don't know, Bo," I said as I watched Tommy's friend carry him out of the store. This time, he was the one going to the hospital.

I happened to run into Tommy a year later and figured, "Here we go again." But he came up to me, stuck out his hand, and said, "I'm sorry. I was wrong." I shook his hand and we actually became good friends after that. You might say we had become blood brothers.

While Stevie did attempt to end that fight and save a life, most often he was joining in and trying to accelerate the bloodshed. Like the night he pulled up to the liquor store at just the right time. I'd been there with a friend named Brian Feeney when two seventeen-year-old girls, dressed in spandex pants and halter tops, came in to buy tonic and cigarettes. As they were walking in, a group of college kids from Weymouth who had just come from the Medieval Manor restaurant drove by in a car and a pickup truck. As soon as they spotted the girls, they started leaning out their windows, whistling at the young ladies. They weren't saying anything lewd, so I just ignored them and took care of the girls. But as they started to walk out, the guys became raunchy and began yelling sexual things to them.

I walked to the door and said, "Get out of here."

A couple of the guys yelled back, "Who are you?"

"I own the place," I told them.

"Well, fuck you," one of the kids told me, getting out of the car.

"Fuck me?" I asked and walked over to the car and hit him before his feet touched the sidewalk.

As he went down, the car and truck quickly emptied as his friends came to his rescue. Just at that moment, Stevie pulled up in his car and jumped out. In a flash, he had hit one kid and knocked him out cold, as Brian ran out of the store and started to fight another kid. While Stevie and Brian were at work, I hit two more and they went right out. The remaining two took off running.

A week later, thanks to two Boston cops, Bob Ryan and Joseph Lundbohm, whose relative had a problem with me, I found myself in court in Southie with my lawyer, Bill Crowe. Lundbohm had gone to the kids in Weymouth and told them I was a gangster and in organized crime, urging them to press charges to protect themselves, which they did. Four of them showed up at the courthouse, and before we went on, they told me that for $5,000 each, they would drop the charges. I told them I was filing charges against them.

Inside the courthouse, my lawyer told me if I paid $5,000 to each of the four kids and also paid for their medical charges, they'd drop the case. "I couldn't care less whether they get paid or you get paid," I told him. "But there is no way everyone is going to get paid."

"Fine," he said. "We're going to court."

When we had our hearing for probable cause, the judge listened to everyone's story. Then he turned to me and said, "Mr. Weeks, there were seven of them. How did you fight seven people?" Even though Stevie and Brian were involved, I was the only one who was charged. It was me they pointed the finger at because the liquor store was in my name.

"Your Honor, I surrounded them," I told him.

He started laughing and said, "I tell you what. I'm going to find you all guilty or else I'm going to dismiss the whole case." The kids suddenly understood that meant they would have records.

"I'm studying law and I go to USC, which is the University of

Southern California . . ." one kid started to explain to him, obviously worried that having a record would hurt a future legal career.

The judge interrupted him, saying, "I know what USC stands for, son." Then he turned to me and said, "What do you want to do, Mr. Weeks?"

"It doesn't matter to me," I said. "I work for myself, so I can't get fired." I wasn't going to be the one to end this thing. It didn't bother me one way or the other.

The judge looked at the kids and said, "Well, the choice is yours. What do you want to do?"

"We'll drop the charges," one of them said, and they all nodded in agreement.

There were numerous times, of course, when Stevie took matters into his own hands and handled the situation by himself. One afternoon Stevie was heading to the escalator at the Prudential Center when he bumped into a kid in his twenties. Stevie said, "Excuse me," and the kid said something smart to him, concluding with "Fuck you." With a crowd watching, Stevie then proceeded to beat the shit out of the kid. Right afterward, when Jimmy and I met Stevie, who was easily twice as old as the kid, he looked just fine. Not the least bit disheveled, he didn't have a scratch on him. The three of us took a ride back to the Prudential, looking for the kid and his friends. Lucky for them, we didn't find them.

A couple of other guys got off lucky, too. Especially when they got into situations they didn't expect involving the three of us. One night in February 1984, about a year after Jimmy, Stevie, and I bought the liquor store, the three of us were in the store when two black kids pulled up in their car, walked into the store, looked around, and then walked out. Once they were outside, they got into their car, turned it around so it was facing out, and bent the license plate so no one could read it. At the time, Stevie and I were talking in the front of the store and Jimmy was upstairs in the office.

When we saw what the two kids were doing, Stevie asked me if I had a pistol. I said, "Yeah, I have a forty-five on me and a forty-four Bulldog under the counter."

When I was giving the .44 to Stevie, Jimmy walked downstairs and said, "What's going on?" We told him the two black kids had come in, then turned their car around and bent the plate. He nodded and walked back up to the second floor and the office.

A few minutes later, the two kids came back in and walked down the middle aisle of the store. One of them had his hands in his coat pocket and I could see the point of a pistol pushing out of his pocket. I was standing next to the counter and Stevie was by the door. Both of us had our pistols behind our backs.

When the two kids came up front, they looked at us and I pulled the hammer back on the pistol behind my back. At the same time, upstairs, Jimmy slid open the sliding glass window, which was a two-way mirror, and stuck the mini-Ruger 14, with a thirty-round clip in it, out the window. A few seconds later, he snapped the bolt and was looking down the barrel at the kids. When they turned around, they looked up at the gun pointing out the window, right at the two of them. Then they looked at me and Stevie, who was starting to laugh. Finally, they looked at each other and one of them said, "I guess we be going," and without another word, they were out the door, in their car, and driving away.

Jimmy came down and the three of us were laughing about the whole scene. When we started talking about it, I said, "How would I have explained this since the three weapons were all registered to me? I mean, they got shot from the right with the forty-five, from the left with the forty-four, and from above with the mini Ruger."

"You were fast," Jimmy said. "Real fast."

Right up until the last time I ever saw Stevie, I never knew exactly what was going on in his mind. Smart, fearless, good-natured, funny, violent, dangerous—he was all of those things. But there was a piece to the puzzle that was Stevie that I didn't fit into the whole picture until the spring of 1997, when I learned about his real relationship with the FBI. Then he became a bit clearer. Or as clear as Stevie Flemmi could ever be to another person.

SEVEN
DRUGS
1980–1990

One afternoon in 1980, I was in the Broadway Appliance and Furniture store with Jimmy and Kevin O'Neil when Billy Shea and Freddie Weichel came in to talk to Jimmy. Billy, who was in his forties, had done time in Norfolk, a state prison in Massachusetts, and other state prisons for armed robbery. Now that he was out of prison, he was looking to figure out a way to make money. As for Freddie, he had a reputation around South Boston as being dangerous. That day, the two of them approached Jimmy in the front of the store to ask if it was all right if they started grabbing all the marijuana dealers in town and putting them in line. From then on, wherever these dealers might be buying marijuana, they would be working for the two of them. Whatever Jimmy wanted out of the business he could have. Jimmy told Billy and Freddie to go ahead and see what they could do. Up till then, it had been small-time people, nickel-and-dime bag sellers, handling things. This was the first time that someone wanted to control all these dealers.

Right away, Billy and Freddie started grabbing marijuana dealers, putting them in line, and taking them over. From that time on, if they were working in South Boston and were selling drugs, they were taken over by Billy and Freddie. Since I hadn't been around during the gang wars of the 1960s and 1970s, all I really knew about Jimmy and the Mafia was that they coexisted. Now drug dealers would have to buy their marijuana from Billy and Freddie, who would be giving Jimmy a large percentage of their profits. No longer would there be any independent drug dealers, just the way there were no independent bookmakers or shylocks. Every once in a while, someone would pop up and go into business for himself, but eventually he would be grabbed.

Billy and Freddie had only been in business a matter of months when Freddie got pinched for a murder he didn't commit. Once Freddie was gone, Billy Shea went back to Jimmy and asked him if I could go around with him to put all these people in line, to make them buy their product off him. When Jimmy asked me if I was interested, I told him I didn't want anything to do with it. I just knew I didn't want to deal with certain people. Jimmy's response was, "Good, 'cause I don't want you involved with it."

Shortly afterward, Billy Shea enlisted Paul Moore as the muscle to go around with him to grab more drug dealers and control a larger portion of the marijuana business. There were few people who could stand up to Moore, one of the toughest kids in town, in a fight. Moore and Billy had only been working together a short time when they happened upon Joe Towers, a marijuana dealer in Southie, who introduced them and their associates to cocaine. Once Towers showed them about cocaine, how to step on it, putting in additives to increase the volume and make more profit, the cocaine business in South Boston really took off. Before then, cocaine had been around, but never on such a large scale as this.

It didn't take long for Billy Shea's network to increase. As he was moving more product, he had more people working for him; as he made more money, Jimmy made more money. In the beginning, they were moving between 7 to 10 kilos of cocaine a week. At the time, the street price was probably between $28,000 and $32,000 a kilo, depending on the purity of the kilo. By the time the person on the street got it, the coke had been stepped on four or five times, diluting it with the powdery substance nasitol, which was a diuretic, then pressed back together because people would want it in rock form. Next it was sold to the drug dealers, who would sell it to their street dealers, who would ultimately sell it to the people on the street.

However, things changed in 1986, when Billy Shea started to spend more time in Florida and pay less attention to business, which resulted in money being misappropriated. One afternoon in 1987, Jimmy and I were driving down D Street when we saw Billy in the D Street projects. Jimmy got out of the car to talk to him while I stood off to the side. Basically, Jimmy told Billy that Billy wouldn't be involved anymore, that he was out of business and that his associates would be taking over. It was a short one-way conversation, since Jimmy had already made up his mind.

Right away, Shea's associates took over and had their people working on the street. The midlevel dealers each paid us a flat monthly fee, somewhere between $1,500 and $1,800 a month depending on the size of their business. Some of the distrbutors, like Shea's partners were paying $5,000 a week. What they were paying for was the right to be in business in different areas of the city. Shea's people shook down drug dealers of various degrees all over New England. Some had been bringing in their drugs by the boatload and would now be paying Jimmy in order to continue doing this. None of them had a choice in the matter. If they didn't pay, he would kill them. They couldn't go to the law, so what else could they do but pay?

There was no change in the origin of the cocaine, which came from different states in different manners. Billy Shea's organization had connections all over the place and often sent people down to Florida to bring it up here by car, truck, or van. The big people, the principals who were allowed to sell the cocaine to the dealers, were making good money. Many different groups were involved, and how much each group or individual made depended on how much effort they put into it. Some people were certainly making millions.

Jimmy, Stevie, and I weren't in the import business and weren't bringing in the marijuana or the cocaine. We were in the shakedown business. We didn't bring drugs in; we took money off the people who did. We never dealt with the street dealers, but rather with a dozen large-scale drug distributors all over the state who were bringing in the coke and marijuana and paying hundreds of thousands to Jimmy. The dealers on the street corners sold eight-balls (the street name for approximately three and a half grams), grams, and half-grams to customers for their personal use. They were supplied by the midlevel drug dealer who was selling them multiple ounces. In other words, the big importers gave it to the major distributors, who sold it to the middlemen, who then sold it to the street dealers. In order to get to Jimmy, Stevie, and me, someone would have to go through those four layers of insulation. While street corner dealers often used drugs, the bigger dealers rarely used their own product.

Marijuana was still a lucrative business, as dealers continued to pay us hundreds of thousands of dollars, sometimes millions. I picked up money from the people who were paying us, either midlevel drug dealers or large-scale importers, depending on how big their business was. Some I went to. Others came to me. I always knew who was supposed to pay me and saw them once a month to get the money off them. If they didn't pay, they were out of business. But that never happened. No one refused to pay us. Once we got it, Jimmy, Stevie, and I chopped up the money.

The marijuana was sold in many other towns across the state. Joe

Murray was the big Charlestown dealer. Mike Caruana, a North Shore dealer from the early 1980s, made so much money off marijuana that he bought gold and was considering minting gold coins with his own likeness on them. One day, however, he turned up missing and was never found. I don't know what happened to him, but he was involved with the Mafia, as well as with Jimmy and Stevie. Only the people who were involved in his disappearance know what happened. Another big-time marijuana dealer was Frank Lepere, from Marshfield, who was paying us millions. And making still more. Some dealers sold both cocaine and marijuana, while others just handled one or the other.

Understandably, collecting involved shakedowns, some of which began in the least likely places. One day Jimmy and I were heading into the Best Chevrolet dealership on Commonwealth Avenue when Mickey G. walked out of a bar across the street. Mickey was a sort of rogue on the fringe of things whom Jimmy had known years earlier. Mickey asked Jimmy what was up and then mentioned that he was heading to get 35 pounds of pot from a high school teacher. In a few minutes, Jimmy had arranged it so that Mickey would bring the guy down to J. C. Hilary's, a restaurant in Dedham, the next day.

When Jimmy, Stevie, and I got to the restaurant, the place was packed with the lunch crowd, but Mickey and the teacher were already sitting in a booth. Jimmy sat down next to the teacher, pinning him in the corner so he couldn't go anywhere. He was wearing glasses and khaki pants and looked like a typical teacher. As I sat down on the opposite side of the table, I opened my coat so the teacher could see the pistol. Jimmy introduced the three of us, and by the time we left the restaurant, the teacher had promised us $100,000. Two hours later, he handed the money to Mickey to give to us. It was a one-shot deal for us. As for the teacher, after that lunch, he got out of the drug business. Real quick.

Another shakedown, in 1988, involved John "Red" Shea (no relation to Billy Shea), who we heard had made a few disparaging remarks about Jimmy and me. When that information got back to us, Jimmy was upset, and since Red was in the drug business, we decided he would have to pay us from then on. We also decided that if he didn't do what we asked him to do, we were going to kill him.

So we had him come down to 309–325 Old Colony Avenue, the end building near a block of stores. Jimmy and Stevie stayed upstairs while we had Red brought down to the cellar of the building. As soon as Red got into the basement, I pulled a machine gun on him and explained what we wanted. It didn't take long to figure out an agreement where he would pay us an amount somewhere between $1,500 and $1,800 each month, depending on his business.

Red was an agreeable and pleasant person, especially when he turned out to be a standup kid in 1990, going to jail for eleven years in the raid that netted fifty-one of our drug dealers. Rather than rat us out, he took it on the chin. If he had known the true story about Jimmy and Stevie, I wouldn't have blamed him if he had given us up then. But he didn't know a thing about it, even in jail, where he got into a lot of fights defending Jimmy. Of all the drug dealers we dealt with, I liked Red Shea the best. He was a tough kid and very honorable—his word was his bond. Although he was never in the inner circle with Jimmy, Stevie, and me, he was a person I would have trusted. I wouldn't say that about a lot of people.

Another shakedown involving a likable person took place one afternoon when I was driving down Dorchester Street and had a chance meeting with a kid from South Boston who was selling cocaine. I knew the kid, who was in his mid-twenties and will remain nameless, from around town and when he used to box. That day, I waved him over and we had a five-minute conversation, during which I shook him down for $12,000. An hour later, I had the money and he was allowed to do his own thing. The kid was basically a street dealer, not large-scale, but he'd been in business a long time. We never bothered him again. Normally people would have paid monthly, but because I did like the kid, it was just a one-time thing. I felt bad about shaking him down, but no one could deal without paying.

Not every drug extortion, however, put money in my pocket. Like the one in 1981 involving an antiques dealer, David Lindholm, who was dealing drugs off the islands of the Cape. The guy was smuggling 1,000 pounds of marijuana a month into Nantucket when Jimmy found out about his little business. Jimmy had someone walk Lindholm into the Marconi Club on Shetland Street in Roxbury, where Stevie was based. Jimmy, Stevie, and I were upstairs in the hall when two guys walked Lindholm in. The guy was a yuppie, average-looking, somewhere around thirty-five, medium build, around five-nine, with wire-rimmed glasses and brown hair, wearing corduroy pants and a sweater.

We had Lindholm stand on a chair while I frisked him to make sure he wasn't wired and didn't have a gun. The guy was shaking with fear while he stood on the chair and Jimmy introduced all of us to him, asking him if he knew who we were. "Yeah," he said softly as Jimmy started laying into him for the marijuana business. He was using his regular voice, going over how the guy wasn't paying anyone and wasn't with anyone, telling him how he had to be with someone so he should be with us.

The guy somehow mistook Jimmy's words as a request, so he answered that he was going to continue not to be with anyone. Jimmy's mood and voice changed real quick. "I'm not asking," he told Lindholm. "I'm telling you."

But the guy repeated that he wanted to continue by himself. He had barely finished saying those words when Stevie hit him with a body shot. He doubled over and fell off the chair, but I grabbed him and picked him up before he hit the ground. As I held him up and sat him back in the chair, Jimmy pulled out a pistol with a silencer on it. I was pretty sure we were trying to shake him down for money, so we wouldn't kill him, and that the pistol was just to emphasize the point that he needed to pay us. The guy perceived no such assurance, so he immediately agreed.

A week later, Jimmy and Stevie told me nothing came out of that extortion, that the law had got wind of it so they had backed away. I had no reason to doubt them, but years later when I got arrested and charged with that particular extortion, I found out that Jimmy and Stevie had actually collected about $1,600,000 from Lindholm in a matter of months. I was a little mad when I found that out and even angrier when I learned that the same thing had happened a few other times. After all, I had put just as much ass on the line as they had and they hadn't given the money to me. But by then everything had changed between the three of us, so in some small way, we were all even.

The only people we ever put out of business were the heroin dealers. Jimmy didn't allow heroin in South Boston. It was a dirty drug that users stuck in their arms, making problems with needles and, later on, AIDS. While people can do cocaine socially and still function, once they do heroin, they're zombies.

From the very beginning, there were serious attempts by law enforcement to get us on drug trafficking charges. One of their biggest efforts had been Operation Beans in 1985. This DEA operation actually began one afternoon in the spring of 1983. That particular day, Jimmy and I had been driving down West Broadway by the D Street projects when a fellow named Ronnie Costello waved us over. Ronnie, who was on the scene and knew a lot of people, happened to be working construction in the D Street projects, putting windows in the buildings and generally refurbishing them. That day, he told Jimmy and me that something big was going on at D and First streets, that all kinds of law enforcement were there. Ronnie got in the back seat of the car, behind me, and the three of us drove down D Street toward First Street, pulling up about a block and half away, where we used binoculars to watch what was going on. All kinds of law, the FBI and DEA, were everywhere, the agents wearing their windbreakers identifying their agencies with big letters across the back. We were there for about five minutes when Jimmy said, "Let's get out of here before someone spots us and thinks we had something to do with this."

As it turned out, we later discovered, the marijuana in the warehouse that had attracted the law belonged to Joe Murray, a large-scale Charlestown marijuana dealer. When Jimmy found out that Murray had been storing his marijuana there, he reached out and had someone bring Murray in for a meeting. At the meeting, he fined Murray $90,000 for storing the marijuana in Southie and putting the heat on us. That was our introduction to Joe Murray, with whom we later became involved in the effort to ship arms to Ireland on the *Valhalla*. Our relationship with this particular drug dealer ended years later when he decided to pack it in. When Murray finally chose to go his own way, we shook him down for $500,000. While no one ever volunteered to pay when they were packing it in, we considered that money their severance pay . . . to us.

Ironically, after he left the business, Joe Murray got killed by his wife, or at least that's who they say shot him. In September 1992, a week before he was killed, Murray had come to Jimmy, Stevie, and me and asked to meet us at Thomas Park, a spot called the Heights by people in South Boston. Here he offered us money to kill his wife and his brother-in-law. Apparently his wife had found out Joe had been cooperating with law enforcement. He was afraid she was going to tell people and he would be outed as an informant.

Before that happened, he was trying to get her killed. We settled on a price of $1 million dollars, $500,000 up front and $500,000 afterward. But Joe decided the price was too steep, and, a week later he went up to his cottage in Belgrade Lakes, Maine, where his wife was. It was reported that he attacked her with a knife but she shot him, supposedly five times with a .357 Magnum, killing him. Too bad he hadn't accepted our price.

The truth of the matter is, Murray had no one with him. While Jimmy, Stevie, and I had a gang, Murray was alone. All along, he had been paying us to be his protection.

Actually, even if he had given us the $500,000 up front to take care of his wife and brother-in-law, we had already decided we weren't going to do anything. And there was nothing Murray could have done about that. But if he'd taken our deal, he would have still been alive because he would have thought we were doing something. Then he would have not left for Maine by himself to take care of his wife. He saved the money, but he paid the price.

But that spring afternoon in 1983, while we were turning the car around, Bobby Darling, a detective with the Boston police, drove by and spotted us. We returned to where we had picked up Ronnie, dropped him off, and proceeded up West Broadway, taking a right on D Street away from First Street toward Fourth Street, then taking a left on Fifth Street. As we were heading up Fifth Street, between F and Dorchester, we could see that Bobby Darling was following us. Jimmy stopped the car and pulled over. Bobby Darling pulled up and said to Jimmy, "Whitey, who was in the car with you? Who was the other fellow?"

Jimmy said, "You're asking me who was in my car with me? Get the fuck out of here." With that, we drove away.

About a week later, we heard that Darling had filed an FIO, a Field Intelligence Observation report, in which he stated that James "Whitey" Bulger, Stephen "the Rifleman" Flemmi, and Joseph Murray, the drug supplier from Charlestown, were observed together, watching the raid from a safe distance. He had lied. He knew who was in our car that day. He had looked right at me and said hi. He knew it was me and Jimmy, but had lied and put in that Flemmi and Murray were in the car.

One afternoon, two weeks later, Jimmy caught Darling out by his condo in Louisburg Square. Jimmy jumped into his car, chased him down, cut him off, and said, "You dirty dog coward motherfucker. You put in that phony FIO report. You lied. You just stepped over the line. If I ever see you round me again, I'll cut your fucking head off."

Darling, who was shaken up, went to Boston Police headquarters and reported the incident. Their reply to him was, "What were you doing over there? That is out of our jurisdiction." When he repeated Jimmy's exact words to him, his commander said, "If I were you, I'd stay away from him." He ended up giving Darling two weeks vacation time.

However, because of that one phony FIO, which was all lies from Darling, who knew exactly who was in the car, a major investigation on us began, an investigation resulting in Operation Beans, which was a play on Boston's nickname, Beantown. Operation Beans, a DEA plan targeting Jimmy, Stevie, and me in an attempt to accumulate evidence to arrest us for drug trafficking, eventually fell flat on its face.

But it didn't take Jimmy and me long to realize exactly what was going on. One afternoon, I was looking out of the variety store when I saw a guy standing around the Old Colony projects, smoking a ten-inch-long cigar. Since I grew up in those projects, I basically knew everyone there. And I knew he wasn't from around there. So I got out the binoculars and studied the guy and another man who was with him. A short time later Jimmy came in, and when I told him what I'd noticed, we both stood there, staring at the guy smoking the cigar and his friend. Over the course of time, we kept seeing the same two people driving by and watching us, along with some additional surveillance on us.

Soon Jimmy started hearing from law enforcement that there was indeed an investigation on us. In the meantime, in the fall of 1984, the *Valhalla* had gotten grabbed, McIntyre had gotten grabbed and disappeared, and the investigations for those events had turned flat. So now the DEA had come in and decided they were going to get us for drug trafficking.

As soon as we started noticing the extra surveillance, I made several trips to a specialty store at 633 Third Avenue in New York to buy some new bug-sweeping equipment. Once I got the new equipment, I used it frequently to sweep both Jimmy's car and his condo at Louisburg Square in Quincy. In both places, I kept getting high readings. In his condo, the readings were by the bow window, yet we couldn't pinpoint the spots. Jimmy thought the law was aiming a laser at the windows to pick up sounds inside, but we couldn't find anything to indicate that that might be the case.

In February 1985, at around four o'clock in the morning, Jimmy and Cathy came out of his condo to go for a walk. They frequently went for walks at that hour. The first thing Jimmy saw as he started to walk out of his front door were two guys in overalls coming around the corner. Immediately, Jimmy ran back into the condo and grabbed his car keys and he and Cathy drove off after the guys. One of the men took off, running into the unit at Louisburg Square that overlooked Jimmy's unit. The other one jumped into a car and bent down under the seat, but his foot hit the brake light. Jimmy pulled up next to the car but couldn't get a look at the guy's face. That was a big tipoff that something was going on concerning his house and car.

A week or so later, I was scheduled for surgery to remove a broken disc in my neck. Over the years, from sports and boxing, the disc in my neck had been deteriorating. Finally, it had broken off and was cutting into my spinal cord, causing me a lot of discomfort and making my left arm go numb. The day before I went into the hospital, I swept the car and got an especially high reading. When I got out of the hospital, I swept the car again and got another high reading. Certain something was going on with Jimmy's Chevy, I took it down to the mechanic on a Friday and showed him where the reading was coming from. After he checked things over, he said the high reading was caused by the car's computer brain, which was sending out a signal that we were picking up.

Monday, I met Jimmy and told him, "I don't like it. There is something in this car. I'm sure of it." This time, when we went back to the mechanic's garage, we were able to figure out that the high reading was coming from the passenger door. After closer inspection, I discovered a small wire hanging down from the lining on the door. When I pulled the lining away from the door, a microphone fell down. Then I saw that the microphone was attached to a piece of a coat hanger that was bent so it could hook onto a bar inside the car door to hold it in place.

Jimmy picked up the microphone and said, "One, two, three testing," and with that about four cars rolled into the garage and agents jumped out with their guns drawn. One of the agents was Steve Boeri, another was Al Reilly, and two others were New York DEA agents. When the agents appeared with drawn guns, I was standing by the car. "Kevin, get away from the car," one of the agents kept insisting. But I wouldn't move because I was holding the piece of equipment I'd used to find the bug and I didn't want the agent to see exactly what equipment I had. "Take your hand out of your pocket," the agent kept telling me, and I kept telling him to go fuck himself.

Finally, after a few more minutes of the agent trying to get me to take my hand out of my pocket, I asked, "Am I under arrest?"

When he said no, I told him, "Go fuck yourself." His next move was to walk up to me, stick a .357 Magnum in my chest, and shove me in the shoulder in an attempt to push me away from the car. Immediately, I shoved him back, and then everybody in the garage became tense, certain there was going to be a problem.

Finally, Boeri turned to Jimmy and said, "Ask Kevin to come over here."

"Kevin, come on over here," Jimmy said.

"Okay," I said, and walked over there while the other agent stood there silently, bullshit because I wasn't intimidated by him and his gun, and because Jimmy had spoken a few words and I had done what he had said.

A couple of other agents went into Jimmy's car and pulled out their transmitter and battery pack. "We know what you're doing," one agent told Jimmy.

"You know nothing," Jimmy told him.

"We know what we know," the agent said.

"You don't got a thing," Jimmy said. With that, all four agents took off. As soon as they were gone, Jimmy and I hopped into the car and shot over to Louisburg Square. When we got to Jimmy's condo, which was three levels, we could see that the plywood beneath the bow window on the first floor had been pulled down. It was obvious that the agents had originally drilled through the side of the window and inserted the microphone from the outside, managing to place their transmitter and battery pack underneath the bow window. But now the transmitter was gone. They had retrieved all their equipment.

Unfortunately, however, an innocent bystander suffered because of the garage scene. The elderly father-in-law of the owner of the garage, who was in his late eighties or early nineties, was there when the agents ran in with their guns drawn. Immediately, they stuck a gun on the owner of the garage, as well as on Jimmy and me, and also shoved the barrel of a gun under the armpit of this old man.

"Leave the old man alone," Jimmy told the agents. "He has nothing to do with anything." But they kept the gun on him. Badly shaken up, as soon as the agents left, the old man went into the hospital, where he suffered a heart attack. Two or three days later, he died. There was no doubt, for his family or for Jimmy and me, that this old man, no physical threat to anyone, had died because of the shock of someone shoving the barrel of a gun up his armpit.

The day after the incident, Jimmy and I were still trying to figure out how anyone had gotten into his car. We knew there were three alarms in the car, one of them a pressure sensor, so that if anyone got in the car, the weight alarm would go off. There was also another pressure sensor under the mats, and the windows and doors were protected with a regular car alarm. Yet, somehow, someone had bypassed all three alarms and never set one of them off. How had they been able to put that bug in the car?

Suddenly, as I was looking at the outside panel on the passenger side,

I thought that maybe it looked a bit off-center. When I pulled it off the bottom of the passenger door, I studied the 8-inch-wide molding that ran around the side. I took it off and, sure enough, there was a hole gaping through the door. The door panel had been wired with copper wiring, which they had obviously used for their antenna. They must have used a hand drill to cut a hole into the outside of the door and then inserted tin snips to make the hole big enough to hold their equipment. That night in February when Jimmy had caught them coming from his car, they must have been trying to change the batteries in their equipment. Since it was so cold out, it would have been necessary to change the batteries every twelve to twenty-four hours.

After all this happened and they removed their equipment, Boeri and Reilly spoke to Jimmy about the people whose condo at Louisburg Square they had rented in order to insert the bugs. "They didn't know anything about what we were doing," the agents told Jimmy. "Please don't hurt them."

"I don't hold them responsible for anything," Jimmy told the agents. "And, besides, you didn't get anything." The agents hung around another two or three weeks and then they left. They knew that we were on our guard and that they weren't going to get anything from us.

All in all, the agents had spent at least six months observing us and trying to get down our movements and our schedules. But we had seen them from the very beginning of their operation. They had thought they were watching us, but we had been watching them. Inept at covert observation, the DEA agents had stuck out like sore thumbs. Jimmy and I couldn't help noticing all the cars driving by the variety store or following us wherever we went. When they were in a car that circled around the rotary three or four times, their faces stood out. When they were in the park with binoculars and we were looking back at them with our binoculars, they stood out. Plus, it was obvious to us from the beginning that these people weren't from the town. Agent Reilly had been the smartest one of all of them, somehow managing not to appear as obvious as the rest. Plus, he had spent time developing an effective plan on how to put the bugs in the car. The problem with his plan was that, unable to use a power source, he'd had to use batteries, which had to be constantly replaced.

But it wouldn't have mattered what the agents had used. The cold fact was that we never talked in buildings or cars or on phones, so nothing could have come of their efforts. Unlike the way the media reported it, the true story of Operation Beans was not that we had been tipped off about it, but rather that the agents had been obvious and we had been aware. Yes, they had succeeded in bugging the apartment and the car, but we never said a word about business in either of those two places, so the bugs did them no good. Jimmy and I always talked outside, never in any enclosed place. No matter how important something was that we had to tell each other, it could wait until we were able to take a walk or go to a place we considered secure. The agents had taken everything into account, except for the discipline, the one issue about which Jimmy never, ever let up. Not then. And, assuming he's still out there somewhere, not now.

Still, the law eventually got to a lot of those involved in the drug traffic. As a result, some guys just packed it in, while others went to prison. In August 1990, the Southie drug bust, a joint effort by the DEA and the Boston police that netted fifty-one drug dealers in South Boston, basically stopped Jimmy's drug business. They got these guys on charges through wiretaps or photographs, along with the confiscation of drugs and records. But this raid and the previous ones did not yield the large-scale information the DEA had hoped for. Everyone had been aware of the ongoing DEA operations for months. We'd watch or hear about the DEA raiding houses, businesses, and garages, trying to build their case, searching for records, products, and anything else they could find. In some instances, they did get records, although never the quantities they expected. One day they even raided the variety store. I was there as they hauled off my computer, where they were certain I kept records of all the drug transactions. But all that was on the computer were records for the videos we rented or sold. Nothing having to do with the drug trafficking business was on that computer or written down anywhere else. That was all in my head.

They tried many more times to bug Jimmy's car, but, as always, they failed to get what they wanted. Knowing they were always trying to do that, I used to make a tiny cut with a razor on the dashboard and on the sun visor. It would drive Jimmy crazy when I did that, but once I saw the dashboard didn't have my slash or if I couldn't see the little white insulation through the blue covering on the visor, I'd know that it had been replaced and had a bug. But I didn't bother to get rid of it. Like I said, we never talked in the car anyhow.

In January 1990, eight months before the fifty-one arrests and indictments came down, the DEA agents were running around South Boston making drug raids. Jimmy and I were driving in the Ford LTD on West Fourth Street when the agents surrounded our car. "Kevin, Whitey," they said, as they approached our car. "We have to retrieve some of our equipment."

I said, "What? The visor?"

They looked at me for a minute and then used a Phillips screwdriver to take the three screws out of the visor and took it with them. Afterward, Jimmy and I drove away and laughed. We knew they got nothing.

But the presence of the law all over the neighborhood and their frequent raids had slowed the business down well before the August 1990 bust. By that time, just about everyone had packed it in and stopped dealing, and drug users were traveling out of town to get their drugs. While there was always someone to pick up the business, it was nowhere near so large a scale as before.

The Southie drug bust itself involved three separate groups: the Paul Moore group, the Red Shea group, and the Hobart Willis group. In

1987, Billy Shea had packed it in, so they didn't get him. But the DEA made the 1990 raids early one morning and continued into the next day, looking for people. They got the majority of them that first morning, and arrested the rest of the three groups the next day. Jimmy, Stevie, and I were the only ones they didn't get. Because we knew the raids were coming down, I used to sleep with a police scanner, tuned into my DEA channel, by the side of my bed. A short time earlier, I'd sent away for some books and papers explaining how to get a list of government channels and had figured out how to punch in the numbers from one frequency to the next. Eventually, I'd been able to figure out what channel was the FBI, the DEA, and so on. Then I'd plugged the channels into the scanner and had them available whenever I needed them. Today, with the evolution of cell phones, people talk more on their cell phones than on the scanner, but at that time, I relied on my scanner.

And sure enough, the day of the raid, at 4:00 A.M., I was woken up by the words, "Good morning, gentlemen. It is now our turn." I could hear the team they had assembled for the raid talking to one another. I jumped out of bed, got dressed, and called Jimmy. A few minutes later, he picked me up and we drove over to the Boston Common. Here we sat on a park bench, listening to the radio and how all the raids and arrests went down, looking over at the bridge where the water is, at the spot where they'd later film a scene from *Good Will Hunting*. At noon, Jimmy made a call and we got word they weren't looking for us, so we went back home.

We didn't know 80 percent of the people who were arrested, for most of them didn't work for us, but rather for the people who were paying us. Some of the dealers were held in jail, while others were released on bail, or got time or probation or house confinement. Hobart Willis got seventeen years. Paul Moore got nine. Jackie Cherry originally got nine years, but they brought him up in front of a grand jury and gave him immunity. When he refused to testify, they gave him an additional eighteen months dead time for contempt. Red Shea ended up with eleven years. But they couldn't get to Jimmy. He was too well-insulated.

Of course, Jimmy lost money once the drug dealers were removed from the streets in the summer raid, but he always had other businesses going on. Knowing I had to build something on the side, I had concentrated on my shylocking and gambling businesses. The drug business had been good while it lasted. But our major involvement with it was over.

EIGHT
JIMMY
TEN MORE MURDERS

Some people might perceive these murders as more evidence of Jimmy's darker side; others would look at them as Jimmy doing the right or only possible thing. Most of the time, it was just plain business: sometimes as payback for informing the FBI, other times to protect business interests; and, finally, just because he didn't like the person. Even though I wasn't around or involved in any of these murders, Jimmy told me about each one at one time or another.

Whatever the reason for the murder, Jimmy had no problem with the execution. His unique streak of violence, which had started when he was a kid, was simply part of his nature. He could stab people, shoot them, beat them with his bare hands or anything lying around, strangle them, hit them with his car, do whatever suited his purpose to inflict harm on someone he felt deserved it.

Paulie McGonigle was one of the victims Jimmy simply didn't like, probably because he'd been with the Mullins gang, on the other side against Jimmy. Paulie's was one of the many deaths that involved unsettled old scores from the gang wars. Jimmy had missed the early part of the gang wars of the 1960s in which eighty-two people died, but when he came out of prison in 1965, he aligned himself with the Killeens and Billy O'Sullivan and some other people from his past, against the Mullins gang with Tommy King, Jimmy Mantville, and Paulie McGonigle, among others. Unlike the McLaughlins and Winter Hill gangs, which were citywide and had players from all over the city, the Killeens and Mullins were South Boston gangs, and their battles from the mid-1960s to the early 1970s were basically a South Boston turf war.

The gang war between the Mullins and the Killeens erupted full-scale after a fight between Mickey Dwyer and Kenny Killeen in 1969. It was a barroom fight, and while Mickey was a boxer, Kenny was more of a barroom brawler. During the fight in the Transit Café in Southie, Kenny bit off part of Mickey's nose. They were able to sew the nose back on, leaving Mickey with a scar on his nose, but that fight brought everything to a head between the two gangs.

Actually, when the fighting really started heating up, Kenny never came out of his house. Even though he was one of the reasons it started, he never wanted any part of the shooting. One night, however, while Kenny was sitting on the porch of his house near Columbia Road and Eighth Street, he was shot at with a rifle. The bullet hit the railing and fragmented, but Kenny got away that time. For the rest of his life, until he died of natural causes in the early 2000s, Kenny Killeen never left his house unless he was accompanied by his wife or a kid. His brother Donnie Killeen had been killed in 1972, but it was yet another lie that Jimmy did the job. Jimmy Mantville and another fellow did it.

Before peace was made between Jimmy and the Mullins gang and they combined forces, two of the Mullins were in a car when they spotted Jimmy driving in South Boston. As they chased after him on East Second and N streets, he jumped out of the passenger side of the car, where he started shooting at the guys across the hood of his car with an AR-15 assault rifle. One of the Mullins, Jerry Roake, who only had a .25-caliber pistol, had a lot of balls and shot back. But Jimmy hit him in the hand, and the bullet traveled up his arm and came out his elbow, completely mangling his arm. After a few minutes, the other guy took off and Jimmy got back in his car and got out of there, too. This was just one instance of these guys trying to kill each other.

Killing Paulie McGonigle, however, took Jimmy longer than he originally expected. Paulie talked a big game, but he wasn't a shooter. Although he never did anything, he kept on stirring everything up with his mouth. So Jimmy decided to kill him. One day, while the gang war was still going on, Jimmy was driving down Seventh Street in South Boston when he saw Paulie driving toward him. Jimmy pulled up beside him, window to window, nose to nose, and called his name. As Paulie looked over, Jimmy shot him right between the eyes. Only at that moment, just as he pulled the trigger, Jimmy realized it wasn't Paulie. It was Donald, the most likable of the three McGonigle brothers, the only one who wasn't involved in anything.

Jimmy drove right over to Billy O'Sullivan's house on Savin Hill Avenue and told Billy O, who was at the stove cooking, "I shot the wrong one. I shot Donald."

Billy looked up from the stove and said, "Don't worry about it. He wasn't healthy anyway. He smoked. He would have gotten lung cancer. How do you want your pork chops?"

I had my own meeting with Paulie McGonigle in June 1974, the day after I graduated from high school. On graduation night, when Bobby Cox, Mikey Raymond, and I threw our big graduation party in the three-decker house we'd moved into for the summer, the 300 kids who showed up scattered around, inside and outside the house, drinking and making lots of noise.

The next morning, around noontime, I was in the back room sleeping when there was a knock on the door. I woke up to hear some yelling at the door. Quickly putting on my pants, I went to the door and saw a small guy threatening my friends. Unlike Jimmy, this guy didn't have the presence of a gangster. Maybe five-eight, he had his hair combed all over to try and cover his balding head and was wearing a silk shirt that opened to his sternum, as well as a gold necklace, platform shoes, and black flared pants. And he was chewing gum. I was eighteen at the time and had no idea who he was, but he looked like something out of Studio 54. The guy was yelling about the party and a friend of his whose grandmother lived nearby. "I'll punch your fucking heads in," he kept repeating. "I'll cut you up and take you all out of here in a garbage bag." I made it clear that I would have no problem punching *his* fucking head in and taking *him* out of there in a garbage bag. With that, he took off.

Forty-five minutes later, there was another knock at the door. When I opened the door this time, I saw Jimmy standing there with two other guys, Pat Nee and Jack Curran, and the same gum-chewing guy from Studio 54. Jimmy looked at me and said, "Do you know who I am?"

"Yeah, I know who you are," I said.

"And you're going to punch this guy out and put him in a garbage bag?" he asked, pointing to Paulie.

"That's not what happened," I said. "He came up here and no one knows who he is. But he's telling us he's going to cut us up and take us out in garbage bags, so I told him I'd punch him out and put him in a garbage bag."

I could see Pat Nee and Jack Curran standing behind Paulie, laughing and shaking their heads. "No more parties here," Jimmy finally said.

"You got it," I said. "It was just a one-time graduation party." Jimmy looked at Paulie and shook his head. And the four of them left.

Five months later, on a November night, Jimmy took care of the right brother. He got Paulie in the car with Tommy King and shot Paulie in the head. Paulie was buried over at Tenean Beach. Less than a year later, Jimmy killed Tommy because they'd had words at Triple O's. The same night Jimmy killed Tommy, he also killed Tommy's friend Buddy Leonard, hoping to confuse the authorities about Tommy's murder.

Before he was killed, Tommy King had threatened a Boston police detective that he was going to kill him. Knowing Tommy's violent reputation and that he was a capable guy, the detective was afraid of him. Jimmy met with the detective, who was a tenacious investigator, and promised to talk to Tommy and make him listen to reason. If Tommy wouldn't listen to him, Jimmy said, he would put himself between Tommy and the detective to defuse the situation and make sure no harm came to the detective. About a week later, Jimmy informed the detective that he no longer had a problem. He told him Tommy hadn't listened to him, but he didn't have to worry about anything, that Tommy would no longer bother him.

The truth was that even though Tommy King had made the threats, when Jimmy met with the detective, Tommy had already been dead for two weeks. Jimmy had ended up using Tommy's death as leverage with this detective. He'd become friends with him by letting him think Tommy was gone on his behalf. It was just another case of Jimmy's Machiavellian side, turning a potentially bad situation to his advantage.

Billy O'Sullivan's death might not have happened if he had listened to Jimmy. Billy O had been with Jimmy against the Mullins and had shot Buddy Roache during the gang war. Buddy, whose brother Mickey later became Boston's police commissioner, ended up crippled and in a wheelchair. In March 1971, not too long after he shot the wrong McGonigle, Jimmy went to New York to pick up guns. Before he left, he told Billy to be careful while he was gone and not to drink. But that night, Billy hung around with Kevin O'Neil down at the Transit Café and ended up drunk. Kevin offered him a ride home, but Billy refused the offer. Heading home, he was chased by a couple of men with the Mullins gang who caught up with him when he tripped on a manhole cover about 200 yards from his house and fell down. While he was lying there, his pursuers shot him to death. If Kevin O'Neil had ended up driving Billy O'Sullivan home that night, he probably would have been killed, too.

The reason for Richie Castucci's murder five years later wasn't any more difficult to understand. A bookmaker, Castucci had been cooperating with the FBI about the Winter Hill gang and bookmaking, shakedowns, and murder. He was also giving information as to the whereabouts of certain members of Winter Hill who were on the lam. Once FBI agent John Connolly informed Jimmy about Castucci's cooperation, Winter Hill put in a bunch of bets with the bookmaker. If they lost, Castucci wasn't getting his money because they were going to kill him. If they won, they would collect the money off Castucci and still kill him. As it was, they lost the bets. A meeting was set up for Castucci to come over and collect the money. When Castucci came over to meet Jimmy and Stevie and Johnny Martorano, Jimmy and Stevie gave him a bag of money and told him to go to the house around the corner to count the money. While Castucci was sitting at the kitchen table counting the money with Jimmy and Stevie, Johnny came in and shot him in the head. They put Castucci's body in a sleeping bag, which made it easier to move him, and deposited it in the trunk of his Cadillac. An associate who had some involvement in the murder actually wanted to be reimbursed for the $17 he had laid out to buy the sleeping bag!

Jimmy O'Toole, a well-known gangland figure involved in armored car robberies, had been aligned with members of the Charlestown-based McLaughlin gang. His murder in December 1973 was hastened by Eddie Connors, who alerted members of Winter Hill that O'Toole was leaving the Bulldogs Tavern on Savin Hill Avenue. Jimmy O'Toole hadn't gone far down Savin Hill and Dorchester avenues when four Winter Hill cars surrounded him, two to block off the ends of the street so no one could get in or out, one to act as a crash car in case the police arrived, and the fourth to serve as a hit car. O'Toole ducked behind a mailbox, which was on a cement pad, not attached to the ground. He kept moving the mailbox from side to side to keep it between himself and the bullets which poured out of the cars. Finally, Joe MacDonald got frustrated and jumped out of the car, walked up to O'Toole, and shot him in the head. Although he was in one of the four cars, Jimmy didn't fire the fatal shot that night. I believe the murder was more payback for O'Toole's involvement in the shooting of Stevie's brother, the Bear, when O'Toole was hooked up with the McLaughlins, than for anything else. The Bear had been hit eleven times but survived.

Eddie Connors, who also had a hand in the rackets, died less than three years later. After he was arrested for a $500,000 armored car robbery, Jimmy and Stevie were worried he wouldn't stand up and might be cooperating with law enforcement. They thought he was starting to talk about his part in the O'Toole murder.

On the night of June 12, 1975, members of Winter Hill sent a message to Connors to give them the number of a pay phone where they could call him. Connors gave the number of a phone booth outside a Sunoco station across from Orbit's department store in Dorchester. He then parked his Lincoln Continental with the motor running and walked over to the booth to await the call. Waiting in the weeds outside the telephone booth on Morrissey Boulevard, Jimmy and Stevie killed Eddie when he picked up the phone. Jimmy had a shotgun and Stevie a rifle, and the first shot Jimmy fired blew Eddie's hand off. After the two of them finished Eddie off, Johnny Martorano picked up Jimmy and Stevie and the three of them took off. As they were driving away, Johnny was obeying the speed limit, and Jimmy said to him, "What are you doing? Pull over." Then Jimmy jumped into the driver's seat and drove off. Quickly.

Roger Wheeler's murder was purely business. A respected millionaire from Tulsa, Oklahoma, and the owner of Telex Corp., Wheeler bought World Jai Alai in 1978 for $50 million. A few years later, however, he began to suspect possible skimming from the company's Connecticut office and started to check things out. When Wheeler started to tighten the reins, John Callahan, a former president of World Jai Alai, broached the subject to Winter Hill that if Wheeler was out of the way, then he could take over and Winter Hill would have a piece of it.

On May 27, 1981, as Wheeler was getting into his Cadillac after a round of golf at the Southern Hills Country Club in Tulsa, Johnny Martorano and Joe MacDonald were waiting in the parking lot for him. While Joe remained in the car, Johnny walked up to Wheeler's car and shot him between the eyes, thus setting off the events for the Halloran and Callahan murders. A major investigation went on after the Wheeler murder, and after a period of time, Winter Hill stopped getting money from Jai Alai.

John Callahan, who was a big man, six feet tall and about 250 pounds, went soon after that, again for business reasons. Jimmy told me that a year after Wheeler's and Halloran's deaths, FBI agent John Connolly told him and Stevie that Callahan was going to be called in front of the grand jury and put under extreme pressure on the two murders. Of course, Connolly denies this. At the time, Johnny Martorano was already down in Florida. But Jimmy and Stevie flew down to New York and Johnny came up from Florida and met them at a hotel at one of the New York airports. Here, they discussed Callahan and whether or not he would stand up when facing the possibility of doing twenty years. It was decided Callahan would have to go.

Shortly thereafter, Callahan flew into Miami International Airport where Johnny Martorano and Joe MacDonald picked him up in a van and asked him if he wanted a drink. When he said yes, Johnny shot him in the back of the head. Then they put his body in the trunk of his Cadillac and left him at the airport. But Jimmy was upset that they didn't bury him. Since the ground in Florida is mostly sand, it would have been easy digging. If they had put him under, no one would have found him, and it would have looked like he had taken off and become another dead end. However, when his body was found in the trunk of his car, the investigation continued.

My father, John Weeks

My mother, Margaret Weeks, in Dorchester

The window over the tunnel was my bedroom window at 8 Pilsudski Way in South Boston's Old Colony Projects.

Here I am as a high school senior at South Boston High, class of 1974.

Rock climbing on Hurricane Island off the coast of Maine during an Outward Bound course, Class H52, fall 1974

Triple O's, the Southie bar at 28 West Broadway where I worked as a bouncer. Jimmy Bulger came here frequently on weekends to discuss business.

Kevin O'Neil, one of the three O'Neil brothers who owned Triple O's. A codefendant of mine, O'Neil was indicted along with me in 1999.

Rotary Variety and the liquor store, both owned by Jimmy, Stevie, and me, were conveniently side by side.

At a Pennsylvania paintball tournament in 1999. My team won both the five and ten man divisions in the ZAP Amateur International Open.

POLICE DEPT.
BOSTON, MASS.
74044 ·)3-28-74

POLICE DEPT.
BOSTON, MASS.
174044 ·)3-28-74·

Brian Halloran, who really did have a balloon-shaped head, was the first murder I participated in. I called it in and Jimmy did the rest.

Michael Donahue made the fatal mistake of giving a ride to Brian Halloran and was killed in the hit.

Anthony's Pier 4 restaurant still exists, right across the street from where the Halloran hit took place.

Boston Herald American

Telephone (617) 426-3000 ★★★ 25 Cents ® Wednesday, May 12, 1982

WEATHER

TODAY
Sunny
High in 70s
Tomorrow
· Mostly sunny
High in 70s
Details: Page 18.

GANG GUNS KILL 2

At least 20 shots were fired from an automatic rifle and a handgun at the two victims as they sat in the car parked outside The Topside, a bar on Northern Avenue near Anthony's Pier 4. The shots came from another car which then sped away.

One victim former Howie Winter associate; second, believed son of Boston cop   Page 5

The front-page headline of the *Boston Herald American* the next day, about the Halloran and Donahue murders on the waterfront

Mob ambush claims 2 in S. Boston

By J.C. KIM
and PAUL SULLIVAN

A 41-year-old Dorchester ex-convict and another man were shot to death in a gangland-style ambush at 6:10 last night in front of a waterfront bar in South Boston.

At least 20 shots were fired from an automatic rifle and a handgun at the two victims as they sat in a car parked outside The Topside, a bar on Northern Avenue near Anthony's Pier 4.

The shots came from another car which then sped away. Police said the two victims may have been "set up" for a mob kill.

One victim, Edward Halloran, 41, of Wells Street, was shot in the chest, abdomen and legs. He was rushed to Boston City Hospital

where he died about 40 minutes after the shooting.

The second victim, whom police did not identify, is believed to be the son of a Boston police officer. He was shot several times and died on the operating table at Massachusetts General Hospital at 8:50.

Halloran, an associate of jailed organized crime leader Howie Winter, was currently free on bail on a murder charge. He was accused of shooting to death George A. Pappas, 34, of Braintree, in a Chinatown restaurant last October.

Investigators believe the Pappas murder was the result of an underworld dispute over drug distribution.

Yesterday's two victims were in a blue Datsun parked outside the Topside at 145 Northern Ave., when

a dark green Chevelle pulled up beside them and a fusillade of shots hit the car, blowing out all its windows.

The Chevelle then sped up Northern Avenue to the viaduct, over the viaduct and away on Summer Street, according to Boston Police Detectives William Mullane and John Parlen.

The Datsun then rolled across Northern Avenue and slammed into a car parked in front of the Port Cafe. One victim was thrown into the street by the impact. Police found him lying in a pool of blood.

The second victim was found slumped over the wheel of the car, covered with blood. Police said a trail of blood about 10 feet long led from the death car into the middle of Northern Avenue.

Halloran leaves a wife and a 10-month-old baby. According to investigators he has faced charges of bank robbery and assault and battery with a dangerous weapon in a long criminal record and was believed to be involved in drug dealing with Pappas.

Ray McCarthy, 22, a bartender at Topside, said: "I heard several shots and dialed the 911 number. As I was talking to police, a series of shots were fired again. I held the phone up and said to the police, 'You can hear it, can't you?'"

SHOOTING SCENE

VICTIM NAMES KILLER

Moments before he collapsed and died of 10 bullet wounds, Edward Halloran, 41, named his killer, it was learned last night.

A witness told police Halloran named a Weymouth man saying: "———— shot me." The suspect is a known bank robber sought by federal authorities.

This information brought the FBI, T-men and members of the Suffolk County District Attorney's office into the case.

Early today they were huddled at the Area C station in Dorchester coordinating efforts to track down the Weymouth man and two companions who were in the attack car.

James O. Welch, Ed Corsetti and Paul Corsetti also contributed to this report.

Tow truck driver Tom Moore hauls away car in which two men were slain.

...e article in the *Herald American* (May 12, 1982) showed the shot-up Datsun

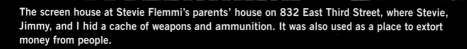

The screen house at Stevie Flemmi's parents' house on 832 East Third Street, where Stevie, Jimmy, and I hid a cache of weapons and ammunition. It was also used as a place to extort money from people.

The pier at Castle Island where Jimmy and I threw off Bucky Barrett's clothes and belongings on an August night in 1983, hours after Bucky was killed in the basement of 799 East Third Street

The *Valhalla* returned to Boston after transferring a shipment of arms to the IRA off the Irish coast.

John McIntyre was killed on November 30, 1984, for informing on the *Valhalla* arms shipment.

The triple-murder house at 799 East Third Street where John McIntyre, Bucky Barrett, and Debbie Hussey were killed between 1983 and 1985.

You have to trudge through heavy undergrowth to get to the Neponset River Bridge, which was a great place to bury a body.

Debra Davis was the girlfriend of Stevie Flemmi, before he killed her in 1981 in the basement of his parents' house. She was twenty-six.

Debbie Hussey, Stevie's "stepdaughter," was killed by Stevie and Jimmy in 1985 at the triple murder house. She was also twenty-six.

On January 13, 2000, investigators unearthed the bodies of Bucky Barrett, John McIntyre, and Debbie Hussey beneath the striped tent across from Florian Hall in Dorchester.

The remains of Paulie McGonigle are placed into the medical examiner's van at Tenean Beach in Dorchester on September 14, 2000.

Stevie Flemmi, Jimmy's partner, who wouldn't hesitate to use murder as a first option in dealing with people

POLICE DEPT.
BOSTON, MASS.

1 7 4 9 2 0 · 1 5 · 0 6 · 74

POLICE DEPT.
BOSTON, MASS.

1 7 4 9 2 0 · 1 5 · 0 6 · 7

Mugshots of Stevie Flemmi, who was arrested in January 1995 and eventually pled out to

A courtroom sketch of Stevie Flemmi at the hearings in front of Judge Wolf in 1997

On the stand at Michael Flemmi's trial about the Mac 10 and Mac 11 machine guns, as well as one hundred other weapons Michael moved for his brother Stevie. My lawyer, Dennis Kelly, is behind me.

This sketch shows me being cross-examined by Tracy Miner at former FBI agent John Connolly's trial in 2002. Judge Tauro is at the bench and Connolly and his wife are at right.

John Connolly and his wife, Liz, entering the courthouse during his trial.

Jimmy and I would walk and talk at Castle Island out of earshot of the FBI. This is only one of two photos of us ever taken together.

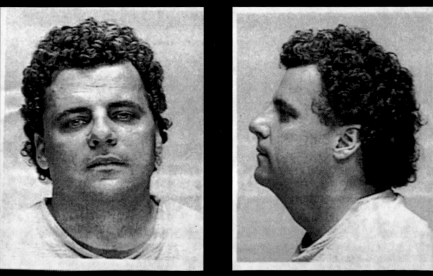

My mugshot from my first arrest in July 1996

RACKETEERING INFLUENCED AND CORRUPT ORGANIZATIONS (RICO) - MURDER (18 COUNTS), CONSPIRACY TO COMMIT MURDER, CONSPIRACY TO COMMIT EXTORTION, NARCOTICS DISTRIBUTION, CONSPIRACY TO COMMIT MONEY LAUNDERING; EXTORTION; MONEY LAUNDERING

JAMES J. BULGER

| Photograph taken in 1994 | Photograph taken in 1994 | Photograph retouched in 2000 |

Aliases: Thomas F. Baxter, Mark Shapeton, Jimmy Bulger, James Joseph Bulger, James J. Bulger, Jr., James Joseph Bulger, Jr., Tom Harris, Tom Marshall, "Whitey"

DESCRIPTION

Date of Birth:	September 3, 1929	**Hair:**	White/Silver
Place of Birth:	Boston, Massachusetts	**Eyes:**	Blue
Height:	5' 7" to 5' 9"	**Complexion:**	Light
Weight:	150 to 160 pounds	**Sex:**	Male
Build:	Medium	**Race:**	White
Occupation:	Unknown	**Nationality:**	American
Scars and Marks:	None known		

Remarks: Bulger is an avid reader with an interest in history. He is known to frequent libraries and historic sites. Bulger is currently on the heart medication Atenolol (50 mg) and maintains his physical fitness by walking on beaches and in parks with his female companion, Catherine Elizabeth Greig. Bulger and Greig love animals and may frequent animal shelters. Bulger has been known to alter his appearance through the use of disguises. He has traveled extensively throughout the United States, Europe, Canada, and Mexico.

CAUTION

JAMES J. BULGER IS BEING SOUGHT FOR HIS ROLE IN NUMEROUS MURDERS COMMITTED FROM THE EARLY 1970s THROUGH THE MID-1980s IN CONNECTION WITH HIS LEADERSHIP OF AN ORGANIZED CRIME GROUP THAT ALLEGEDLY CONTROLLED EXTORTION, DRUG DEALS, AND OTHER ILLEGAL ACTIVITIES IN THE BOSTON, MASSACHUSETTS, AREA. HE HAS A VIOLENT TEMPER AND IS KNOWN TO CARRY A KNIFE AT ALL TIMES.

CONSIDERED ARMED AND EXTREMELY DANGEROUS

IF YOU HAVE ANY INFORMATION CONCERNING THIS PERSON, PLEASE CONTACT YOUR LOCAL FBI OFFICE OR THE NEAREST U.S. EMBASSY OR CONSULATE.

REWARD

The FBI is offering a $1,000,000 reward for information leading directly to the arrest of James J. Bulger.

www.fbi.gov

August 1999
Poster Revised November 2000

Jimmy was put on the FBI's Ten Most Wanted List in August 1999 for eighteen counts of murder. There is a $1 million reward for information leading to his arrest. And he's still on the run. . . .

Years later, H. Paul Rico, a former Boston FBI agent who worked security at World Jai Alai, was charged with first-degree murder and conspiracy to commit murder in Wheeler's death. Investigators accused Rico of aiding Johnny in the murder, but Rico died in custody in Oklahoma before he was brought to trial. The truth was that Rico had done all the legwork. He had told Johnny where Wheeler was going to be, what he drove, and what he looked like. Basically, Rico had set up the murder.

Approximately a year after Rico died, John Connolly was indicted for Callahan's murder and charged with first-degree murder and conspiracy for allegedly providing information, the tip to Jimmy and Stevie, that prosecutors said led to Callahan's death.

Ten murders, ten violent deaths. Jimmy might have been responsible for only nine of them, but any way you look at it, the world was left missing nine criminals and one innocent businessman.

NINE
JIMMY AND SOUTHIE

Jimmy had his own unique sense of morality. Even though he spent so much of his life involved in violent crime, he still believed that certain crimes could not be committed, certainly not on his turf, anyhow. And he never hesitated to help someone he felt needed his help.

But even when he felt compassion for someone in need, Jimmy could appreciate the same morbid, black humor I enjoyed. For instance, one day, Jimmy, Stevie, and I were driving up Broadway in Jimmy's dark blue Ford LTD when we noticed this lady coming down the street in a motorized wheelchair. Jimmy stared at her for minute and said, "I wonder what that poor lady does in the winter."

I looked at him and said, "Snow tires."

Laughing, he said, "You dirty bastard. Don't you have any sympathy for anybody?" We had lots of those sick laughs.

But heroin dealers were one subject about which Jimmy had no sense of humor. We didn't deal with them. Jimmy wouldn't let them in town. Even though cocaine and marijuana were well established in Southie, if we found out anyone was selling those drugs to a kid, they had a problem. We went after them, too. However, as long as Jimmy was in charge, heroin never took root and was never going to.

If we found out about a heroin dealer, Jimmy and I let them know they had to get out of town. If they didn't, I beat them up. It might have taken more than one business visit, but they always left. In the rare cases when they didn't leave after a beating, we told them on our second visit we would kill them the next time. Then they left.

There were some exceptions, of course. Like the Kivlan brothers, Al and Pat. Unfortunately, the Kivlans, both ex-boxers in their forties with broken noses and scar tissue around their eyes, never listened to anyone. In 1990, a girl Jimmy knew came to the store and said her daughter couldn't play in her own backyard because of the needles there. Jimmy and I went over to her house on F and Silver streets, a two-family house whose yard abutted the three-decker house where the Kivlans lived on the first floor. The houses were just up the street from where a Metropolitan District Commission cop lived. The girl showed us the needles and told us that every time the police came, the Kivlans got rid of the stuff and the cops couldn't find a thing. The MDC cop told us the same story. Whenever he called the cops, everyone in the house was gone by the time they got there. The next day, they were back in business. The Boston cops told us directly that they couldn't catch the guys.

One Friday night, we came to the house, and when people started pulling up, we told them to get the fuck out of there. On Saturday night, we came back and saw the same people pulling up. When they started to go into the house, Jimmy and I got out of the car and I beat up two or three of them. "You're getting off easy with a beating," Jimmy told them. "Next time we see you here, we'll kill you."

When nothing changed the next night, Teddy Devins and I went over to the Curley Lumber Yard on Monday and bought some sheets of plywood. Then we drove the truck over to the Kivlans' house, stood on the bed of the truck, and, with people still inside the house, started to nail the plywood over the windows. The brothers were too scared to come out, but as we continued nailing, we could see one of their wives, stunned, looking out at us. When we finished, we spray-painted the plywood with the words, OUT OF BUSINESS NO DRUGS.

Later that day, we caught up with Al Kivlan and his brother on G Street and Fourth and told them they had twenty-four hours to get out or we would kill them. By Tuesday, they were gone from the house on F and Silver. For good. A day or so later, the MDC cop and some other neighbors came down to the store to thank us. They told us we had done what the Boston cops hadn't been able to do. Obviously, we used different tactics than the Boston cops.

Another heroin dealer who needed some persuasion to move out of Southie was some kid in the Old Colony project. When we heard people complaining about noise at all hours of the night in one building there, we considered it unacceptable. There were little babies in that building. And residents had older kids who couldn't sleep because of cars pulling up and doors slamming loudly at all hours of the night. The first time we went into the building, the dealer jumped out the side window and took off. On our next visit, we caught up with him and told him that was it. He was out of business. Things died down a little bit, but a week later the heroin dealer was back in full swing.

The third time I went up to the house, I knocked on the door, the dealer answered, and I gave him a beating and knocked him out. But he still didn't learn. Shortly afterward, we heard that he had started dealing again. One afternoon, Jimmy and I were driving down East Ninth Street in the Old Colony project when Jimmy noticed him walking on the sidewalk. Jimmy just pulled the car onto the sidewalk and ran him over. The kid ended up in the hospital with some broken bones in his legs, but he moved out of Old Colony. How many times do you have to tell someone to get out before he finally gets the message?

One angel dust dealer needed a little extra persuasion, too. He lived in the Old Colony project, right down the street from where my mother lived on Pilsudski Way, and was selling dust to everyone. People started coming into the variety store to complain that he was even selling to kids who were getting messed up on the shit. So Jimmy and I drove down and waited for him to come out of his house. Then we grabbed him, put him in the back seat, drove him around terrorizing him, and then told him he was out of business and to get the fuck out of town. A short time later, we started to hear that the kid was back in business. Obviously, he didn't realize we knew he was starting up again, because one afternoon he walked into the store. But as soon as I saw him, I went to stand in back of him and blocked the door. He took off running and screaming and calling so much attention to himself that I had to let him go.

The next day, Jimmy and I met down at the variety store, and as we exited the store to get to the car, we saw the kid coming across Old Colony Avenue. He was halfway across the street, standing on the median strip, yelling, "Whitey, Kevin, I'll pay youse if you let me stay in business. I'll give you half my money, half the money I make."

Jimmy turned around, saying, "You little motherfucker," and took out a knife, but the kid took off running again. A few weeks later, he got pinched for drug dealing. Law enforcement tried to get him to say he was paying us to sell drugs, that we were shaking him down so he could sell his angel dust.

"No," the kid told them, "they were going to kill me if I didn't stop selling. They told me to get out of town." That was the only good thing the kid did. He told the truth.

Still, the cops continued to ask us for help with people selling heroin. "You guys can do things we can't," they kept telling us. So we'd go down and drive the dealers out of town, but then we started to hear that the same cops were grabbing the people afterward. "We know you're paying Whitey and Kevin," they'd tell the dealers, and try to get them to admit that. So we backed away from running people out of town if the police or even a Good Samaritan asked us. We figured there was a good chance it was a setup.

There was very little prostitution in Southie. It was pretty much restricted to Boston's Combat Zone downtown. But whenever Jimmy and I saw anyone doing that, we went after them. I'd say over twenty-five years, it happened maybe two or three times. But when it did, we took care of the guys who had grabbed young girls and were trying to pimp them. We'd get ahold of the guys and tell them to get the fuck out of town. That was just one of the things we were against.

But we never ran out of people we wanted to run out of town. One especially despicable creep was this guy in his late thirties or early forties, who we all called Wheels because he was in a wheelchair. One Saturday in the early 1980s around two in the afternoon, I was standing on Broadway across the street from the South Boston Savings Bank with Jimmy, Kevin O'Neil, and Bobby Ford, who used to run a booking office in Southie for Jimmy. We looked over and saw Wheels bumming money off people. An alcoholic, the guy could get up and walk, but he preferred to shuffle his feet to push the chair and spin the wheels with his hands, pretending he was a cripple. That way, he could beg for money for wine. He'd typically ask a guy for change and wouldn't say a word if the guy said no, but if a woman refused him money for wine, he'd be swearing and grabbing onto her dress. That afternoon, the piece of shit was swearing at one particular woman in her fifties who had a grandchild with her, calling her everything in the book.

Furious as I watched him degrade the poor woman, I walked across the street and grabbed the back of his chair by the handles. I intended to push him down the driveway behind the bank into the parking lot, but he put his feet down, grabbed the wheels, and stopped me dead. I couldn't move him. So I threw the wheelchair and him over onto the ground. Then I picked up the wheelchair and smashed it on the street. Wheels was on the ground yelling, so I gave him a boot in the back. When I walked back across the street, the three guys were doubled over, laughing with tears running down their faces.

"What's so funny?" I asked.

"You look like the meanest prick in town," Jimmy told me in between bursts of laughter.

"Fucking asshole can walk," I said.

"Yeah, we know, but they don't," Jimmy said and pointed to the people across the street. Sure enough, all the people were trying to help him up. They thought that poor old wino was being picked on.

"Let's get out of here," I said.

One night two weeks later, Kevin O'Neil and I were driving around when we saw Wheels in front of the Marion Manor Nursing Home in Dorchester, doing his same thing, going after women who were leaving from work at the nursing home. This time I jumped out of the car, came up behind him, pulled up the hood on my sweatshirt, and threw Wheels out of the chair. Then I pushed it up to Fourth Street where Kevin had parked the car and dumped it into the trunk. A few streets later, I took the chair out of the trunk and tossed it into someone's backyard.

A week later, Bobby Ford saw Wheels on Broadway. Bobby did pretty much the same thing I did, except he drove over to the Summer Street Bridge, where he threw the chair into the water. That, we all figured, was the end of Wheels and his wheelchair.

A year later, Jimmy and I were walking into Store 24 on West Broadway when someone came up to Jimmy and said, "Hi, Whitey, how you doing?"

Jimmy stared at him for a minute and then yelled out, "Wheels!"

The guy was all dressed up with khaki pants and a nice shirt, his hair cut neatly and his face clean-shaven. "I've been sober for almost a year," he told us. "I'm doing good." A perfect example that even the worst prick can change.

There were times, however, when Jimmy wasn't around, when I was called upon to take care of some of these pricks, particularly when they were messing with people who mattered to Jimmy. Like with Nancy

Stanley, Theresa's daughter. Jimmy was out of town when Nancy came down to the variety store, upset about some guy named John who had just gotten out of jail and was bothering her. First thing I did was call him and tell him I heard he was looking for a job. I asked him if he had a driver's license and said he could have a job delivering liquor. I told him to come down to the variety store, which was next to the liquor store, to see me.

When the guy, who was probably around five-ten and 220 pounds, came into the store, I had him follow me downstairs to the office. As soon as we got there, I turned around and cracked him a right hand, splitting him open over both his eyes and breaking his nose. Then I stomped on his knee till it cracked. Finally, I hit him and broke his ribs. While John was moaning in pain, two of us dragged him upstairs and threw him on the floor. As he hobbled toward the door, a woman who worked at the store saw him on the floor and thought he'd been in a car accident. She started to dial 911, but someone told her, "Kevin did it," and she hung right up. John managed to stagger into his car, but before he drove away, I came over to tell him that if he came near Nancy again, I'd kill him. I saw him a few weeks later on crutches. But he never came anywhere near Nancy again.

There were countless times when Jimmy performed generous acts toward those in need, not for notoriety, but because he thought it was the right thing to do. He was an extremely generous guy. No one, except the people he helped, knew exactly what he did. But he thought nothing of paying the rent for families in need, or buying bicycles or coats or food for needy kids, or cars for families who needed to take their kids to school. Many times he found jobs for people who needed them. At Christmastime he'd buy gifts for children and their families, and he always gave money to St. Augustine's food pantry. If he saw an old lady having trouble trying to cross the street, he'd get out of his car and stop traffic to help her cross. If he saw a woman carrying boxes, he'd put her in his car and drive her home.

If someone was bothering a family, he'd say to me, "Let's take a ride," and he'd stop by to help with the situation, as well as to look around and see if anything was broken. If he saw the family needed a new refrigerator or some furniture, he'd go right down and buy whatever they needed and have it all delivered to them. If he heard about anyone picking on girls or mothers who were living in families without brothers or fathers, we'd go down and grab those guys. "Pretend she's my mother or sister," he'd tell the bullies. "And then go ahead and bother her again and see what I do. The only reason you're picking on her is that you think no one will come after you. But I will."

But we didn't help every resident of Southie whose kid was being picked on. For example, one woman Jimmy knew well came to us to complain about a guy who was bothering her daughter. "Will Kevin give the kid a beating?" she asked Jimmy, while I was standing right there.

Jimmy looked at her and said, "What about your two sons? Why don't they go after him?"

She turned around, looked at me, and said, "Oh, no, they could get in trouble."

"Oh, and Kevin can't?" Jimmy said. "You want Kevin to stick up for your family and you don't want your own sons to get involved because they could get in trouble? Sorry, we can't help you." And the two of us walked away. It would have been a different story if she didn't have any sons, but that woman had her own boys to take care of the problem.

Certainly, Jimmy made sure no one took advantage of his own family. One night when he was living with his elderly mother at the Old Harbor project, he heard some kids playing basketball outside. After midnight, he went down and told them to knock it off. When the kids ignored him and continued playing, he went out with a knife and stabbed and flattened the ball. One of the kids started saying stuff to him, so Jimmy turned around and stabbed him, too, opening up his stomach. Then he put the kid, who was in his late teens or early twenties, into his car and drove him to the hospital.

He'd get especially angry when he heard about someone in Southie being robbed by residents of the town. "Don't rob off people who have less than you," he'd tell the thieves. "Go to Newton or Wellesley, anywhere they have more money than here. But leave your own people alone." When he heard about a young boy in Southie who was raped, he sent the whole family to Disneyland.

He also had a strong sympathy for gasoline station attendants. He'd pull in for gas when it was freezing out and take off his gloves and give them to the kid who was pumping his gas. "Keep them," he'd tell the kid. "You're out here in the rain and snow." And he always tipped the kid who was pumping his gas. "You give five dollars to some asshole behind the bar who opens a bottle of beer for you," he'd say. "Well, this kid is out there freezing his ass off and working a hell of a lot harder than the kid in the bar."

Whenever he came across a cause he believed in, he didn't hesitate to help out. Like with Charlie Ross, a longshoreman on the Boston waterfront whose family lived near ours on Pilsudski Way and whose daughters I went to school with. In the 1980s, Charlie was picketing the *Globe* with a few other members of the Ancient Order of the Hibernians because of a cartoon that was hurtful to the Irish. The cartoon depicted a rat plunging an explosive devise, wearing a shamrock top hat and dressed up as a leprechaun. Charlie wanted the *Globe* to retract the cartoon and make a positive statement, rather than to infer that all Irishmen were rats because of the IRA. Jimmy and I donated $200 to Charlie's cause, money that Charlie turned over to the families of the political prisoners in Irish prisons like Long Kesh and Maze.

Jimmy's loyalty to friends had no limits, even if the friends lived far from Southie. Two such friends were from Alcatraz, where Jimmy served time from 1958 to 1963. Jimmy often wore the belt buckle engraved with "Alcatraz, 1934–1963" that FBI agent Nick Gianturco had given to him. Clarence Carnes was a close friend of Jimmy's during his years there, and the two of them had been involved in fights. Carnes had come to Alcatraz in 1945 at age eighteen, the youngest inmate ever imprisoned there. He'd been part of the May 1946 escape attempt in which six prisoners killed two guards and the Marines were called in to restore order. Carnes was spared the death penalty that two of the escapees received because he had not taken part in the murders of the two guards.

After Carnes died in 1988 and was buried in a pauper's grave outside a Missouri prison hospital, Jimmy made arrangements to have his body exhumed and buried in a Native American funeral in Oklahoma. Jimmy had the funeral home take care of the details, and then he and Theresa flew out to Oklahoma, rented a car, and drove to the burial ground. The arrangements cost him $15,000 to $20,000.

The stories that Carnes was gay and died of AIDS were bullshit. He was an alcoholic, which was why he had gotten into trouble in the first place. At age sixteen, drunk, he'd held up a gas station and killed the attendant, for which he received a life sentence at Oklahoma State Reformatory. After an escape attempt there, he was transferred to Leavenworth and later sent to Alcatraz.

Even when he was eventually paroled, Carnes violated his parole and ended up back in prison where, on a dialysis machine, he died at age sixty-one from cirrhosis of the liver, not AIDS. At the Native American funeral ceremony, Jimmy met Carnes's relatives, who thanked him for what he'd done.

Carnes wasn't the only friend from Alcatraz whom Jimmy remembered. During a visit to Alcatraz after his release, Jimmy met Whitey Thompson, a former inmate who was now giving tours there. Thompson had been at Alcatraz from 1958 to 1962, but he hadn't been a high-profile inmate, and he and Jimmy hadn't known each other. None of the different guys from Alcatraz whom Jimmy had kept in touch with remembered Thompson, either. But when Thompson told Jimmy he was writing a book about his experiences at Alcatraz, Jimmy gave him $1,500 toward the book.

In 1989, after Jimmy got a copy of the finished autobiography, titled *Last Train to Alcatraz* and later retitled *Rock Hard*, he was furious. Whitey Thompson had written about another inmate, Alvin Karpis, referring to him as Creepy Karpis, the name law enforcement, which liked to give people nicknames to make them seem more sinister, had hung on him. Karpis had been with the Ma Barker gang and had served time in Alcatraz from 1936 to 1962.

Jimmy told me Karpis's own explanation of how he'd been captured in 1936. J. Edgar Hoover had declared him Public Enemy #1. When the feds finally surrounded Karpis and threw their guns on him, Hoover was around the corner hiding behind the bushes. He yelled out to his men, "Is it safe? Do you have him?"

"It's all right, boss," they told him. When they had subdued Karpis on the ground, Hoover came out from the bushes and put the handcuffs on him. That way, he could say he was the one who got Karpis.

No one who knew Karpis ever called him "Creepy." But one time Karpis and another guy were digging an escape tunnel in a narrow passageway, down by the boiling-hot steam pipes. It was so hot that the two guys would strip down to their underwear and go in to dig the hole. When they came out, they were so filthy and covered with dirt that they jumped right into the shower. After one guard saw the two of them together in the wide-open shower, he reported they were homosexuals. In his book, Whitey Thompson wrote that Karpis was a fag.

Jimmy knew Karpis well, and he took exception to that statement. Furious that he had given money to Thompson to get his book started and that he had written all kinds of lies in it, Jimmy flew back out to Alcatraz. This time, he waited for Whitey Thompson to come around and give his tours. There was no doubt he was going to kill him. After he couldn't find Thompson at Alcatraz, Jimmy found out that he was living in Washington, so he traveled up there to find and kill him. Thompson was just lucky that Jimmy had to stop tracking him up there and return to business in South Boston. If it weren't for that, Jimmy, who was a hunter, would definitely have found and killed him. As it turned out, Karpis wrote two books about his experiences in Alcatraz, *Public Enemy #1* and *On the Rock*, before he died in Spain in 1979. Thompson died on June 7, 2005. Hmm, I wonder where Jimmy was that day . . .

TEN
STIPPO

The story of Stippo's Liquor Store is a classic example of how the media latches onto a false story and runs with it, never letting the true facts get in the way of a good story. This had all the elements of a terrific crime story: a hard-working, law-abiding young husband and his adoring wife, their two beautiful, innocent little daughters, a highly successful liquor store, and two ferocious mobsters who threaten the lives of this perfect family in order to seize the store. The trouble is, except for the innocent little girls, every other detail of the story is a lie and I said as much under oath. Here is the true story, the one happily ignored by the media for more than twenty years.

In the fall of 1983, Stippo, whose real name was Stephen Rakes, and his wife, Julie Miskel Rakes, were given money by his parents to buy a run-down Texaco gas station at 295 Old Colony Avenue near St. Monica's Church. The Rakes's plans were to turn the gas station with its two service bays into a liquor store. Shortly after that, Stippo purchased a liquor license at auction for $5,000, which he transferred to 295 Old Colony Avenue. Although he planned on opening Stippo's Liquor Mart on Thanksgiving, it didn't open until a week or two before Christmas.

Local liquor stores in South Boston shared an unwritten understanding that liquor would be marked up 33 percent, while wine would go up 50 percent. The prices of beer would run all the same across the board. There might be a twenty-five-cent difference here or there, but basically the prices were pretty level. However, when Stippo opened the door, he was undercutting everyone, only marking everything up 5 percent.

Shortly after he opened Stippo's Liquor Mart, Stippo started receiving bomb and death threats. Someone was calling up the store, threatening Stippo, his wife, and his father, who was a friend of mine, saying they were going to blow the place up and kill them all. At the time, Jimmy and I had already opened our bar at F and Second streets, originally called the Old Time Tavern, which we'd renamed Court's Inn.

Stippo's sister Mary, who was a friend of mine and Jimmy's, came down to the bar one Friday afternoon and asked me if Jimmy was there. When I told her he would be in shortly, she said she was supposed to meet him there. After he came in, the two of them sat down in a booth and had a conversation. Then he called me over and told Mary, "Don't worry. I'll take care of it."

After Mary left, Jimmy explained to me about the death threats Stippo and his family were getting. Jimmy and I both liked Mary and her father and mother, who were good people, so we left the bar and went down to the liquor mart to talk to Stippo. His father was down there but his wife, Julie, was home. Apparently, Stippo told us, she was scared about receiving the threats and didn't want to be down there anymore. Jimmy said we'd look into it and find out who was doing it and make it stop. When we asked him if he had any idea where the threats might be coming from, he said no, but he did tell us that he had previously been partners in a liquor store at Dorchester and West Ninth with the Luongo brothers, and it might be them.

After Jimmy and I left Stippo's store, we went to the package store owned by the Luongos and talked to two of the three brothers who were there. After a forty-five-minute conversation, we were convinced the Luongo brothers had nothing to do with the bomb threats. But they were open about the fact that they didn't like Stippo and that there had been hard feelings when they had parted ways. They also told us Stippo had been stealing money off them and had previously tried to buy a liquor store on the same block as their store. The Luongos said that when the owner refused to sell it to him, the store had mysteriously burned down. There was no doubt that Stippo did not have a good reputation in town and that more than one piece of property he had owned went up in flames. He'd even been investigated by the arson squad, although nothing ever came of it. But still it was clear that the Luongo brothers, despite their dislike of Stippo, had not made the bomb threats.

After we left the Luongos, Jimmy and I decided to go our separate ways for supper and meet later in the evening. On his way home, Jimmy drove up to Perkins Square and went into the Bayview Liquor, a store owned by the Barrys. When I met Jimmy later, he informed me that the people there didn't know anything about the bomb threats. During the week, the two of us went to a couple of other places, but we couldn't make any headway. No one we talked to knew anything about the bomb or death threats.

The following Monday afternoon, Jimmy and I were driving down Andrew Square when an old friend of Jimmy's yelled out, "Hey, Sonny," using an old nickname Jimmy had since he'd been a kid. Jimmy pulled over and introduced me to Domi Musico, who owned a liquor store and also a bar near Andrew Square, not far from where Stippo had opened his store.

We were talking small talk for a little while when, out of the clear, Domi said, "So, do you believe that cocksucker Stippo opening up and undercutting everybody? But that's all right. I keep calling him up and telling him I'm going to blow the place up and kill them all."

Jimmy and I looked at each other and started laughing. We had just stumbled onto it. Then Jimmy looked at Domi and said, "Domi, you can't do that. His father is a friend of Kevin's."

"I'm not going to do anything," Domi said. "But I want that cocksucker to have some restless nights like I've had."

"Don't do anything," Jimmy told him again.

"I won't do anything," Domi promised Jimmy. "I just hate him."

Later that evening, we went back to Stippo's and told him we had found out who was making the threats and that he didn't have any more problems. "It's all taken care of," Jimmy assured him. Stippo was pleased and thanked us. And that was the end of it. Or so we thought.

The following week, after Christmas, Mary came back down to Court's Inn and sat in a booth with Jimmy. After they'd been talking for a while, Jimmy called me over. "Stippo wants to sell the liquor mart," he told me. "He wants to know if we're interested. A legitimate business wouldn't be a bad idea. What do you think?"

Mary was still there but I said, "It doesn't hurt to listen."

That night, Jimmy and I went down to Stippo's. He and Jimmy started talking, but Stippo didn't want to talk in front of his wife, who was down at the store at the time. He asked us to meet him later at his house on East Fourth Street. I knew the house well, from when I used to visit its former owner, Marty McDonough, a high school hockey referee who worked as a liquor salesman and was a real nice guy, a legitimate guy. Later that evening, when Jimmy and I went up to his house, Stippo told us he wanted to sell the business, that he needed to get out, that it was too much for him, and that he was in over his head. Basically working on a 5 percent markup, he'd only had the place three weeks, but he couldn't keep it going any longer.

I set up another meeting with him for the next night, when I would go over the books with him. When I went to his house for the second meeting, he showed me the books. Then I met him again, this time with Kevin O'Neil, who was in the liquor business. Even though I had a bar, Kevin had been in the business much longer than I had.

On my fourth visit, Jimmy and I went to Stippo's house and the three of us agreed on a price of $100,000 for the store, along with a note Stippo would carry for $25,000 to make it look legit. The $100,000 was cash, the $25,000 on paper. When Jimmy and I were leaving Stippo's house that night, Jimmy said, "You know Stevie is going to want a part of this."

"I have no problem with that," I told him.

The night we were going to give Stippo the money, I brought $30,000 in cash to Theresa's house, all one-hundred-dollar bills. Jimmy took the $30,000 in hundreds downstairs and came back up with $30,000 in twenties and tens, having replaced my money with his. Obviously, he wanted to keep the hundreds for himself. Then he took $70,000 from him and Stevie and put that in a brown paper bag, along with my $30,000, and we went to Stippo's. I don't have a clear recollection as to whether or not Stevie was with us that night. But when we got to the house, Stippo let us in and we sat down at the dining room table. Stippo's two little girls were running around the house, and when one came over to us, Jimmy picked her up and put her on his knee, commenting on how pretty she was. As soon as the money was on the table, Jimmy told Stippo to count it.

At that point, Stippo turned around and said, "I don't know about this. My wife doesn't really want to sell." He started hemming and hawing, but knowing Stippo the way I did, it seemed clear to me that he was trying to shake us down for more money. What he wanted was for us to sweeten the pot. I think he figured that since we were so interested in the store, he could get more money out of us. Here we had already agreed on a selling price and he was trying, at the last moment, to get more money out of us.

But it wasn't happening. "We agreed on this price," Jimmy told him. "The money is here. And you're not getting any more out of us." With that, I took a gun out of my belt and put it on the table. His daughter, who was sitting on Jimmy's lap, reached over and touched the handle of the gun. Jimmy pushed the gun back over to me and told me to put it away, removing Stippo's daughter from his knee and letting her stand up on the floor.

Stippo then called his sister-in-law, who was babysitting, and told her to take the kids into the kitchen. Once the kids were gone, we started talking, and the tone wasn't pleasant. "Listen," Jimmy told Stippo, "we had a deal. We agreed upon a price and now you are trying to get more money out of us. You were the one who came to us to buy the store. We didn't come to you."

Finally, Stippo agreed and Jimmy told him to count the money. Stippo took the $100,000 and counted ten stacks of $10,000, each one made up with two stacks of $5,000 each, one by one. We counted the money, too, and then Stippo put $25,000 off to the side and put the remaining $75,000 back in the bag.

After we shook hands, we had him give us the keys to the store right then. Knowing Stippo as well as we did, we wanted those keys that night so he couldn't go to the store and remove some of the stock before we got there the next day. Then we made arrangements to meet him there the next morning, when he would show us how to work the alarm and open the store. He had told us there was approximately $65,000 in stock in the store and that he had paid for the walk-in chest, the electrical work, and all the construction.

The next morning, we met him there, and opened for business shortly afterward, in January 1984, changing the name to Rotary Liquors. For the next three days, Stippo came down to help out, showing me how to run the place and introducing me to the salesmen who were coming in. Then he informed me that he and his wife were taking the two kids to Disney World for two weeks.

After Stippo left, I had Kevin O'Neil come down to the store and go over the stock with me, showing me which beers and wines sold and those for which there was no big demand. While he was there, I told him that I didn't think there was really $65,000 in stock there.

"What you have to do is get the beverage journal," Kevin told me. "Then you need to take an inventory of everything you have in the store, match it against the prices in the book and the post off, since when you buy stuff in quantities you get discounts. Then you'll know how much stock you have."

After I did all that, I realized there was only $35,000 to $38,000 in stock, definitely not the $65,000 Stippo had claimed. Then the bills started coming in from the liquor distributors. It appeared that Stippo hadn't paid any of them, so the second week I was there, I had to come up with $47,000 in cash out of my pocket to pay the bills. Not only had Stippo lied about how much stock was there, he had walked out with the first three weeks' receipts of approximately $33,000 and never replaced the stock. Next, the salesman from Lennox Martell came in, looking for payment on the walk-in chest. Shortly after that, Murphy Electric, who did the electrical work, asked for money for their work, followed by Brian Burke, who did the construction, was also looking for his money. I soon realized that Stippo hadn't paid for much of anything except the $5,000 license for the store.

Approximately a week later, Jimmy and I started hearing ridiculous stories about Stippo and us. According to these reports, Stippo was dead, we had threatened to kill him, we had hung him over the bridge, and we had stuck a gun in his daughter's mouth. All kinds of lies were circulating around town. His own sister Mary came down to the store to tell us about them, but we'd already heard them. Mary got Stippo's number in Florida and we called him from the store. When I told him about everything that was being said, he told me he'd be back in two weeks. I told him he had to come back soon and put these rumors to rest. When I let Jimmy know Stippo would be back in two weeks, he took the phone and said, "Get back now." He also said we'd pay for his airline flight up and back.

Two days later, Stippo came back, without his family. Jimmy and I met him and the three of us stood in front of the liquor store for an hour, so people could drive by and see him. Then we drove up to Perkins Square and we stood out front there, talking with Stippo, so, again, people driving by could see him. We offered to give him the money for the flight back, but he said, "No, I've got it," and wouldn't take it. He went back to Florida and that, we thought, was the end of it.

However, when Stippo returned from Florida, the stories persisted. According to our friends, Julie's sister was telling everyone that we had threatened her sister's family. The story that got us the maddest was the one that we had stuck a gun in the little girl's mouth. We would never harm a child. I had a son of my own. And Jimmy would never do anything like that. So Jimmy and I drove Stippo over to the Saltonstall building where his sister-in-law worked. He called her outside and basically told her to shut her mouth.

But things got even more stirred up when Julie went to her uncle, Joe Lundbohm, a Boston cop, and told him the same thing, the lies that we had threatened to kill Stippo. Yet the truth was that we had never approached Stippo; he had approached us. But Joe Lundbohm went to the FBI and John Connolly, who told Jimmy what Stippo was saying and that his wife had gone to her uncle because of the lies Stippo had told her. The one thing Stippo had not told his wife was that he had reached out to us. He did tell her, however, that he only got $67,000 when he really got $100,000. Jimmy and I never blamed Julie for any of this. She was only repeating the lies her husband had told her.

John Connolly told Joe Lundbohm that Julie and Stippo would have to get wired up. Stippo was afraid of being wired up, because he knew that when he started talking to us, he would have to lie to verify the story he had told his wife. Once he started a conversation with a lie, we would have been on our guard and would have known something wasn't right. If he told us nonsense while he was wired, we would have said, "What are you talking about?" and it would have come out that he was a liar.

Even though John Connolly, acting yet again as the FBI agent that

Jimmy was paying for information involving us, had told us what was going on with Lundbohm, we never acted on it. And we never killed Stippo because the whole incident finally died down. After things quieted down, Joe Lundbohm and his partner Bob Ryan used to hang around the liquor store trying to catch us doing something illegal. Even though he couldn't do that, Lundbohm did manage to bring me up on charges involving the fight with the kids from Weymouth outside the liquor store.

Although I continued to run the liquor store and the situation did go away, Jimmy and I got a lot of unwanted and unnecessary notoriety because of all the inaccuracies in the press. The media played the story as if Stippo was the victim, and they were able to reach millions of readers and listeners a day with that lie. Basically, there was nothing we could do about that. How many people could we talk to in a day? There was no way we could defend ourselves against the press.

A short time later, Stippo opened a jewelry store with his wife and father-in-law on East Broadway which, unbeknownst to the two of them, was selling hot jewelry. Some of the thieves had already come down to me and asked me to sell the stuff, but I told them I had nowhere to sell it and didn't buy it from them. So they had all gone to Stippo's store.

Stippo's father, James, continued to come to the liquor store every day to see me. There was no doubt he disliked his own son and blamed him for remortgaging and forcing them out of the house that he and his wife had lived in on Jenkins Street. Still, James told me how he and his wife had a meeting with their other kids and made them all promise never to do anything to Stippo so long as they were alive. Stippo's own family hated him.

Both in 1991 and 1995, when the federal government was looking to indict Jimmy and me, Stippo got called in front of a federal grand jury. Both times, he actually told the truth about what had happened, saying that he was the one who wanted to sell the place to Jimmy and that he had asked Jimmy and me if we were interested in buying it. Unfortunately, Julie told the opposite story, the one he gave her about the gun and their kid, passing along the lie about how we had extorted Stippo. Again, it wasn't her fault. That was the only story she knew. By then the two of them had gotten divorced and lost the jewelry store, and there was bitter infighting between them.

Ultimately, in May 1996, Stippo got indicted for five counts of perjury and two counts of obstruction of justice. He was telling the truth, but by then it was too late. Just before he went to trial on those charges, Stippo came down to the variety store, looking to borrow money off me. He said he needed it to pay $750,000 to his lawyer. This was an outright lie. But it didn't matter. I gave him shit. If he'd told the truth to his wife in the first place, neither he nor I would have been in difficult positions then. I should have listened when members of his family had told me, "Kevin, be careful around him. You never know what he's going to do."

After Stippo was found guilty of perjury and he was awaiting sentencing, he made a deal with the government, cooperating against Whitey and me. This time, he told them the story he had told his wife, 99 percent of which was a lie. The only truth to his story was the fact that the gun was on the table when he was trying to shake us down for more money. Because I had put that gun on the table, the government charged me with racketeering, one of the twenty-nine charges leveled against me in my racketeering indictment in 1999. They said the presence of the gun showed we were extorting Stippo. In truth, however, he was extorting us, trying to get more money out of us.

If Stippo had originally gone in front of the grand jury and kept his mouth shut, the most they could have given him was the duration of the grand jury, minus the time it was already sitting. Being the standup kid that everyone knew him to be, he would have gotten eighteen months, but instead he decided to cooperate with the government. As it turned out, he got probation and never went to jail. I guess the eighteen months was too much for him.

So, was it extortion or not? Because the gun was put on the table, the government said yes. But knowing Stippo the way I and everyone else did, I knew he was trying to get more money out of us, and there was no way that was going to happen. Still, in the end, the media continued to portray Stippo as the poor victim. Yet if anyone was the victim, based on the lies that were told to her, it was his wife. None of us ever held her responsible for anything. Julie filed a $28.5 million civil case against us in 2002, but it was dismissed.

In the end, Stippo did get $100,000 from us for the sale, plus $8,000 of the $25,000 note. I didn't pay him the complete $25,000 because he had lied about what he owed. But it was his other lies that the media ran with, ignoring the fact that he did not have the best reputation in town, a fact we knew from the very beginning. They also ignored the fact that we had no intention of buying a legitimate business, that we had our bar, which was enough for us. Even the maroon Dodge Caravan that Stippo bought was part of a media lie. The press said we bought him the car to get out of town, but he bought it himself with the money he got from the sale of the property.

Both of Stippo's sisters, Trish and Mary, gave interviews to the *Boston Herald* in April 2005, concurring that Stippo was in debt over his head and had come to us for help. "Stippo couldn't even get beer for the store," Trish told investigators and reporters from the *Herald*. "He owed every liquor distributor in the city." At last one paper got something right.

One other little detail should be mentioned. After all this happened, Stippo's younger brother Joseph married my sister Karen. He's a great guy. So much for the family being afraid of us.

ELEVEN
THE MEDIA LIES

There were a lot of things that brought out Jimmy's violent nature, but the one that never failed to enrage us was the name Howie Carr, a piece-of-shit reporter. I called him Howie Coward because he hid behind his computer at the *Boston Herald* and the microphone of his Boston radio talk show, writing and speaking words he would never dare say in person, one-on-one, to whoever he was writing or talking about. Lots of reporters and radio hosts write and speak untrue and nasty things, but Howie never has a good word to say about anybody. His radio show attracts the same crowd as Jerry Springer. As far as I am concerned, Howie Carr and his big mouth have no journalistic value. He's just one of those loudmouths who like to dig up dirt on people and invoke controversy.

Jimmy certainly wasn't the only one Howie attacked with his computer. In one of his hate-filled, vindictive, venomous columns for the *Herald*, he wrote about Vinnie Mancuso, an eighteen-year-old kid from Southie whose mother was suing the city of Boston because the cop who shot her son on May 16, 1986, was drunk when he killed Vinnie. I knew Vinnie, who was a car thief but was never violent. Joe Quinn, the cop who shot him, was referred to on the street as Cuckoo Quinn. He claimed Vinnie came at him with a knife, yet somehow Vinnie ended up with a bullet in the back of his head as he tried to run away. After that Quinn retired from the police force and eventually died. In his column, Carr called Vinnie a member of the FFA (Future Felons of America). Very funny. Making fun of a dead kid.

It's not right to take cheap shots at people in every column. If you have a problem with someone, say it to his face. But that's not Howie Coward's way. He prefers to creep behind closed doors and write stories in which people who understand what's going on can see he is not even close to being on target. He should have been a writer for a supermarket tabloid. Like so many other reporters, Howie is big on using the little catchwords, like "alleged," or "reputed," or "sources say," so he can get away with anything he wants to say.

His own personal life could be material for another hate radio talk show. Maybe they could talk about his first marriage and how it ended in divorce. My greatest revenge is knowing that this guy has to look in the mirror every morning and see he is a coward. And the rest of the day, he gets to live the life of a coward.

In the late 1980s, when Howie was working at Channel 56 in Boston, Jack Hynes, one of his coworkers at the television station, stopped by the liquor store. "Why doesn't Howie ever come in here?" I asked Jack. "The coward drives by here three or four days a week just to get a look at us. You tell Howie that if he comes in, we got a fresh Dumpster out back waiting for him. Just like with Robin Benedict." I was referring to a high-priced call girl who was killed by a college professor in 1984. Benedict's body was disposed of in a Dumpster.

One afternoon, probably five years after that, Jimmy, Stevie, and I were standing outside the liquor store. Howie pulled up in a blue foreign sports car across the street from where the three of us were standing. The minute I spotted him, I walked between Jimmy and Stevie and started running across the street. As the blue car took off, a puff of black smoke rose out of the tailpipe.

The next day, sitting safely behind his keyboard at the *Herald*, Howie wrote an article about Jimmy standing outside the liquor store, referring to him as "the diminutive weightlifter." Jimmy read the article and just laughed at the coward's latest column. "He didn't have the balls to get out of the car to face you," he said. "And now he's going to write about us."

Over the years, Howie has made a career of writing about the Bulgers every chance he gets. Even if the article has nothing to with either Jimmy or Billy, he puts them in. Without this subject, he would have little to talk or write about. His hatred of Jimmy and Billy probably started with Billy, who never was the darling of the press. Jimmy told me that once when Billy was talking to an elderly lady, Howie tried to interrupt, asking him repeatedly, "Can I ask you a question, Mr. President?"

Billy, who knew exactly who Howie was, turned around and said, "Who are you?"

"I'm from the press," Howie answered him.

"Well, do you vote in my district?" Billy asked him. When Howie said, "No," Billy told him, "Well, you just wait until I'm through talking to my constituent. Then I'll talk to you."

Howie never waited.

Jimmy, however, did make some serious attempts to get together with Howie. One, in particular, was at Howie's house in Acton. Jimmy and I staked out the house, driving by a few times to take pictures of it and to get the layout. The reason for our visit was simple: We were looking to kill him. We didn't like him because he was a piece of shit who wrote nasty stories about people. The guy was an oxygen thief who didn't deserve the right to breathe.

Jimmy's first plan was to fill a basketball with C-4 and blow it up the second Howie came out of his house. His second plan was to wrap a detonation cord around a tree in front of his house when Howie was home. The cord, a quarter of an inch thick, would contain C-4. When it exploded, it would take down the tree, which would take down the house. But both plans had too much risk of killing Howie's kids, so we had to pass on them.

My idea was just to shoot him. So, one day, I went down to his house at five in the morning and lay in the graveyard across the street. I was holding a high-powered rifle with a scope on it, waiting until he came out. Somewhere between seven and seven-thirty, Howie walked out of the house, holding the hand of his daughter, who was probably around seven or eight. There was no way I was going to kill him in front of his daughter or take a chance on hurting her, so I passed on it. I would have liked another chance to finish the job, but Jimmy got busy with some other stuff and told me to forget about him.

Even though Carr is a maggot and a piece of shit, if we had killed him, it would have been like Alan Berg, the Denver radio talk show host assassinated by a white supremacist with a Mac-10 as he got into his VW. Law enforcement would never have stopped until they tracked down Carr's killer, just the way they did with Berg's. His murder would have been an attack on the system, like attacking freedom of the press, the fabric of the American way of life, and they would have spared no expense to solve the crime. But in the long run, Jimmy and I got sidetracked and the maggot lived. Still, I wish we'd killed him. No question about it.

In November 1999, Howie came to my arraignment. When I was walking by him, he said, "Do you have anything to say?"

"Yeah," I said. "Howie, be fucking nice."

In his column the next day, he wrote that I said, "Howie, be nice." He couldn't even get those four words right.

I was later informed they would be calling Howie Carr as a witness at my bail hearing. However, he didn't get the chance to offer his thoughts about how dangerous I might be to him, since I didn't go for a bail hearing.

Another reporter who earned Jimmy's wrath was Paul Corsetti, also from the *Boston Herald*. Disgusted with the articles Corsetti was writing about him, Jimmy found out where Corsetti hung out and drank. One night in the early 1980s, dressed in a suit, Jimmy had me drop him off at the Dockside, a restaurant bar at Faneuil Hall. While I stayed outside in the car, Jimmy went in to find the *Herald* reporter.

When he saw Corsetti sitting at the bar, Jimmy went over and said, "Do you know who I am?"

Corsetti said, "No."

"I'm Jim Bulger," Jimmy told him. "And if you continue to write shit about me, I'm going to blow your fucking head off."

The next day, Corsetti reported the meeting to the Boston police. He was issued a pistol permit within twenty-four hours. The cop who gave him the permit told him, "I'm glad my last name is not Corsetti." A couple of days later, Jimmy found out about the scene with the cop and was glad to hear how uncomfortable he had made Corsetti.

But Corsetti was just one more example of *Herald* reporters who report stories that are inaccurate. These reporters are not the only members of the media who are careful never to allow the truth to get in the way of a good story. The story about state trooper Billy Johnson was another perfect example of that tactic.

That story began in September 1987, when Jimmy had me pick up him and Theresa to take them to the airport. They were planning to fly to Montreal to visit Theresa's daughter Karen, who was married to hockey star Chris Nilan. It was around five in the afternoon, but by the time we got to the airport, Jimmy was already in a bad mood. We'd been halfway there when Theresa had realized she'd forgotten her license and birth certificate, so we had to go back for them. He'd started screaming and yelling and was plenty aggravated when we finally arrived at Logan.

Once we got inside the terminal, I walked him down to the check-in counter. While we're in line, he put his bag on the conveyor to the X-ray machine. A security woman saw the bag, grabbed it, and said, "You have a large amount of money here. I'll have to take a look."

Immediately Jimmy grabbed the bag out of her hand and said, "Fuck this shit. I'm not going anywhere." She promptly called security, and when a security guard arrived, he started to go after Jimmy. Walking a good way behind Jimmy, I banged into the security guy and knocked him over the counter. At that moment, Jimmy was trying to take off his money belt. But he had a knot in it, and as he was trying to pull the belt off, the knot kept getting tighter around his waist. Calling out, "Kevin," Jimmy finally snapped the money belt off and handed it to me. That was the only the mistake he made. Actually, in all the years we were together, that was the only mistake I ever saw him make. But his calling out "Kevin" gave the authorities my identity. Knowing who Jimmy was, they could easily figure out by my physical description that he was calling Kevin Weeks, not Kevin O'Neil.

When I headed out of the airport, one of the security guards tried to follow me through the revolving doors. As I stepped out, Jimmy stuck his foot into the door, trapping the guard inside the middle door. Walking across the street, I saw two state troopers who had parked their car in front of mine. "Beautiful night, isn't it?" I said calmly to them.

"Yeah, it is," one of the troopers answered. Then I got into the black Chevy and drove away. As I pulled out of the airport, I put on the police scanner and drove back to the variety store. There was nothing on the scanner about the Logan incident.

Back at the airport, the officials found that both Jimmy and Theresa had less than $10,000, the specified amount a passenger is allowed to carry. "You can't fucking hold me," Jimmy told them. "You got nothing on me." As it turned out, even though the officials could have made up any charge they wanted, said he assaulted a guard or charged him with disorderly conduct and made him go to court, they didn't charge him with anything.

A couple of hours after I left, after a lot more swearing from Jimmy, the officials released the two of them. When I met Jimmy down at the variety store later that night, I gave him back the $80,000 in the money belt.

But the media screwed up the simple facts of that case. Both Howie Carr and Peter Gelzinis reported that Jimmy had a suitcase filled with $500,000 that he was trying to bring into Montreal. But the inaccurate facts didn't stop there. On September 25, 1998, William Johnson, the state trooper who had initially detained Jimmy and Theresa, committed suicide in a New Hampshire field. The media tried to blame the trooper's death on Jimmy, insisting that Billy Bulger, who was president of the Massachusetts State Senate, had taken revenge on Johnson by demoting him. But that simply wasn't true. Other troopers told me the guy had mental health issues. Even though the trooper had plenty of problems before he met Jimmy, it made a much better story to link his suicide to the scene at Logan eleven years earlier.

Most of the time, the *Boston Globe* wasn't as inaccurate as the *Herald*. They just knocked the people from Southie during busing. They also liked to describe me in all their stories as "Whitey's surrogate son," another example of the media putting labels on people they wrote about. Jimmy and I were friends, not like father and son. Even though he was the boss, he always treated me equally, like an associate, not a son. The reporter who seemed to do the most research and put real effort into getting the true story without having been there was Shelley Murphy, who had been at the *Herald* for ten years when she went to work for the *Globe* in 1993. But Jimmy and I usually just ended up laughing at most of the news stories, as time and time again the media had it wrong, over and over holding to their pledge to never let the truth get in the way of a good story.

When Jimmy and I, along with two of our friends, won the lottery, the press had another field day. The truth of the story is that in December 1990, Jimmy and I walked into the liquor store and saw a friend of ours, Pat Linskey, buying Mass Millions season tickets. When Jimmy asked him what he was doing, Patty said he was buying tickets as extra Christmas gifts in case he forgot friends and people who worked down at the store. Jimmy and I offered to help him pay for the tickets, but he said, "No, I have it."

During that week, the three of us gave out the tickets to friends and relatives as last-minute gifts, telling everyone, in a more or less joking manner, "If you win, we're partners." But no one ever expected to win.

Almost eight months later, on July 26, I was up in New Hampshire with family playing golf for the week. When I got back to the liquor store that weekend, I got a call from Pat saying that his brother Michael had hit the lottery for $14.3 million. That night, Patty and I met Michael, who said to Patty, "We're partners." Patty told Michael he was partners with me and Jimmy, and Michael said, "I don't care what you do with your 50 percent. I know what I'm doing with mine." So Michael got 50 percent, and Pat, Jimmy, and I shared the other 50 percent, with the three of us receiving $119,000 apiece before taxes for twenty years.

At that time, there was no love between Jimmy and Joe Malone, the state treasurer. Actually, if Danny Aiello and Jerry Cooney, a one-time heavyweight contender, mated, their son would look just like Joe Malone. Joe had the machine at the liquor store taken out. At the lottery headquarters, they checked their machine, and all the balls that were used to draw numbers were weighed to see if we had somehow rigged it. It was a waste of time. The drawing was legit.

At a press conference, Joe said that the only winner who could have caused him more trouble would have been his mother. The press was certain that somehow Billy had put the fix in for his brother and that it was all part of an after-the-win scheme to launder dirty money. Again, they were wrong. But the truth also was that it caused us more heat than it was worth.

The media also worked hard trying to make up stories about Jimmy's sexual orientation. But there wasn't any truth to any of those stories. One photo of Jimmy that often appears in the press shows him bare-chested except for a vest, wearing a cowboy hat and holding a gun. It's supposed to equate him with the Village People, when he really was with a woman.

The photo was taken when he and Theresa were on vacation and they went into a vintage costume place where you put on old-fashioned garb and have your photo taken. They never show the part of the photo where Theresa is dressed as a saloon girl. It's just easier for the press to take Jimmy's part of the picture out of context and leave Theresa out of it. Actually, Theresa has the complete photo and won't release it. She's saving it for when she writes *her* book.

Despite their continuous attempt to grab pictures of us, Jimmy and I were pretty alert and managed to avoid nearly every photographer who hounded us. There is one photo of the two of us, however, that continually accompanies articles about either one of us, and is usually shown on the Whitey Bulger episodes of *America's Most Wanted*. This one was taken by a *Globe* reporter who happened to stumble across the two of us one summer day when Jimmy and I were walking around Castle Island. I was wearing a white T-shirt with FILA across its front and Jimmy had on a Boston Red Sox cap. The minute we spotted the photographer, with his footlong telescopic lens stretched across the roof of his car, Jimmy and I both gave him dirty looks. Then, as I started running toward him, the photographer jumped into his car and took off. For all the years the photographers hounded us, that was one of only two photographs they ever got of the two of us together.

There was one incident, however, in which Jimmy and I managed to use the media to further our own interests. In 1990, we were interested in the race for governor of Massachusetts and were anxious to do whatever we could to hurt the campaign of lieutenant governor Francis X. Bellotti. Jimmy had never liked Bellotti and particularly blamed him for the failed investigation into the fire that took place at the Hotel Vendome on June 17, 1972. During the fire, nine firemen lost their lives when the southeast section of the hotel collapsed. Jimmy always believed that the investigation was whitewashed because Franchi Construction, which was doing the renovation of the hotel, was a political contributor to Bellotti. It had been reported that some of the support beams were illegally taken out and should never have been removed during the renovation. Jimmy and I were told by firefighters who went into the hotel the night of the fire that the building wasn't structurally sound to begin with.

Bellotti had always been after Jimmy, making it a personal matter, trying to embarrass Billy's political career through his brother. So Jimmy was determined to do whatever he could to make sure that Bellotti didn't get his party's nomination in the race for governor. During the campaign, Jimmy and I used to go around town and along the expressway at night spreading our particular message of "Remember John Coady" on sidewalks. Late at night, I hung over the overpasses or climbed the walls, spray-painting in fluorescent orange and black the places where the cars went by with the words "Remember John Coady," while Jimmy waited in the car.

John Coady had been the deputy revenue department commissioner in 1982 when Bellotti's office probed the Revenue Department. During Bellotti's investigation, a state tax examiner, Stanley Barczak, made allegations against Coady. Seven weeks after Barczak's testimony, on July 30, 1982, Coady committed suicide in his North Andover home. Many people believed Coady had done nothing wrong and that Bellotti's relentless pursuit had made an innocent man commit suicide.

Our campaign to discredit Bellotti may well have ended up costing him votes. A week before the election, people started to talk about John Coady, and the *Globe* wrote stories about the graffiti appearing all over town. It was enough to stimulate the media's interest in John Coady, even though they had no idea that Jimmy and I were behind the whole scene.

But for the most part, the media devoted far too much space to printing lies about Jimmy and me. I assume that most people would prefer to stay private, rather than have their names in the newspaper. We were no different.

TWELVE
IN THE WIND
1994–1996

I was standing by the end of the counter next to the lottery machine at Rotary Liquors at 295 Old Colony Avenue, the store we'd bought from Stippo ten years earlier, when John Connolly walked in. It was around three in the afternoon on Tuesday, December 23, 1994. Connolly, who modeled his appearance after John Gotti, was wearing an expensive suit and tie, his hair carefully coiffed, dressed as sharply as when he'd been an FBI agent. He'd retired from the FBI in 1990 and was now working as head of corporate security at Boston Edison, a nice benefit from his years at the FBI. Although I'd see him riding around South Boston, he rarely came into the variety store next door, where I usually worked. If he was looking for Jimmy, he'd go to the liquor store, but most of the time he'd be talking to Kevin O'Neil. "Is the other guy around?" he asked this time, referring, of course, to Jimmy.

He looked a little anxious, like he had something on his mind, but I told him Jimmy wasn't around. When he asked for Stevie, I told him he wasn't around, either. We made some small talk before he said, "Then I've got to talk to you."

The two of us headed down to the walk-in beer chest and walked inside. This was the perfect place for a private conversation since it would be hard to bug because of the dampness, along with the humming of the fans and the whirring noise of the compressors. And we would also be out of sight of anybody hanging around down there.

"The indictments are imminent," he told me as soon as I closed the door to the chest. That wasn't exactly a surprise. We'd known for months that a grand jury had been sitting in Worcester considering the extortion of the Jewish bookmakers, like Chico Krantz and Jimmy Katz, who were paying rent, another word for protection money, to Jimmy and Stevie. We knew the indictments would be for bookmaking, extortion, gambling, and money laundering. "They're trying to put them all together over the holidays," Connolly continued. "That way they can pinch them all at once."

That made sense. Stevie would be at his mother's and Jimmy at Theresa's over the holidays. They could scoop them both up, and whoever else might be around visiting their families, on the same night. Obviously, they were trying to put whoever else was named in the indictments in position over the holidays and arrest them. But I wasn't certain exactly who the others might be.

And I wasn't worried about my involvement in the case, since I had nothing to do with the Jewish bookmakers. I also knew that for the past year or two, Jimmy and Stevie had been receiving weekly updates about what was going on with the grand jury, which had already received a couple of extensions. They knew what people were saying there from their sources in law enforcement, as well as from people who had been summoned there. They'd held the grand jury out in Worcester to try and cut down on leaks, but it wasn't working. In all the information they were getting, my name had never been mentioned. Jimmy knew the whole cast of characters involved, the bookmakers and everyone else the grand jury was targeting, as well as the witnesses they were calling in. And he'd been maintaining a lower profile than before. Normally, Jimmy was pretty elusive, but he'd been even more so for the past year and a half. He'd also been taking more trips than usual, getting out of town when the heat was turned up.

In 1993 and 1994, before the pinches came down, Stevie and Jimmy were traveling through the French and Italian Riviera. The two of them traveled all over Europe, sometimes separating for a while. They'd be gone two or three weeks at a time. Sometimes they took girls; sometimes just the two of them went. They would rent cars and travel all through Europe. It was more preparation than anything, getting ready for another life. They didn't ask me to go, not that I would have wanted to.

Jimmy had prepared for the run for years. He'd established a whole other person, Thomas Baxter, with a complete ID and credit cards in that name. He'd even joined associations under Baxter's name, building an entire portfolio on the guy. He'd always said you have to be ready to take off on short notice. And he was.

Stevie, however, was, as usual, all over the place. He wasn't curtailing any of his activities or anything. Over the past two years, Jimmy had been especially upset with Stevie's traveling back and forth to Cambridge and Brookline, meeting with Frank Salemme at the Busy Bee restaurant. Frankie went back to the 1960s with Stevie and had made a successful bid in the late 1980s to take over the New England Mafia. Recently, however, Frankie had taken off after he and his son got indicted for some scam in Hollywood on a movie production. But for years before Frankie went on the lam, Stevie had headed to the other side of town during the day and then came back over to meet with us in Southie around four-thirty in the afternoon.

Jimmy kept saying, "What are you doing? You're over there with him and then you come over to us. You make it look like one big gang and you're the liaison between Frankie and us. You're making us one big target."

"No way, Jimmy," Stevie said. "I'm just staying on top of things."

"Are you making money with this guy?" Jimmy asked him. "Do you have anything going with him?"

"No," Stevie said.

"Then why are you over there?" Jimmy asked.

"We're friends," Stevie told him.

"Yeah, well, they're getting pictures of you and Frankie together, and then the feds are taking pictures of you leaving and meeting with us here," Jimmy said.

But it had been useless for Jimmy to talk to Stevie. He continued moving around, not changing any of his activities just because a grand jury was investigating him. Stevie wasn't as keenly attuned to the law as the two of us were. Many times they were on him for days and he didn't have a clue.

One October afternoon in 1994, a few months before the indictments, Stevie picked me up at the variety store just to take a ride. I hopped into the car with him, and we drove downtown toward Andrew Square and took a left onto Boston Street. As we did, I turned the visor down so I could look in the mirror and immediately picked up four cars following us: a van, a Trans Am, a red Camaro, and a Ford LTD. We hadn't gone more than three blocks from the store when I picked up the law behind us. As we pulled into a gas station on Columbia Road, two of the cars started to pull over, one across the street from us, one behind us, while the other two kept circling up and down the block.

"Look at those cars, Stevie," I said as I pointed out all four to him.

"Holy shit," he said. "I didn't see one of them. You have good eyes."

I said nothing. He drove me back to the store. I got out.

"Only four people in the FBI office know about these indictments," Connolly went on to tell me that December afternoon in the beer chest. He'd heard it from Dennis O'Callahan, the SAC, or Supervising Agent in Charge, of the Boston office. "So, where are Stevie and Jimmy?"

After I talked to Connolly for a while to make sure I had it right, I told him I'd beep Jimmy and try to get hold of him. By then it was three-thirty. When Connolly left, I went next door to the variety store and beeped Jimmy. He called me back a couple of minutes later and told me he was going shopping with Theresa. I told him to swing by and pick me up. In a few minutes, he picked me up in his blue Ford LTD and I got into the back seat and the three of us drove to Neiman Marcus in Copley Plaza. Always aware the car might be bugged, I didn't say a word about the indictments or Connolly while we were in the car.

When we got to Copley Plaza, Jimmy told Theresa he was going to talk to me. She stood by the entrance to Neiman Marcus while Jimmy and I walked toward the back of the car, which he had parked illegally at the sidewalk. I told him exactly what Connolly had told me. There was no change in his facial expressions as I explained how O'Callahan had told Connolly that the feds had plans to arrest him and Stevie over the holidays. And how only four people in the FBI office knew that.

"Have you gotten hold of Stevie yet?" he asked me and I told him no, that he was the first one I'd called. He said he'd call Stevie and I should, too. Then he called over to Theresa, who was still standing in front of Neiman Marcus. The two of them talked privately for a few minutes, and then the three of us drove off and he dropped me off at Preble Street near the variety store. "I'll call you later," he said before the two of them took off, and I went into the store. I realized he might be gone for a while. Things were changing.

Around five-thirty, Stevie finally showed up at the variety store. He looked the same as always, black leather jacket, black gloves, dungarees. I told him the same thing I'd told Jimmy. Jimmy hadn't reached him, so it was the first time he'd heard about it. I also told him that Jimmy had already gone. Stevie didn't seem panicked. "My guy is right on top of it," he told me. "I'll be hearing from him." He left the store, assuring me he had plenty of time. I repeated that only four people knew and that maybe his guy wasn't one of them.

A week later, Stevie came back in the store and I said to him, "What are you doing? Stevie, you've got to take off."

"My guy is right on top of it," he told me again.

"Stevie, I told you there are only four people who know. Take off for a couple of weeks. If anything comes down, you've got a head start. If nothing happens, you had a vacation."

Stevie got a little upset, and we started arguing. He kept telling me his guy knew everything and I was telling him there were only four people who knew. Finally he said he had a couple of things to do and then he would take off.

I heard nothing from Jimmy that week or the next, but I felt more interest in me, obviously, since I was the only one left in South Boston. I continued doing my loan-sharking and my usual business activities, but there was no ignoring the stronger presence of the law. Before the indictments, Jimmy and I had always joked about FBI agent John Gamel, a former Worcester weatherman, six-eight, with black hair, thick glasses with oversized black rims, and a mustache, a real geeky kind of guy who always wore the same brown trench coat and tried to blend into a crowd. But he looked like a huge bookworm, a big goof. At Castle Island, Jimmy and I would be watching him and laughing because he stood out like a giraffe walking among people.

We also knew that since the grand jury had first been convened, they had round-the-clock surveillance on us. There were three different teams, each one working eight hours on us. We got to know lots of their faces. It didn't matter how many different cars they drove, we remembered their faces. South Boston is a small community, so it wasn't that hard to spot the undercover cops. People overestimate the law. They figure that once they're on you, you can't do anything. But that's not true. It's not that they're so great at what they do, it's just that the criminals can be lazy at what they do. And if a criminal makes one mistake, he's gone. Most criminals don't put enough effort into not being caught. The law can make a thousand mistakes, and they still get their check every week. And time is always on their side. They have all the time in the world.

But I'd gotten really good at losing the law whenever I wanted to. I'd hop on the T, go one or two stops, then hop on another train and go a few more stops before getting off and getting into a waiting car. Or I'd make my way through the projects on foot, snake through a few buildings and tunnels, come out the other side, and jump into a car I'd parked there earlier. Or I would drive down a one-way street, hop out, and have another car waiting. When they had a plane on me, I would drive to Logan Airport where there was restricted airspace and their plane couldn't follow me.

Sometimes Jimmy and I would be flying down the highway in the left high-speed lane, and we'd suddenly swing over three lanes and fly off an exit at high speed. Other times, we'd be in the right lane on the highway, going 25 miles per hour. Anyone who is behind you who is not following you would get upset and swing by and pass you. But the law would slow down and try and stay behind you at a distance. Or they'd get ahead of you and wait at a rest area for you to pass. Those were just things we learned over the years. Like how the law would use magnets to try to put transmitters underneath the car's bumper, sort of an early form of LoJack. But we'd always check the bumpers and find them. Then we'd take out the battery and leave the empty transmitter in place there. When I think about all the work Jimmy and I put into not getting caught, I can barely imagine how much money we could have made legitimately, probably with a lot less effort. But with Jimmy gone, I wasn't curtailing my activities, and was basically living the same life, although without his presence. But no matter where I went, I felt the presence of the law.

On Thursday night, January 5, 1995, I was down at the L Street Tavern, which my friend Bobby Cox owned, playing whist with some friends. This was the place used for *Good Will Hunting,* where Matt Damon always hung around. In the movie, Damon had the middle booth. But the end booth was my booth, right next to the jukebox. When I walked in, anyone sitting there would get up so my friends and I could play cards at our designated card table. Anyhow, that night, Stevie's younger brother Michael walked through the door and motioned to me. As the two of us walked outside together, he told me, "They just pinched Stevie."

"What's he doing still around, Mikey?" I asked him. "I told him to take off two weeks ago."

"I know, I know," Michael said.

"Jesus, what was he thinking?" I said. "He should have taken off."

"I know, I know," Michael kept repeating.

When I started to look around, all I could see were all sorts of new cars driving around. The faces in the cars were all staring at me as the undercover agents kept circling the bar. It was an even stronger presence than I'd had in the past two weeks since Jimmy took off. "Mikey, you brought the law with you," I told him as I started to point out the circling cars to him. "Just look at them. I'll catch you later."

I walked into the bar, grabbed my jacket, and walked out the side door. A friend met me at L and Seventh streets and gave me a ride to another friend's place. I wanted to get hold of Jimmy and let him know what was happening. I hadn't had any reason to contact him for the past two weeks, but now I did. I kept beeping him from my friend's apartment in Southie at G and Broadway, and finally, around midnight, he called me back. "How you doing?" he asked me.

"Fine," I said, "but they just pinched Stevie. And red's all around." Red was the universal warning sign for danger. When we used it, it meant the law was around. "And they're looking for someone else."

"I heard it on the radio," he told me. "I just got back to Massachusetts, but now I'm making a U-turn. I was coming back tonight." He was probably taking Theresa home for a visit. We talked for a couple of minutes about nothing much and then he said, "Call you later," and he was gone.

As it turned out, Stevie was actually indicted on Monday January 9. He'd been arrested on Thursday night on a complaint, and was charged with something just to hold him and prevent his taking off till the indictment was handed down. On January 9, the indictment came down for Jimmy, too, as well as for six others, including Bobby DeLuca, Jimmy and Johnny Martorano, Frankie Salemme and Frankie Salemme Jr., and George Kaufman. Now that he'd been indicted for racketeering, extortion, money laundering, and gambling, Jimmy was officially wanted and in the wind. He was gone.

Over the next six weeks, Jimmy and I had a lot of phone calls. Since he was on the lam now, he'd had to get rid of his beeper and was using calling cards at pay phones to call me at numbers I would give him. I'd never have him call me at the same number twice. He'd always tell me exactly when he would call, and he was never a minute late with each call. I never had a number to reach him at.

The next time I saw Jimmy was in the middle of February 1995. He'd made arrangements to drop off Theresa at her daughter Karen's house in Hingham and pick up Catherine Greig. Theresa wasn't well suited for life on the run, and after two months she was ready to come home and see her four kids. Cathy was much better equipped for that kind of life. She had no kids and had been devoted to Jimmy since the early 1980s. Cathy was very intelligent, and always upbeat and pleasant. A good person, she treated everybody in the same nice manner. She had two toy black poodles, Nicki and Gigi, that she and Jimmy loved and were always walking. Cathy was a dental hygienist, but thanks to caring for Nicki and Gigi, she'd become expert at grooming dogs as well. They had been together as long as I had known Jimmy.

Cathy lived with Jimmy—when he wasn't living with Theresa—in a house in Squantum. In mid-February, Jimmy made arrangements for me to meet Cathy at 7:30 P.M. at the bottom of the Golden Gate stairs that run down from Thomas Park in South Boston. When I drove up, she was coming down the stairs. Her sister Margaret had dropped her off and taken Nicki and Gigi. Cathy gave me her usual big smile and hopped in my black Pontiac Bonneville and we took off. I'd driven around for an hour before I met her, to make sure I was clean and there was no law following me. As always, Cathy looked attractive and well put together. Blond and blue-eyed, she had a lovely smile, a pretty face, and nice bone structure to her face. And she kept herself in good shape. That night she was wearing warm clothes, no hat, and a big smile, and carried an over-the-shoulder type of weekend bag as her only piece of luggage.

We drove around for another hour to make sure neither one of us was being followed before heading over to Malibu Beach in Dorchester. There were two parking lots on the beach, one on the Morrissey Boulevard side, where I was to park, and the other on the Savin Hill side, where Jimmy would park.

Cathy and I were on the walkway heading from the Morrissey Boulevard side to the Savin Hill side, about nine, when Jimmy appeared out of the shadows of the cold, clear February night. Trying to surprise us, he strode calmly out of the darkness. But Cathy saw him right away and picked up her pace. I could see a few other people around, but no one was paying us any attention. At first Jimmy didn't show any outward emotion, but as he got closer, he gave us a wide smile.

"How you doing?" he asked simply, and Cathy went right to him and gave him a big hug. The two of them embraced a long minute, making a dramatic scene, sort of like out of *Casablanca*. He was wearing a Stetson hat, a black leather jacket, and dark jeans. He and I shook hands, and the three of us walked over to the Savin Hill side of the parking lot. Jimmy seemed nice and relaxed and in a good mood, like he didn't have a care in the world. We got into his black Mercury Grand Marquis, me in front with him driving and Cathy in back, which is how we usually sat when we were out with women.

We drove around South Boston and Dorchester for an hour or so, just to see the town and stuff. Jimmy was joking around for a little bit and then we talked about what was going on with the case, how Stevie was doing and why he hadn't taken off. Jimmy had spent nine years in prison, including a stint in Alcatraz, so he knew how hard it would be for Stevie, who'd never been in prison before. He felt that was one of the reasons Stevie hadn't fled, the fact that he had no idea what prison was like. He was worried that left to his own devices, Stevie would self-destruct.

Actually, eight years earlier, back in 1987, Jimmy had wanted to pack it in. He was approaching sixty and figured it was time to retire. He'd had enough of it all. He wasn't sure what he would do, maybe travel. He certainly didn't need any more money. It would have been fine with me. But Stevie had wanted to stay active and Jimmy was hostage to him.

Now, even though Jimmy had been gone less than two months, it was obvious that he was preparing to stay out as long as he had to. I knew it would work for him. He'd prepared for this for years. And he had no bad habits, no vices. He didn't drink or gamble or use drugs. Things would have been different if he did any of those things. Plus, most important, he was extremely self-disciplined and would never let his guard down. It takes a lot of money to stay out there, but I imagined he had taken care of that. Driving around that night, I did ask him if he needed money and he said he was all set.

Finally, Jim drove me back to my car and I gave him a new phone number where he could reach me whenever he needed me. He said he'd call me. And then I got out of the car and Jimmy and I had a handshake and the two of them drove off.

Although the indictments had been served and Jimmy was officially a fugitive, I had pretty much the same routine as before, although it was less restrictive and more relaxing without him around. I'd stay home till around noon. Then I'd shower and shave and go down to the variety store around 1:30 and stay till 6:00 P.M. People would come down to see me and complain. I'd hear about people being bothered, kids breaking into houses, relatives beating up family members, the basic day-to-day complaints. As I'd always done, I'd have to deal with each situation. I'd grab the people who were preying on weaker people and tell them to stop it. I'd find the guys who were robbing in Southie and send them to Newton or Wellesley. "Don't go robbing your own people," I'd tell them. "Go to the richer towns. They have more."

Parents who were having trouble with their kids would ask me to talk to the kids and help keep them out of trouble. Some kids were trying drugs or getting into fights all the time or stealing cars. I'd go to the house or see the kids on the street or when they came into the store and tell them, "What you're doing is building up a record where you will end up doing time in jail. Everything you're doing is foolish. You're not making any money doing what you're doing. It's not worth it." I didn't have a record, but I had a reputation and the kids might listen to me better than they would to their parents. I sponsored some basketball and hockey teams, giving money to each team so they could buy uniforms and equipment. The community wasn't as close as it had been when I was growing up, with a lot of people leaving and a lot of outsiders moving in. It was actually a tougher place now, and it wasn't easy for a kid to stay out of trouble.

Lots of people were coming up to me and saying, "Tell him I said hi." I couldn't say okay because if one of these people were working for the law, it would show that I had knowledge of Jimmy's whereabouts or had contact with him. Then law enforcement would indict me for aiding and abetting.

If I saw his brother Billy, I'd say, "Everybody is doing good," and he could draw his own conclusions. I would never want to jeopardize Billy or put him in a compromising position. I considered it plausible deniability. I was saying something without saying the words.

But most nights, around six, I'd leave the store, get dinner, and head back out afterward. Most Tuesday nights, I'd play pool in a league for four hours or so. Thursday nights, I'd play cards. They were friendly games where we would enjoy the action and have some fun while killing a night.

Obviously, I wasn't making as much money as before, since my operation was smaller now. I still had a few drug dealers and bookmakers who were paying me or giving me a cut. I had my gambling and loan-sharking businesses, as well as the sports business with guys working for me to take bets on football games. But after the indictments, we'd pulled our horns in. Things were a lot quieter on the streets in Southie.

I was also visiting Stevie in Plymouth once a week at the beginning, and then maybe every two or three weeks. But he was calling me every night asking me when I was coming up, talking about the case and what was happening in court. I didn't like talking on the phone at all. I was afraid he might say something accidentally on the phone, where every conversation from prison was recorded. I felt like he was making me a target by calling me every day.

When I visited him in Plymouth, we'd sit separated by the glass partition and talk on the phone. There would be no physical contact. Despite what some of the newspaper reports said about Stevie, things were pretty bad at Plymouth. The food was terrible and he had lost weight. You had to remember that Plymouth was a federal holding facility, where you're being detained until trial. It wasn't a state joint like Norfolk where things were much better and you had more facilities, and there was more to do to occupy your time.

But Jimmy had been right about Stevie. He wasn't doing well in prison. Whenever we'd talk about Jimmy, he'd always say, "It's better for my case that the other guy is out there. Tell him to stay free." There was no doubt that the whole atmosphere of the trial and everything would be changed if Jimmy had gotten caught. It would be more of a media event than it already was.

Although I was hearing from Jimmy pretty regularly, at least once a week, and often two or three times a week, I had no idea where he and Cathy were. And I wouldn't ask. In May 1995, he called to ask me to meet him "at the lions" in New York. So I took the Amtrak out of Dedham to Penn Station, and had no trouble getting on the train without being followed.

When I got to New York, around one o'clock, I met Jimmy and Cathy "at the lions," which referred to the two statues of lions in front of the main branch of the New York Public Library, on the corner of 41st Street and Fifth Avenue. Cathy looked great, as usual. She was still taking good care of herself and seemed as happy and pleasant as ever. Jimmy wore boots, a dark three-quarter-length jacket with a drawstring at the waist, slacks, a baseball hat, sunglasses, and no gloves. No change in his appearance from how he dressed in Southie.

Sometimes Cathy would stand off to the side to give Jimmy and me a chance to talk privately. Mostly we talked about the case and what was happening. He was now using his ID as Thomas Baxter and was confident about the way things were going. He'd heard from whoever else he was in contact with now that the case on him was falling apart, thanks to bickering between the state police and FBI. Also, some of the people involved in the case, like George Kaufman and Chico Krantz, were sick and might not make it to trial.

Then the three of us took a long walk, just three more assholes blending in with the rest of the assholes walking along the streets of New York. We stopped at a restaurant in one of the hotels and had an early dinner. After dinner, I turned around and came back on the train.

In late June 1995, I had to take off and get out of town for the summer. Paul Moore, a South Boston drug dealer who was paying us money, had been arrested and had started to cooperate. I had had dealings with Paul and knew there was an excellent chance I would get indicted. So I took off for the summer. I went to New Hampshire, to the Lake Winnipesaukee area, and had a great time for myself. I had three different places to stay at, including one owned by my wife's uncle. There were reports that I wasn't around, and anyone looking for me would have had a hard time finding me. I spent my days swimming off the dock, cruising around the lake in a maroon-and-white Chaparral boat I bought with a 350-horsepower inboard/outboard motor.

Since there weren't many pay phones available for use in the Lakes Region in New Hampshire, it wasn't easy finding numbers to give to Jimmy to call me at. So I got myself a pair of hand phones, like the ones the linemen from the telephone company use, from a friend who worked for the telephone company. I'd find out the phone number of a local business. Then at night, when the buildings were closed, I'd clip the handset onto a junction box on the outside of the building where the telephone line came in, and Jimmy would call me there. The building was always closed then, so no one else was around and I could talk to him as long as he wanted, usually ten or fifteen minutes. I managed to do this at maybe four different buildings near the lake, so the two of us could stay in touch that summer. Every once in a while I'd sneak back into South Boston and take care of what I had to do and then head right back up to New Hampshire.

Finally, the first week in September, the superseding indictments on Jimmy and Stevie came down but I wasn't mentioned. I came back to Boston a week later, relieved to have escaped another round. It was easier to talk to Jimmy at different pay phones back in South Boston. Every time we talked, he sounded great, upbeat, and not at all worried about his case. "A rolling stone gathers no moss," he would tell me, which I assumed meant he was moving around the country, using calling cards in lots of different places to call me.

Finally, in the spring of 1996, a year since I'd last seen him, he asked me to meet him again in New York, "at the lions." The purpose of the visit was simply to touch base with one another. I took the train and again had no trouble eluding the law. When I met him and Cathy at the public library, they both looked great. She had natural blonde hair, but it looked like she had lightened it a bit. It was obvious he was still keeping in shape. The two of them looked completely relaxed, like they were on vacation. He wasn't one of those people who showed a lot of affection in public. He felt that was all for show, so they didn't walk around holding hands. But you could tell he cared for her. And there was no question she cared for him.

It was a nice late May day and the three of us walked around Bryant Park behind the library and talked about what was going on with the case and in Southie. Then we grabbed a sandwich and a tonic from a nearby sandwich shop and walked around some more. Finally, around six, we headed back to Penn Station. Jimmy and Cathy walked me right down to the platform, where the three of us shook hands and I hopped on the train back to Boston. As always, when I was on the train, I didn't allow myself to fall asleep, feeling the need to stay awake and be aware of my surroundings.

Right after that visit, I got some important news I needed to share immediately with Jimmy, but it turned out to be five weeks until he next contacted me. I'd only been back in Boston a few days when it got back to me that Theresa was dating that piece of shit Alan Thistle, who everybody knew was an informant for the FBI, the state police, and the Boston police. It was also well known that he was a drug user.

As soon as I heard that news, I just showed up at Theresa's house on Silver Street in South Boston around seven at night and rang the bell. Theresa seemed a little surprised to see me, but let me in. She'd always been a beautiful woman, and dressed in dungarees and a long-sleeved white blouse, she still looked stunning. She was around fifty-four or fifty-five, with platinum-white hair. Right away, I said, "So, what are you doing going out with Alan Thistle?"

"*He's* with Cathy," she answered me. "I have my life to live."

"There's plenty of guys out there to go out with. Why him?" I said.

"He's an informant for law enforcement. He's just pumping you for information."

I knew Thistle worked for John Gamel and I'd always thought that he might be wired up. Once Thistle had asked a friend of mine what kind of watch he had. "If I get enough money off the FBI, I'm going to buy a watch like that," he told my friend.

Before my friend could answer, I jumped in and said, "It's a cheap one, not expensive." I didn't want him to have any info at all. I knew he would try and use the fact that my friend had a gold Piaget in a negative manner. You just had to measure every word you said to this guy.

Before Jimmy took off in 1994, while the investigation was going on, Thistle had approached me and another fellow and told the two of us he was getting $1,500 a month from Gamel. "Yeah, I know what he looks like," I told him. "He's always trying to follow us around."

"Well, if you want to pay me, too," he said, "I can be a double agent for you and Jimmy. I can let you know what they're saying and what they're doing." He went on to tell me that they were bugging the benches where we sat at Castle Island.

"We're not interested," I told him. "We're not doing anything."

But that night at her house, Theresa kept defending him. "Everything you tell this guy, he's going to go back and tell law enforcement," I kept repeating. I was there close to three hours, trying to explain to her that she shouldn't go out with this guy, that he was bad business.

Finally, when I got ready to leave, she said, "Well, it's too late."

"What do you mean it's too late?" I asked.

She told me to come downstairs and follow her into the kitchen. In the kitchen, she lit up a cigarette. Jimmy hated her smoking, and she never smoked in front of him or me. I could see she was nervous, and her hands were shaking as she pulled out a card and handed it to me. The card said, FBI SPECIAL AGENT JOHN GAMEL. As I looked at it, she said, "I already talked to him. He came by the house and I told him everything.

Where Jimmy and I were in New York. The name Thomas Baxter that he was using. Everything." Even that she and Jimmy had stayed with a relative of mine in upstate New York. I could see she was real excited and nervous, but I needed to find out everything she had said about the six weeks she and Jimmy had been together on the run, especially about the ID that Jimmy had developed back in 1985 and had just started to use. "All right, relax, calm down," I said gently. We were both standing up in her kitchen. If Thistle had walked in at that moment, I would have broken his jaw for him, but he didn't. "Don't worry about it. We'll figure it out."

We talked for a few more minutes, although she didn't have much more to add. Then I said, "I'll get back to you," and left. Hell hath no fury like that of a woman scorned. It certainly hadn't made Theresa happy when Jimmy dumped her off and took off with Cathy ten minutes later. I never talked to Theresa again after that. There was no reason to.

Unfortunately, there was nothing I could do but wait for Jimmy's call. After I saw Theresa, I visited Stevie at Plymouth and told him what she'd had done. Since it wasn't safe to talk about most subjects on the prison phone, we both used pads of paper to write each other messages that we would hold up to the glass partition. After we were through with each message, we would scribble over it in case anyone got hold of the piece of paper. Jimmy had always been just as concerned with writing things down. The two of us hardly ever wrote anything down, but the few times we did, we would burn the piece of paper or rip it up into small pieces and throw it out the car window while we were driving down the highway.

"You've got to reach Jimmy," Stevie wrote to me that visit, but, of course, there was nothing I could do for those five weeks, except hope he didn't get caught using his Baxter alias.

Finally, on July Fourth weekend, he called and I told him Theresa had given him up. "Thank God, at least I know," he said calmly, not sounding the least bit rattled. "I'll call you back."

When he called back a few days later, he told me to take some photos of his younger brother Jackie, which he could use for a new ID. He also told me he'd grown a mustache, which was a big change from his usual clean-shaven look, so I should make sure Jackie had a mustache in the photo. I talked to him for a few minutes about taking out Alan Thistle, since Thistle was dating Theresa and was working for the FBI and everything. But he said no. Going out with Thistle would be Theresa's punishment.

So I went to Jackie's house at 17 Twomey Court in South Boston with a blue cotton sheet, a phony mustache, and a Polaroid camera, and took a bunch of photos of Jackie, using the blue sheet for background. I chose the four best and spent a good month putting together the documentation necessary to get Jimmy a new Social Security number, driver's license, and birth certificate.

In August, on the night Jimmy was supposed to call me back at eight, I waited at the phone number I'd given him, but he didn't call. He was very punctual and it wasn't like him to be even a minute late. When he finally called me at exactly nine, I figured out that he had to be in the Midwest, probably the Chicago area, with the time one hour behind us in the East, and he had gotten confused with the time difference. "You probably know where I am now," he said when I told him I'd been waiting an hour.

"I've got an idea," I said, and he told me to meet him in Chicago at Water Tower Place in two days and to bring the pictures of Jackie. I rented a little blue foreign car and drove out there with a girl. Pam and I were separated by then. After I made sure there was no one following us, we stopped overnight in South Bend, Indiana, near Notre Dame. The next day we met Jimmy and Cathy near Water Tower Place, a big modern building in Chicago. It was a beautiful late summer day and the four of us first had something to eat at an outside café. Afterward we walked around in downtown Chicago. The girls walked and talked together so Jimmy and I could walk alone. As always, no one recognized him.

When we were walking that afternoon, Jimmy told me how he had been in Louisiana, and had rented a place down there. He'd ended up befriending this family where the husband was kind of lazy. The guy was a carpenter by trade, so Jimmy bought him all kinds of carpentry tools. They were such nice people that he also bought appliances to help them out. He even went craw fishing with the guy, throwing out the nets and stuff. He ended up spending around forty grand on that family. I just laughed as he told me this story. It was typical of Jimmy to do the unexpected. There he is, on the run, and he's taking care of other people. That's Jimmy.

He also told me how he and Cathy were walking down the street in that Louisiana town one afternoon and the sheriff who was directing traffic stopped the cars to let the two of them get by. "Hi, Tom," the sheriff greeted him, as friendly as could be. Jimmy smiled back and he and Cathy just kept on walking.

But even though Jimmy and Cathy looked terrific and I could tell he was still working out regularly, there was a sense that things might be coming down. At one point, while the two of us were walking, he told me, "If anything ever comes down, put it on me." I said nothing in response. I didn't understand at the time why he was thinking that. I also figured he was in touch with others, although we didn't talk about it and I never knew for sure.

But the IDs turned out to be all wrong. Jimmy's mustache looked nothing like the one I'd put on Jackie. The fake one was much bigger than the pencil-thin one Jimmy now wore. So we went shopping and bought a Polaroid-type camera and some blue sheets and headed to his hotel to take new photos. He hadn't been able to get a room in a nice hotel, so he'd had to settle for a crummy one. In the room, we took a bunch of photos that worked fine. He'd done his homework and had four new names with addresses and social security numbers, which we could use on the second set of IDs. One of the aliases was Shackleton, the name of a man he befriended in the Illinois area and and whose ID he had acquired. I have no idea how it happened, if he gave the guy money or what. He chose the photos he liked best and compared them to the size of my license picture to ensure they would fit into the frame. Once he was satisfied with them, we were ready to head out for dinner.

Around nine, we walked over to a nearby Japanese restaurant. It was a warm, pleasant summer evening and Jimmy and I wore regular slacks and shirts. Cathy, dressed in white pants, a blouse, and a light jacket, walked on ahead with the girl I was with. Three black kids in their early twenties walked by and started to stare at the girls. They were saying something to the girls, but they were mumbling so Jimmy and I couldn't really hear them.

Jimmy burst out, "What are you looking at, you motherfuckers?" Out came his knife and out came my knife, and we ran right toward them. The guys took off running down the street. I don't think the girls realized what was going on with the guys, but they saw us pull out the knives. That's Jimmy, too. On the run and still aggressive. Not taking shit from anyone. We had a good laugh about that scene during dinner.

When we walked into the restaurant, Jimmy said, "Every day out there is another day I beat them. Every good meal is a meal they can't take away from me." It was strange talk from him, but a few minutes later he was acting as if he didn't have a care in the world.

We sat in the back of the restaurant at an ordinary table. Jimmy asked the waiter what he recommended and then checked with the three of us. Finally, Jimmy ordered some chicken dishes, some meat dishes, and some vegetable dishes. We had a couple of beers with the meal. It was a relaxing, pleasant meal with good food and friendly conversation.

After dinner, we walked the few blocks back to his hotel. We shook hands and I told him I'd be leaving early the next morning. He said he'd give me a call. Chicago was busy and there weren't that many hotel rooms available, but I'd gotten a room earlier that day a few blocks away from his hotel. That room also turned out to be a shithole, even shabbier than Jimmy's. After ten minutes we checked out, along with the cockroaches that had their suitcases packed, too. The two of us headed back to South Bend and spent the night in a motel on the main drag there. By the next night, we were back in Boston.

Back home, I finished the IDs and gave them to a friend I trusted to bring them to New York. There was too much heat on me to make the trip myself. While looking for Jimmy, the law had increased the surveillance on me a notch or two. But Jimmy knew I was sending someone I trusted, so it was no big deal. As it turned out, Jimmy wasn't happy with the finished IDs. He called me to complain that there was no date of issue on the licenses. "They don't put date of issues on Massachusetts licenses anymore," I told him. "If they put one on and a cop stops you, he's going to pick it right up that it's a phony."

He finally accepted what I said and then we talked for a while about the case. From what both of us had heard, it looked as if the case was actually falling apart. George Kaufman, the liaison between the Jewish bookmakers and Jimmy and Stevie, had died. He'd been a real sweetheart, but he had a heart attack from his diabetes. At least he died of natural causes.

A few months later, in mid-November, Jimmy asked me to come back down to New York. It took some careful arrangements, switching cars and stuff, but I was able to elude the law and take the train down. Again, I met him "at the lions." He and Cathy looked exactly the same, like two hassle-free tourists in New York. We talked about the case for a while and I showed him my driver's license and how there was no date of issue on it.

It was a cold November day and we headed out to a restaurant in a nearby hotel. On the way, he stopped to ask a street cop for directions. Cathy stood next to him while he talked to the cop, but I moved to the side. If the cop recognized Jim, I knew I'd have to crack him. I felt a surge of adrenaline that I might have to bang this guy out so Jimmy could take off. But the cop just told us to go down a few blocks and take a left. I knew this was all part of Jimmy's belief that the best defense is offense. When we were walking away, he said, "The best place to get lost is a big city. People are just walking around thinking about their own problems. You don't stand out there." If he wanted to, however, he knew how to disarm people with his personality and mannerisms. Otherwise, he would terrorize them. There just wasn't too much in the middle of those two sides.

I had known all along, however, that it would not be easy for anyone to capture Jimmy. If he saw them coming, he would take them with him. He wouldn't hesitate. Even before he went on the run, he'd always say, "Let's all go to hell together." And he meant it. I also knew Jimmy wouldn't go to trial. He would rather plead out to a life sentence than put his family through the embarrassment of a trial. If he had a gun on him, he'd go out in a blaze of glory rather than spend the rest of his life in jail. But I don't think they'll ever catch him.

I'd always thought he could end up traveling around Europe. I figured that if he ended up in Germany, there would have to be a new Third Reich. If he took off for Mexico, the entire village would be speaking English. It's not like he would ever conform to them. I also knew he would be smart enough to avoid putting himself in the position of killing anybody. But then again, if anybody fucked with him, he'd kill him.

Most of that day and evening in New York, however, Jimmy was upbeat, and seemed to treat his life as if that day was just another adventure, one he'd been planning ahead for since the early 1980s. But there was also a strange feeling, something hard to explain, but just a little bit off. I understood that I was the only one he trusted completely. When I look back at everything, I think he had some insight about Stevie, that he had a feeling how Stevie was going to react to everything. And that was why he was acting so different that day.

At the end of our dinner, he seemed more aware of everything around him. His tone was a little more serious, and there wasn't as much joking as usual. He repeated the phrase he'd used before that a rolling stone gathers no moss, which told me that he knew he was going to be on the move again. I got the feeling then that he was resigning himself to the fact that he wasn't coming back. Up until then, I always believed he thought there was a chance he'd beat the case. However, at that point there was something different going on with him. I didn't fully understand all the aspects of his case. It would be another six months before it all became clearer. Yet at that moment, at that restaurant in New York, I sensed that he had moved to a new place in his mind. It was over. He'd never return to South Boston.

After dinner, the two of them walked me to Penn Station. The three of us sat in chairs and talked for over an hour as I waited for my train. When they announced my train, I got up. Jimmy walked me over to the gate where the guy took my ticket and we shook hands. He said, "I'll be in touch." And that was that. I walked onto the train and figured he would call. But he never called again. I think about him a lot. I figure he's out of the country now. I hope they never catch him.

THIRTEEN
FBI AND THE LAW

For years, I had assumed that FBI agents John Connolly and his boss, John Morris, the supervisor of the Bureau's organized crime squad in Boston, were on the take. Jimmy and Stevie were always giving them money and gifts in exchange for information about what the law was doing. Jimmy even had three nicknames for Connolly: Elvis, because of the way he combed his hair; Neighbor, since he and Jimmy had once lived in the same building at Bay Shore Drive in Quincy; and Zip, because Jimmy and Connolly shared the same zip code.

Although I had little to do with Connolly until after Jimmy was on the run, I knew a bit about him. Eleven years younger than Jimmy, he was also a son of Irish immigrants, and had grown up in the Mary Ellen McCormack Housing Project, a few doors down from the Bulger family. I'd even heard stories about how Jimmy had once bought an eight-year-old John Connolly a vanilla ice cream cone, after convincing the little boy he wasn't a stranger, and a few months later, had broken up a fight where Connolly was being pummeled by an older kid. Connolly, however, had apparently been more impressed with Billy Bulger and later told me that it was Billy who had convinced him to continue his education at Boston College. He'd started working for the FBI in the

Organized Crime Unit in New York and came to the Boston office in 1973.

From what I saw, Connolly was a likable guy, always laughing and amiable with a nice personality. He liked nice things and owned a house up at Thomas Park in Southie, where he lived in the top two floors of the house and rented out the downstairs apartment. But there were times when I'd seen Jimmy get angry when he thought Connolly was spending too much money. Like when the FBI agent bought a boat, a 40-footer or something, with a nine-and-a-half-foot beam and twin engines. Jimmy was bullshit because he felt that Connolly was being too ostentatious, that he was flashing too much cash. How could he explain it? Connolly would say that he was single and could spend the money on himself, but Jimmy didn't buy that answer and was always telling him to tone it down.

All I knew about FBI agent John Morris was his nickname, Vino, given to him because he liked wine. The only time he got to drink expensive wine was when Jimmy and Stevie gave it to him. Jimmy told me that one night while he and Stevie were at Morris's house in Lexington, Morris had asked them for $5,000 to help with a problem he was having with his daughter. Jimmy and Stevie took the money out of their pockets and handed it to him. Even before Jimmy told me that story, I had known Morris was on the take.

Jimmy also told me about a brainstorm Morris had in 1975. He'd planted explosives in the car of a Revere loan shark, Eddie Miani, as part of his clever plan to scare Miani and develop him into an FBI informant. The bomb wasn't actually hooked up to go off, but it was a real one and the Revere police considered it an attempted murder case. But Morris's plan didn't work out and the attempt to recruit Miani was unsuccessful.

I certainly got to know Connolly a lot better than Morris, but that didn't happen till some years passed. The first time I met him was in 1978 at the L Street Bathhouse in Southie, a building on the beach where people used to work out, with a private area for members to sunbathe and swim in the ocean. That day, I had just finished working out with Johnny Pretzie and was walking out of the building when Connolly was heading in. I'd seen Connolly around but had never spoken to him. He stopped the two of us, Pretzie introduced us, and we shook hands and said, "Hi, how are you?"

That was pretty much all that ever passed between the two of us until six years later, in 1984, when Connolly came into the liquor store, walked over to me, and asked, "What's going on?"

I didn't really answer him, but when Jimmy got back to the store, I said to him, "Can you imagine that cocksucker asking me what's going on?"

Jimmy snapped back at me, "That guy is a friend of ours. Don't ever talk about him like that. You want him to think that's what we say about him?" I figured he was corrupt and we were paying him for information from the FBI, and Jimmy must have just wanted me to be careful not to disturb that relationship. Of course, at that time I had no idea whatsoever of the real bond between these two men.

After Connolly had retired from the FBI in 1990, Jimmy told me about a trip the two of them had taken years earlier, to Mexico, most probably to get out of town during the Blizzard of '78. Apparently Jimmy had been driving and they had had an accident. He didn't get hurt, but Connolly ended up with a black eye. Wonder if that might have made anyone look twice. Here was an FBI agent and Boston's most notorious criminal vacationing together.

While Jimmy and Connolly always appeared to have an amicable relationship, Jimmy had reason to be mad enough to take care of Morris. In 1988, four *Globe* reporters, Gerry O'Neill, Dick Lehr, Christine Chinlund, and Kevin Cullen, published a four-part series on the Bulger brothers, with one installment devoted to the "special relationship" between Whitey and the FBI. It got back to Jimmy later that during an interview with Gerry O'Neill at Venezia's restaurant in Dorchester Bay, Morris had told the *Globe* reporter that Jimmy was an informant and said how dangerous he was, adding that Connolly and Bulger were close, perhaps too close. Morris had also described a dinner at Stevie's mother's house with Billy Bulger, Jimmy, Morris, and Connolly.

Although the word "informant" wasn't used in the actual *Globe* series, it was implied by the mention of "special relationship" in the sentence: "And the Federal Bureau of Investigation has for years had a special relationship with Bulger that has divided law enforcement bitterly and poisoned relations among many investigators . . ." When Jimmy read the published article in the *Globe* in September 1988, he was bullshit. But no one believed the story, and we figured it was probably just another way of getting back at Billy Bulger through his brother; smearing Billy's reputation by proximity after a recent probe of a downtown office development deal at 75 State Street. I certainly did not believe it because I knew the FBI was giving us information and telling us everything that was going on. The idea that Jimmy or Stevie would be giving them information was unthinkable. After all, we were the ones paying them.

Years later, it wasn't hard to figure out why Morris would leak such information. He had been corrupted by Jimmy and Stevie and compromised as an FBI agent and handler. He was also so terrified of Jimmy's violence that he feared for his own life. Afraid that he was in over his head, Morris was worried that someone in organized crime was planning to kill him. Jimmy felt that Morris had put out the information that Jimmy was an informant in the hopes that someone would now try and kill Jimmy and Morris's problems would be over. Eventually, Morris admitted to the agency that he had leaked the information and was given a two-week suspension after the article appeared in the *Globe*.

Jimmy had always known that Morris was afraid of him. He also knew that Morris was jealous of Connolly. Years earlier, Connolly had gotten some sort of a grant to attend a special program at Harvard, and Morris had felt slighted that he had been passed over for the privilege. But Jimmy's wrath at learning that Morris had told stories about him to the *Globe* was huge.

But it was typical of Jimmy not to act on his anger right away. Rather than show his hand to a weak weasel like Morris, he filed the information away for future use. Never forgetting that Morris was the leak, seven years later, Jimmy put it on him. In October 1995, while he was on the lam, Jimmy called from out of the state to tell me exactly what he had done. He had spent a little time calling around and had finally located Morris at the FBI Academy in Quantico, Virginia. When he first tried to call him there, an operator at Quantico told him that Morris was busy. "Tell him Mr. White called," he told the operator, certain Morris would get the reference to "Whitey." "Tell him I'll call back."

An hour later, Jimmy called back, and this time he got Morris on the phone. "You started this fucking thing," he told him. "Use your Machiavellian mind and straighten this out. Because if I go down, I'm taking you down with me."

It had to terrify Morris that Jimmy, on the run, had found out exactly where he was. Morris, of all people, knew what a dangerous man Jimmy was. And now he knew that Jimmy Bulger could find him no matter where he was. When I told Connolly about the conversation, he laughed and said, "He had a heart attack a couple of days ago. He died twice on the table. It must have been some phone call." But instead of retracting the *Globe* story or dying on the table, Morris recovered enough to seek immunity from prosecution and, years later, went on to testify against John Connolly.

As for my relationship with Connolly, things changed drastically between the two of us in 1996. Two years earlier, in December 1994, Connolly had come to the liquor store to tell me that Jimmy and Stevie were about to be indicted. But once Stevie was in jail and Jimmy was gone, I saw a great deal more of Connolly. Our frequent meetings, which probably numbered more than three dozen, began in 1996 and continued until I got pinched in November 1999. The first meeting took place in Harvard Square when Stevie, who was locked up in Plymouth, gave me the number to call to reach out to Connolly. Stevie wanted me to find out what was going on with the investigation, what the state police and DEA were doing. Connolly informed me that the DEA and state police, who were working together, were not getting along with the FBI, that cooperation was at the lowest point ever. He said he'd try and find out more and would let me know. The next time I visited Stevie at Plymouth, I gave him that information.

At our next two meetings, which were at a restaurant/bar in Cambridge called Finnigan's Wake, John and I were basically talking about witnesses and the case they had against Jimmy and Stevie. He kept telling me that the feds had a weak case, that they had nothing there, that the case was going to fall apart. We also discussed witnesses, their health and which ones had already died. When I wanted to set up a meeting or speak to Connolly, I would call his office and say it was Chico calling. If he wanted to get in touch with me, he would call a relative of mine, who would call me up and tell me that my girlfriend was looking for me. That was my relative's way of joking with me.

After our first few meetings in Cambridge, the rest of my meetings with Connolly were held in the evenings at the Top of the Hub restaurant on the fifty-second floor of the Prudential Building, where Boston Edison had its business offices. We'd meet around five-thirty, eat, and talk. At each meeting, he continued to keep me informed about the different witnesses. Chico Krantz's health was failing. Another bookmaker, Eddie Lewis, was also in bad health. George Kaufman had already died of natural causes. Frankie Salemme Jr. had also died. The only thing Jimmy Katz had said was that he believed the money he gave to George Kaufman was going to Whitey and Stevie, which wasn't a really damaging statement. More and more, we continued to hear that the case was falling apart.

One fall day in 1996 while I was visiting Stevie, he wrote down a number and held it up to the window for me to write it down. "Call the number," he told me. "Get ahold of Eric. Ask for Dick. Say you're a friend of Paul's." That night, I followed his instructions and set up a meeting with Dick for the following Thursday night at the old Braintree Drive-In. That night, Dick walked out of a small blue foreign car with his rottweiler. About five-ten, in his mid-sixties, he was heavyset, with silver hair, glasses, and a pudgy round face. "Are you Dick?" I asked him.

"You must be the infamous Kevin Weeks," he answered.

"I don't know about that," I said, "but I am Kevin Weeks."

This Dick was the man Stevie had always referred to as Eric, but I had never known his real name. Stevie spoke about Eric a lot, about how he was a state police officer and was tipping him off about the joint state police, DEA, and FBI investigation. In actuality, he might have been more important to Stevie than John Connolly. Jimmy had several other sources in the FBI, but Dick was the only one connected to the state police.

Dick was in a sensitive position where a lot of information on the investigation and its budget approval went directly across his desk. At our first meeting, I talked to him about the investigation and what was going on with the state police. After he put the dog back in the car, the two of us stood outside in the cool fall night and continued to talk. I hadn't been afraid of the dog. I had a pistol with me and would have shot him if there had been any problem.

That night, Dick reaffirmed what Connolly had told me, that the FBI and state police were at their lowest point of cooperation. He said he would find out what he could and get back to me. I met with him about a dozen times, usually in the same place. He told me he had a counterpart in the Rhode Island State Police, as well as some other sources, and he was going to see what he could find out about the investigation. I told Stevie whatever he told me and repeated the information to Jimmy whenever he called.

But with each new meeting, I got the feeling that Dick didn't know much and was jerking me around. It seemed to be a waste of time to meet with him, but Stevie wanted me to continue. One night, Dick and I were talking about books and I told him I was reading a book by Vinny Teresa called *My Life in the Mafia,* and he told me he was in the book. I went home that night and finished the book. In it, the only mention of anybody in the state police was a Richard Schneiderhan, so now I knew Dick's and Eric's real name.

After our twelfth meeting, I decided the meetings were a waste of time. Dick was giving me bits and pieces, but for the most part I felt he was trying to distance himself from the whole thing. He'd gotten a lot of money over the years from Stevie but now, with Stevie in jail and Jimmy on the run, there was nothing they could do financially for him. He was just placating them with lip service and nothing more. Jimmy used to brag that he could ask six FBI agents to jump into his car with machine guns, but Schneiderhan was Stevie's one state police connection. Eventually Schneiderhan was arrested and convicted. His final stay was recently denied and he's going to have to go to jail now for eighteen months.

However, in the spring of 1997, less than a year after I had started to meet with Connolly, I got some news that literally shattered my world. One night while I was home reading a book and watching the ten o'clock news on Channel 56, I heard that Stevie Flemmi had gotten up on the stand at the evidentiary hearings in front of Judge Wolf and announced that he and Jimmy were FBI informants and had been given immunity from prosecution, that they had been told they could commit any crime short of murder. I dropped the book I had in my hands, put my feet down on the floor, and leaned forward, yelling, *"What the fuck?!"*

Stunned, there was nothing I could do except sit there on my couch, flipping the channels and waiting until the eleven o'clock news to make sure I had heard it right. When that broadcast repeated the news, I kept shaking my head in disbelief as I got up to grab a beer and kept flipping some more, waiting for the two o'clock news and any reruns I might get. All I kept thinking was, *Did I get it right? How could that be possible?* After the two o'clock news, I turned off the TV, still unable to believe that I had heard it right, unable to understand the whole thing. It made no sense. We *killed* guys because they were informants. And now I was learning that Jimmy and Stevie were informants themselves.

The next day I went out and got a paper, and there it was in black and white. Jimmy and Stevie, FBI informants. For twenty-five years, I had believed that Jimmy was corrupting the FBI through greed and money, paying them for information to help us. But I couldn't deny what I had just seen and read. Sure, I knew that the media all too frequently got it wrong or outright lied. But this time Stevie had said on the stand, under oath, that he and Jimmy were FBI informants. The words had come right from his mouth, not from a reporter's pen. It was incomprehensible. I thought about how intelligent Jimmy was, how he had always turned percentages in his favor. But we had always said the criminals take the good with the bad. You don't give up your friends. I knew that a lot of criminals had connections in law enforcement and that they were given information in return for money and favors. But it was not supposed to be the other way.

I had really liked and respected Jimmy. He had treated me well. But I couldn't understand this. You just don't cooperate with law enforcement. If you have enemies, you don't talk about them to law enforcement. Rather, you take it to the street and handle it that way. You don't rat on them and sic the law on them. You don't eliminate the competition that way. Much later, I came up with my own theory on why Jimmy might have become an FBI informant—that he had been coerced into it by crimes he had committed with Stevie—but on that spring day I was still reeling from the shock of finding out that twenty-five years of my life had been a lie.

After I got the papers, I went down to the store and talked to Kevin O'Neil, who was as shocked as I was. In disbelief himself, Kevin had no idea what was going on. I tried to find a few other people and see if they had heard what I had. Some people hadn't heard it and those who had had no idea what was going on. But most of the people around us couldn't believe it. The only thing all of us knew was that we were the ones getting info. A few said they had suspected it but could never prove it. I had never even *thought* it.

But the one thing I knew for sure was that I now had a problem. People would be thinking I had something to do with these two guys being informants. No one was saying anything, but from that minute on, I was walking around with two pistols to protect myself. I made sure I had plenty of firepower, usually carrying two .45s or two .38s. I kept the pistols in my waistband or inside my coat pocket. I wore a coat with the pockets cut out so when my hands were inside the coat, they were actually on my pistols.

The night after I heard the news, Stevie called me at eight, the way he usually did. As always, there was the recorded voice informing us that the call was being taped. Stevie was in his usual cheerful mode, having just finished another day in the hearings. Everything was hunky-dory. Nothing was wrong. "What's going on?" I asked him.

"Oh, that thing you heard was nothing," he told me. "Wait till the whole story comes out."

The next day I went up to Plymouth to see him. At that time, I was usually going once a week, as was his brother Mikey, his sons, Stevie Junior and Billy, and Phil Costa. I sat down opposite the glass partition separating the two of us and picked up the phone. "What are you doing?" I asked Stevie.

"I know what I'm doing," he told me. "Don't worry about it."

"Do you know you put a bull's-eye on my back?" I asked him. "I've been around you all these years and now you're putting a bull's-eye on me?"

"You weren't involved in all that," he said. "You don't have to worry. It's nothing. Wait till the whole story comes out."

"Stevie," I said to him, "it's all over the news that you and Jimmy are informants."

"Well, we never said anything about you," he said.

That's when I put the phone down and said, right into the glass partition, "How could you? Everything I did, I did with the two of you." He couldn't give me up without giving himself up.

The next time I saw John Connolly at the Top of the Hub, he, too, told me to wait until I heard the whole story. "The Mafia was going against Jimmy and Stevie," he said. "So Jimmy and Stevie went against them." He had a three-inch-thick leather case with him, filled with the 302 reports the field agents filed regularly that he had written up on Jimmy and Stevie. Obviously, since he had retired from the FBI seven years earlier, he had made copies of the reports for his own personal files. There were lots and lots of them, but he took out all the papers and I started going through them. The reports discussed things about the Mafia, but there was also stuff about friends of ours, about Irish guys, members of Winter Hill, guys Jimmy and Stevie had given up.

I looked at Connolly and said, "They were giving up everybody."

"No, they weren't," he said, pointing out some letters on the pages I was holding. "Look at the bottom of each report. See? 'Not to be disseminated without case agent's approval.' No one could see them without me. I had to approve anyone looking at these reports."

But I knew that was bullshit because some of those people had already been arrested for the same exact crimes that were listed in the reports.

"There's nothing in there about you," Connolly told me as I continued, incredulous, to read over hundreds of reports. Again, those words didn't mean anything to me because everything I had done, I had done with Jimmy and Stevie. There was nothing they could say about me without incriminating themselves.

As I read over the files at the Top of the Hub that night, Connolly kept telling me that 90 percent of the information in the files came from Stevie. Certainly, Jimmy hadn't been around the Mafia the way Stevie had. But, Connolly told me, he had to put Jimmy's name on the files to keep his file active. As long as Jimmy was an active informant, Connolly said, he could justify meeting with Jimmy to give him valuable information. Even after he retired, Connolly still had friends in the FBI, and he and Jimmy kept meeting to let each other know what was going on. I listened to all that, but now I also understood that even though he was retired, Connolly was still getting information, as well as money, from Jimmy. As I continued to read, I could see that a lot of the reports were not just against the Italians. There were more and more names of Polish and Irish guys, of people we had done business with, of friends of mine. Whenever I came across the name of someone I knew, I would read exactly what it said about that person. I would see, over and over, that some of these people had been arrested for crimes that were mentioned in these reports.

It didn't take me long to realize again that it had been bullshit when Connolly had told me that the files hadn't been disseminated, that they had been for his own personal use. He had been an employee of the FBI. He hadn't worked for himself. If there was an investigation going on and his supervisor said, "Let me take a look at that," what was Connolly going to say? He had to give it up. And he obviously had.

I thought about what Jimmy had always said. "You can lie to your wife and to your girlfriends, but not to your friends. Not to anyone we were in business with." Maybe Jimmy and Stevie hadn't lied to me. But they sure hadn't been telling me everything.

Soon after that, Stevie actually mentioned my name at his hearing in front of Judge Wolf. When he took the stand, he was asked, "How are you corresponding with John Connolly now?"

He answered, "Through Kevin Weeks."

When I read it in the paper, I was bullshit. It was the first time my name had been brought up in the courtroom. Nice of him to put another fucking bull's-eye on my back when I was out there helping him. I had no choice but to continue to help Stevie because if he flipped on me, I was gone. I was getting life. I was hostage to him, walking a thin line because I had to placate Stevie in what he was doing in his case, while on the street I had to distance myself from him. But after that day in the courtroom, I realized Stevie didn't give a fuck about me. All Stevie was worried about was Stevie.

A short time later, Stevie asked me to help him get some evidence suppressed that was being used against him. In particular, they were tapes of Stevie and Frankie Salemme that had been obtained through a roving bug that had been placed in a house at 34 Guild Street in Medford. On October 29, 1989, the tapes had secretly recorded, for the first time ever, a Mafia induction ceremony for four made guys.

Stevie alleged that there had been no need to set up the roving bug, which is the most intrusive form of surveillance available. The need for a roving bug had been based on the fact that the FBI didn't know where the induction ceremony would take place. However, the truth was they had known seven to ten days beforehand exactly where the ceremony would be. But the FBI was so paranoid of leaks in the office getting back to the Mafia that they lied to U.S. Attorney Diane Kottmeyer, the strike force chief who was overseeing the case, and said they didn't know where the ceremony would take place. They also didn't inform the judge that they had informants who were going to be at the ceremony who could have been wired up. It was just another case of the ends justifying the means. Stevie wanted to show that the FBI had broken the law and, therefore, everything obtained on the roving bug should be thrown out.

Stevie wanted me to find out exactly when the FBI had gone to the Department of Corrections to make sure Vinnie Federico, who was one of the four men scheduled to be inducted, was granted a furlough from MCI-Shirley so he could attend the ceremony at a relative's house on Guild Street. Stevie also wanted the names and file numbers of the Top Echelon informants, the high-ranking members of organized crime, that the FBI had used to get that authorization for the roving bug. When I asked Connolly for the names of these informants, he told me four of them were his, including Jimmy, Stevie, Sonny Mercurio, and a made guy from Boston who later died of cancer. The fifth one, a made member of the Rhode Island Mafia, Anthony "The Saint" St. Laurant, belonged to Bill Shea, the FBI agent from Rhode Island. When I got the identities of all five informants, along with the rest of the information, from Connolly, I told it to Stevie when I visited him at Plymouth.

Personally, back in 1989, I had never known anything about the induction ceremony. Jimmy and Stevie had been involved, but I never heard about it till it was over. About a week after the ceremony took place, Jimmy and Stevie had been talking about it, saying how the feds got the whole ceremony on tape. They had heard how someone who was leaving had said, "Only the ghosts know what happened here tonight."

"Oh, yeah," Stevie had said to Jimmy, "only the ghosts and the feds."

When I had heard them talking about it like that, I figured they had learned what had happened from the feds and were not personally involved. Since at that point I didn't know the true relationship between Jimmy and Stevie and the FBI, as far as I knew, it was a one-way street and the feds were giving us information. Now I understood that Stevie and Jimmy's involvement in the ceremony must have boosted their importance as FBI informants. As it turned out, the evidence intercepted at Guild Street was presented to the grand juries that indicted Stevie.

At one of our meetings at the Top of the Hub, Connolly showed me a letter he had drafted on a legal pad to U.S. District Court Judge Mark Wolf. Wolf's hearings in the racketeering case against Jimmy and Stevie were still going on, but Stevie's lawyers were not making any headway in their attempts to set up a pretrial hearing in front of the judge. They were getting nowhere in their attempts to get the charges dropped against Jimmy and Stevie and to get their cases thrown out. In Connolly's letter, the source—three unnamed Boston police officers—falsely accused retired Detective Sergeant Frank Dewan of fabricating evidence against Bulger and Flemmi. Dewan had been a zealot, obsessed with getting Stevie and Jimmy. Everything that happened in the town, Dewan blamed on us. And 99 percent of the time he was wrong. But if he saw someone talking to us, that guy was automatically an associate. If a cop from the neighborhood waved to us, he was corrupt. If someone got killed, we did it or we ordered it. He saw Jimmy's handprints on everything that happened, and that just wasn't true.

Connolly's letter included examples of how the government had corrupted its case by planting evidence to get us. He included the story of John Morris planting a bomb under Eddie Miani's car in 1975. John gave me the letter to read over to see if I had any ideas or anything else to put into it, and I added a few things to it. I added the story of David Lindholm, a known drug dealer we had shaken down whose nickname on the street was Little Lies because he was known not to tell the truth.

Connolly typed the phony letter on his computer on the Boston Police Department stationery that I got for him from a source I had there. The three-and-a-half-page letter succeeded in convincing Judge Wolf that the government was using illegal evidence to get us. At the time of the letter, there were only two or three days left before the judge had to make his ruling, and the letter prompted him to grant Stevie a pretrial hearing right away.

Eventually, Connolly was convicted of obstruction of justice in writing the letter to the judge, but at the time it did succeed in convincing the judge to allow the hearing. The whole scene makes me wonder how things work when the situation is reversed and law enforcement uses the media to leak stories so they can create talk on the street. That way they can gather evidence even though the initial evidence they put out is blatantly false. When the law does that type of planting, it is not considered illegal, but, rather, a tactic, a tool of the investigation. When someone like Connolly does it, it is merely illegal.

Jimmy had told me stories about FBI agents, but in all these stories, they were the ones giving us information. In one such story, FBI agent Dennis Condon had set up Edward "Punchy" McLaughlin, one of the three Charlestown McLaughlin brothers, during the Winter Hill-McLaughlin gang war. In October 1965, Condon approached McLaughlin and told him, "Tell your brother to calm down."

McLaughlin turned around and said, "Worry about your own brother, the fucking drunk."

A night or two later, Condon called up Stevie and told him exactly where McLaughlin got the bus every morning. The next day, Stevie showed up at that bus stop, holding a paper bag from which he pulled out a gun, walked across the street, and shot and killed him. That night, Condon called up Stevie and said, "Nice shooting." Frank Salemme later testified that FBI agent Paul Rico, who was Condon's partner, had also given him and Stevie information about McLaughlin's whereabouts.

Rico helped Stevie many more times, but he had been especially helpful in 1968 when Stevie had been on the lam for the Fitzgerald car bombing, letting Stevie know when it was safe for him to return to Boston in 1974.

Years later, in the early 1990s, federal prosecutor Jeremiah O'Sullivan was leading an investigation against Jimmy and Stevie and Winter Hill. Jimmy told me how John Connolly ran into O'Sullivan one day in Post

Office Square. O'Sullivan said to Connolly, "There is an investigation going on with your boys."

John turned around and said, "They already know that."

"How could Jimmy know that?" O'Sullivan asked. "It was funded by my office." Obviously, O'Sullivan didn't know about Connolly's two-way relationship with Jimmy. But the truth was that O'Sullivan was tipping off Connolly about the investigation. During the Wolf hearings, when O'Sullivan was scheduled to testify about his role in the investigation, the federal prosecutor suffered a heart attack, which couldn't have come at a better time for him. After the hearings were over, he made a speedy recovery.

During these hearings, Stevie testified that John Morris had given him a tape recording in the 1980s. He felt that the fact that Morris gave him this tape would help support his claim that he was working with the FBI, that, in fact, he was listening to tapes with the FBI agent. Stevie was also blaming everything on Morris, testifying that Morris gave him the tip-off about the imminent arrest, which, of course, wasn't true. He was trying to keep Connolly's identity in the tip-off secret when in fact Connolly was the one who told me about the coming indictments. When I was meeting Connolly at the Top of the Hub, he gave me the tape that Morris had left behind, which I then gave to Stevie's attorney. In fact, if Stevie had just told the truth about Connolly in the first place, it would have helped his case instead of hurting it.

Of course, Stevie had expected Connolly to say something to help his case. Perhaps that was why he was trying to protect him about the tip-off. However, on April 30, 1998, during one of his two courtroom appearances during the Wolf hearings, Connolly, afraid of incriminating himself and being charged with crimes, had invoked the Fifth Amendment after every question he was asked. He refused to bolster Stevie's contention that the FBI assured him and Jimmy that they could commit crimes short of murder, so long as they provided information on the Mafia.

Lehr and O'Neill, the *Globe* reporters who had written the four-part series on the Bulger brothers, went on to write a book, *Black Mass*, based on the Wolf hearings. In their book, maybe 50 percent of the facts came out, and a lot of times they were taken out of context. These so-called experts didn't know anything that really happened with Jimmy and Stevie and me, but they still said certain things about me. I'd love to give these guys the opportunity to say these things to my face, like a man, but that will never happen. Dick Lehr is a professor at Boston University. I'd like to meet him one-on-one with no one else around besides the two of us. Then he could tell me what he thinks of me and I could show him what I think of him. I've always believed that if you have a problem with someone, you knock on his door and say, "You have something to say to me? Okay, now what do you want to do about it?"

Kevin Cullen, another *Globe* reporter who worked on the 1988 four-part series, handled things real bravely. After his involvement in the series and the subsequent word that Jimmy would kill him, being the tough guy he was, Cullen fled to Europe. He became the London bureau correspondent. I wonder if this expert on the Bulger case is out there now, looking for Jimmy in England.

Even today, it's hard to try and figure out what happened between Jimmy and Connolly. Connolly was an affable guy, but Jimmy had exposed his dark side and their roles had become reversed. Instead of Connolly being the handler and Jimmy the informant, Jimmy had become the master and made Connolly his puppet. I had seen so little of Connolly before Stevie got arrested in early 1995. But then, until I learned the truth about Jimmy and Connolly, I had assumed he was just a corrupt FBI agent taking money to look out for Jimmy's interests. Once I understood their true relationship, FBI handler and FBI informant, I saw the power Jimmy had over him and understood how deeply Jimmy had corrupted him.

But my days of meeting Connolly and visiting Stevie to help him with his case were coming to an end. I would soon have my own case to take care of, and the three of us would no longer have anything to discuss. If I had known earlier what the real relationship had been between the two of them, I would have gone my own way a lot sooner. But even knowing the truth about Jimmy, I couldn't hate him. Though I had been shocked and furious over what I learned about him, it's still hard to be around someone for twenty-five years and not like him. Besides, you had to admire Jimmy. He beat them at their own game.

FOURTEEN
ARREST, PRISON, AND RELEASE

On November 17, 1999, around three in the afternoon, I was walking down N and Sixth streets, heading to my car to go down to the variety store, when agents from the DEA and state police called out, "Kevin."

"Yeah," I said.

"Have you got a minute?" one of them said. "We want to talk to you."

"I'm heading down the store to get a cup of coffee," I told him. "I'll meet you down there."

"No, we want to talk to you here," the agent said. I could see other agents in cars around the street, as well as some walking around. They were all over the place.

"Am I under arrest?" I asked.

"No," he said.

"Then I'll meet you down the store," I said.

As I started to walk away, he got on the radio and talked to someone else. Then he turned around and called out my name again. This time, he said, "Kevin, you're under arrest."

When he handcuffed me, he asked me if I had any weapons.

"I have a knife in my back pocket," I told him.

"Thanks," he said, and reached in and took it out. Two agents from the DEA and State Police Task Force then put me in a car as other official cars drove by. A few minutes later, Dan Doherty from the DEA and Tom Duffy from the state police, acting as professionally as the other two agents, took me out of that car and put me in the back seat of their car. They drove me over to the DEA headquarters in a building over by City Hall, where they seated me in a room.

It wasn't a surprise that I was being arrested. The night before, on November 16, I had been at the Teamster's Pub for a billiards league. When I came out of the building with a friend of mine, we got in my car on Third Street. I took a left on D Street, and was driving up D Street when a van came through the lot where the gas station was. I could see that the driver of the van was burning me, looking at me hard. Immediately, I recognized him as Dave Lazarus from the IRS. He had been all over town lately, asking questions about me and giving everybody he talked to his card. He drove down the street behind me and I saw him making a U-turn. I had my scanner on and could hear him and his fellow agents talking about me. Then I spotted two or three other cars all converge and begin to follow me. At the time, I had two pistols on me. After I ran the red light through the intersection of Broadway, I took a left on Fourth Street, floored the car, and, without stopping for traffic, headed across Dorchester Street. As I took a right onto G Street, I could hear them saying on the police scanner that they had lost me. I went down the street and dropped off the friend who was with me, handing him the two pistols I had on me. He jumped into his car and took off with no problem. They weren't following him. They were following me. Later on, I parked my car and walked back to my house. That was it for the night.

When I came out of my house the next afternoon, they were waiting. At the DEA headquarters, they gave me the twenty-nine-count indictment. That also didn't surprise me. I had heard that they had grabbed Kevin Hayes, and they were trying to get him to cooperate against me. I had talked to a friend of mine who knew Hayes well and he had told me, "Don't worry. He'll never cooperate. He'll never say a thing."

"Are you sure?" I had asked my friend. "Because this guy can put me away." I was prepared to take Hayes out, but my friend told me he was friends with Hayes's wife.

"Don't worry," my friend said again. "He'll never say a word against you." It turned out that Kevin Hayes did give the DEA and the state police the Predicate Act in the last five years, meaning he told them about a criminal act that had occurred in the last five years, with which they were able to indict me on a RICO charge. They said I had kidnapped Hayes, which was not true. He had come in of his own will. Besides, the guy weighed 400 pounds. There was no way I could have kidnapped him. Hayes also told them that there had been two Igloo coolers in the room, the kind you use for sandwiches and cold drinks, and that I was going to put him in the coolers after I chopped him up. If I had ever chopped up his 400-pound body, I would have needed a freezer truck for all the pieces.

I was kept at DEA headquarters for about three hours. At first the agents tried to make a deal with me, telling me, "Kevin, you don't have to go away. You can work with us."

"You have nothing," I told them.

Finally they said, "Bring in the other guy," and brought in Kevin O'Neil. I had heard all along that they were going to indict me and Kevin, but I felt bad for Kevin. He had nothing to do with anything Jimmy, Stevie, or I were doing. For him, it was guilt by association. Eventually he pleaded guilty in October 2000 to a superseding indictment charging him with racketeering, extortion, and money laundering. He was sentenced in September 2004 to a year and a day in prison. He also had to pay a $10,000 fine and $25,000 in restitution to Ray Slinger, the guy who lied about the body bag.

A couple of years earlier I had spent a weekend in jail, so this wasn't my first time in jail. I wasn't that concerned about what they had on me. When I carefully read the indictment, which included racketeering, extortion, money laundering, conspiracy to distribute drugs, and two charges of using a firearm in commission of a crime, I knew half the charges were bullshit ones that I could beat, and that a lot of them were repetitive.

That night, Kevin O'Neil and I were taken to the state police barracks at Logan Airport, where they locked us up in separate cells. There was no need to call my family. People who knew I had been arrested had certainly called them already.

The next day, on November 18, I was taken to the Federal Court in Boston, where I was arraigned. Then Kevin and I, along with some other prisoners, were put in a van and driven to Wyatt Federal Prison, a federal holding facility in Rhode Island. The feds didn't want me in Plymouth because that's where Stevie was. Once we got to Wyatt, we got processed and put in a cell block. I made my first call to my sister, who told me my mother had just died that day. I had known she was sick but I hadn't thought she was near death.

Two days later, on November 20, I was picked up in Rhode Island and driven to the wake at the O'Brien Funeral Home in South Boston. I was shackled and handcuffed as the marshals led me inside. They had already blocked off traffic so no one else could drive into the street. I was alone with the casket for about ten minutes with the marshals right beside me, along with Jackie O'Brien, the funeral home director. Then I was led back to the car and driven back to Rhode Island. Here, I was in a five-man cell with two guys from the Dominican Republic, one from Colombia, and another from Venezuela. They were all very respectful and kept asking if there was anything they could do for me.

That night, I rolled over and went to sleep, but I didn't sleep great. The next day, I was brought to a bail hearing at the federal courthouse in Boston, where I was bound over without bail. Whenever I went into

Boston for a hearing, I was awakened at 4:00 A.M. and driven up to the courthouse, where I would sit in a holding cell until my turn before the magistrate. Then I would be driven back the same day. Back in Rhode Island, I had visits from my brothers and my wife, Pam.

A couple of weeks after I was arrested, my lawyer got me a copy of Judge Wolf's 661-page ruling that he had released on September 15. It was a shock to see everything there, to see exactly what Jimmy and Stevie had been doing over the years. I'd seen Connolly's reports that he had written on Jimmy and Stevie, but I hadn't known exactly how many years those two guys had been informants, Stevie since 1965, Jimmy since 1975.

One day after a visit in Wyatt, I was walking downstairs waiting to be brought out of the visiting room when an inmate asked me, "Are you Kevin Weeks?"

"Yeah," I told him.

He introduced himself and then I knew he was a made guy from Rhode Island. "Kid, what are you doing?" he asked me. "Are you going to take it up the ass for these guys? Remember, you can't rat on a rat. Those guys have been giving up everyone for thirty years."

At the time, I was still thinking things over. At forty-three, I was looking to make a plea for fifteen years. Later on, my attorney, Richie Egbert, came up to see me. "Hi, Richie, how you doing?" I said as we shook hands and went into the little room where lawyers can visit their clients.

Right away, he said, "Kev, I don't know what to tell you."

"Well, how does it look, Richie?"

"Not good," he said. "We can beat half these charges, but every charge they find you guilty on, they're going to give you the max. They're so mad at the other two, at Whitey and Stevie, and with Whitey gone, they're going to look to give you the max on whatever they can. The maximum sentence."

"What are we talking about?" I asked him. "How many years, Richie?"

"You don't want to know," he said.

"Just tell me, Richie," I said. "What are we talking about—for years?"

"You're gone," he said. "It's over. If I was you, I'd do some thinking. I'm not telling you what to do, but it's over." Then he informed me he might have a conflict of interest with another client who was involved in the case and he wasn't sure he could represent me.

Soon after that, I met with another attorney, Charlie Rankin. He came up to Wyatt on a Friday and we sat around for a while and talked about the case. He basically told me the same thing Richie had said. On every charge, they would give me the maximum. "For me to represent you, by Monday, you'll have to give me one hundred and twenty thousand dollars for the bail hearing," he told me. "Then it will be twenty thousand dollars a week for the case. And you'll pay all expenses, for transcripts and appeals, for everything like that."

Right then, I was thinking, *He's talking appeals*. This guy thinks we're going to lose. "How long will the trial last?" I asked him.

"Four to six months," he told me.

"So you're talking around six hundred thousand dollars," I said. "For that, what are you guaranteeing me?"

"No guarantees," he told me.

"What about time?" I said. "I'm going to give you six hundred thousand dollars and you can't even tell me what to expect out of this?"

"No guarantees," he said again.

That Monday, they brought me to Boston to the bail hearing at the federal courthouse. When I was sitting in the holding cell, I looked over and caught a glimpse of Bobby DeLuca, dressed nicely in a suit, sitting in the cell next to me. Bobby was one of the original people who got indicted in 1995, along with Jimmy and Stevie and Frank Salemme and Jimmy and Johnny Martorano. He was Stevie's codefendant in the case. I had gotten to know him when I was visiting Stevie at Plymouth and had always found him to be a real nice and honorable person. Out of everybody who got indicted at that time, he was one of the only ones who didn't cooperate. He went and did his time. That day, he was pleading out guilty and getting sentenced, taking a ten-year sentence on top of the five he already had.

Anyhow, while we were in adjacent cells, he called out, "How you doing?" and the two of us shook hands through the bars. We couldn't see each other well, but we talked for a couple of hours. Right away, Bobby said, "Stevie is a selfish bastard. He don't give a shit about anybody but himself. That day he mentioned your name in court, we all told him, 'What the fuck are you doing mentioning Kevin's name? He's the only guy out there helping you. And you just put a bull's-eye on his back.'"

As it turned out that day, my bail hearing got postponed, so nothing happened and I was brought back to Wyatt. Charlie Rankin later informed me he was going to put the bail hearing off.

I did receive some good news, however, when I learned that my case and bail hearing had been assigned to Judge Harrington. That pleased me because I knew the judge was good friends with John Connolly and that Jimmy knew him. If I had a shot with any judge, he was it. When I was in the courtroom that day, along with Kevin O'Neil, waiting for Judge Harrington to enter, Tom Duffy and Steve Johnson from the state police served me a piece of paper. I noticed that the agents all had smiles on their faces when I was given the paper. I looked at it and read that Judge Harrington had recused himself.

Back at Wyatt a few days later, I received a letter from Stevie. The last time I had seen him was during my last visit to Plymouth the end of October or beginning of November 1999. He had sent the letter to a family member of mine who had forwarded it to me. At the bottom of the handwritten note, Stevie had written, "My case is going good and good luck with yours." In other words, "You're on your own." I didn't expect anything from him, but I hadn't expected that. He had certainly chosen his words poorly.

In the meantime, there was news about Johnny Martorano, who had been in Plymouth with Stevie and Salemme and Bobby DeLuca. As co-defendants in the case, it had been advantageous to have both Johnny and Stevie in Plymouth so they could go over everything about their case, which they had been planning to fight together. But everything changed after Johnny learned what Jimmy and Stevie had been doing, which was probably a little before I heard about it on television. After that, Johnny had weighed his options. One option had been to kill Stevie right there in the cell block, which he was certainly both mad enough and capable enough to do easily. Another option was to cooperate. I bet it was a hard choice, but Johnny came to the same decision I eventually did: What am I protecting them for? These two have been giving everyone up right along. What am I going to do? Go to prison for life just to be able to say I am a standup guy? Johnny ended up cooperating, admitting he killed twenty people and implicating Jimmy and Stevie in multiple murders, in exchange for a fourteen-year sentence.

Although I'd only met Johnny Martorano a few times, I'd been brought up on the stories about him during the gang wars of the 1960s and 1970s up through the early 1980s. All I knew is that if you were going to go after Johnny Martorano, you'd better be in a tank. Now, here was this guy who was a legend in Boston, who had been involved in twenty murders with Jimmy and Stevie, and he had decided to cooperate against them.

A few years later, in June 2004, I ended up writing a letter to Judge Wolf on Johnny's behalf before his sentencing, explaining that when a man of Johnny's stature decided to cooperate against Jimmy and Stevie, it made my choice a lot easier. "After the life I led, trying to tell right from wrong, good guys from bad guys was very confusing. Then I realized that John Martorano seemed to know what to do. If it was right for him then it was right for me."

But when I was still trying to decide what to do for myself, I learned that Frankie Salemme was trying to make a deal. I did a lot of thinking and talking it over with my family. I also spoke to Kevin O'Neil, who also ended up cooperating. "Listen, I'm gone," I told Kevin. "It's over."

"And we don't owe them a thing," he said.

By late December 1999, I had decided to make a deal, to cooperate. In January 2000, I was brought up to Boston for an interview. By then the government had appointed me a new lawyer, Dennis Kelly, who was very articulate and knowledgeable. He'd been a federal prosecutor and knew his way around the federal system. We talked about some of the crimes I might or might not have been involved with and if maybe we might be able to find some bodies. At the second meeting, the agents and prosecutors said that before they made a deal with me, they wanted me, as an act of good faith, to go out and recover some of those bodies. At the time, I didn't have any plea agreement or anything, but Dennis told me I should do it.

"If I give these people these bodies," I told him, "they can use these bodies against me. I have nothing to sign now."

"Kevin," Dennis told me, "they have dealt with people before who have lied and double-crossed them. This time they want to make sure you can deliver what you are telling them before they make a deal with you."

So on January 13, 2000, I showed them three bodies. That day, I had them bring me back to the place where, fifteen years earlier, on Halloween night, Jimmy, Stevie, and I had reburied Bucky Barrett, Johnny McIntyre, and Deborah Hussey. When we got there that cold January day, the snow-covered area was being prepared for a building, for a credit union of some sort, and all the landmarks were gone. The woods and the bushes were bulldozed down and everything was barren around where they were going to put the new building.

I laid down in the snow, just as I had done when I had been lying in the same spot with the machine gun in 1985. I figured out from the angle of the front door of Florian Hall the exact spot a few feet away where

Jimmy, Stevie, and I had put the bodies. After I told the law enforcement where to dig, I was driven back to my cell in Rockingham County, New Hampshire, where I'd been transferred from Rhode Island a short time earlier.

That night, I was looking out my cell window at the TV in the common area and all of a sudden I saw my picture on the news. They showed scenes of the agents recovering the bodies. I went and sat down on my bunk and said to myself, "What the fuck have I done?"

About a half-hour later, the guards took me out of my cell to the pay phone. Tom Duffy from the state police was on the phone. "Kevin?" he said.

"Yeah," I answered.

"You hit the ball out of the park," he said.

"What do you mean?" I asked.

"We went down with the backhoe to exactly where you said the bodies would be," he told me. "And that's exactly where they were. Now we believe you. Now we can talk."

The next day when the door opened and I came out of my cell, not one person said a word to me except, "Hey, how you doing?" and they had all seen it on TV. The night before I'd figured I was going to have a problem when I came out of my cell because it was all over the news that I was cooperating, but it turned out that there was no problem at all.

Over the course of time, now that my credibility had been established, agents and investigators from all over the country kept calling me in and interviewing me. I met with agents from the Joint Task Force, Violent Fugitive Task Force, DEA, state police, IRS, and Justice Department, along with investigators from Oklahoma and Dade County, Florida. Initially they didn't want the FBI included because of corruption considerations, but when the Justice Department got involved, they brought in FBI agents, not from Boston, but from out of state. Now that they had the bodies, the agents and investigators wanted to know how they got killed and exactly what crimes I was involved in.

I was kept in Rockingham County Jail in New Hampshire from January 2000 to April 2000. In April, they moved me to Stafford, County, New Hampshire, where I stayed until September 21. On that day, I was moved to Allenwood, Pennsylvania, where I would serve the remainder of my sentence. In the beginning, I was brought to the federal courthouses in Boston and Worcester for interviews, and then returned to my cell in New Hampshire. From January 2000 until July of that year, I was taken down at least once a month to be interviewed. And when I left for Allenwood, I continued to be interviewed, sometimes being brought back to Boston, but most times I had agents coming down there to see me.

The deal I would be offered would be based on whatever information I gave. While my court-appointed lawyer, Dennis Kelly, was there for the initial meeting, he did not accompany me to my interviews. The investigators wanted to know my criminal history. Of course, I had no notes and everything I had done was in my head. The agents were always professional, writing down everything I said. People on the street might have thought I ratted about anything and everything, but the focus was on Jimmy and Stevie and their connections in law enforcement. All I talked about were the crimes I was involved in. The police asked me about a lot of other murders and I'd say they might have occurred, but I wasn't there. I didn't hurt anyone who was still out on the street. All I could tell the agents was what I, not anyone else, was involved in.

Dan Doherty from the DEA and Steve Johnson from the Massachusetts State Police were the agents in charge of me the whole time. Always respectful, professional, and businesslike, they never lied about the sentencing and never made any promises or anything. Although I did not know what was ultimately going to happen, we talked about crimes and things they had heard. Most often they had heard different stories, but I said, "No, this is what happened. I'm not going to lie or embellish."

They listened and the only comment they made to me was, "Kevin, it is what it is."

Several agents commented that my stories never changed. That's because I was there to tell the truth. And the good thing about telling the truth is that your story never changes. You don't have to remember what you said to one person or the next. It's when you make up one lie that they can tear you apart. At that point in my life, it was either the truth or nothing.

In July 2000, I received three letters of immunity: from Suffolk County, Massachusetts; Dade County, Florida; and Tulsa, Oklahoma. I wasn't involved in the murders in Tulsa, Oklahoma, or Dade County, Florida, but I wanted to be sure that I couldn't be held culpable in those crimes after the fact. Once I had my immunity taken care of, I was able to work on my plea agreement, which took seven months to negotiate. They ended up adding five murders to my charges on the superseding indictment. When I was initially indicted in November 1999, my offense level came in at level 43. Your offense level goes from 0 to 43, while your criminal history level goes from 1 to 6. The more arrests and convictions you have, the higher your criminal history level. When my additional charges came in, I was enhanced one point for each murder, including Bucky Barrett, John McIntyre, Deborah Hussey, Brian Halloran, and Michael Donahue, with a total of five points, and four more points for managerial position, which brought it from 43 to level 52. But because of my plea agreement, my offense level was brought back to level 43. Still, it was overkill. Level 43 is as high as the guidelines go, even though your level can be enhanced a few more points. But any way you look at it, I was facing life imprisonment.

The agents kept on interviewing me, and in October 2000, I led them to three more bodies. I knew where one was, but as for the other two, I told them I had only a 50–50 chance of finding them. The 50–50 chance referred to the location, which was the spot Jimmy used to look at with his binoculars from his bay window. I had been around him so long that I knew him well enough to understand he was only looking at that spot for two reasons: he was either looking for a place to put somebody or he was looking at a place where somebody was already buried. As it turned out, someone was already buried there: Tommy King. Johnny Martorano had killed Tommy in Jimmy's car in 1975, after Tommy and Jimmy had had words at Triple O's.

"But Tommy King was buried in a marshy area," one of the guys kept saying.

"Tommy King got killed up the street," I told him. "And if you walk over there, you'll see the marshy area. There's a fifty–fifty chance he will be there." Two weeks later they found his body.

A few weeks before they found Tommy King, they found Paulie Mc-Gonigle. That location I had no problem with, since Jimmy had told me Paulie was buried on Tenean Beach in Dorchester.

The third body was Debra Davis. They had info that she was near Tommy King's body, so they gave me credit for discovering her body, too. But she had been buried at low tide, so they had to wait for the tide to go out before they could find her along the Neponset River, a few weeks after they found Tommy.

Even though Davis's family and the family lawyer had been informed that I had no involvement in Debra's death, that I had never met her, and if it wasn't for me her remains would never have been found, the family lawyer still came after me civilly. They were trying to blame me for her murder, even though they knew I had nothing to do with it, and sued me for wrongful death. Like everything, it all comes down to money. That's all they wanted.

As of the writing of this book, the suit has been stayed by my bankruptcy case.

The only arguments the agents and I ever had in the entire process of my cooperation concerned Stippo. Basically, there was one agent who believed Stippo and what he had to say, while the rest of the agents disagreed with him. Those agents had their doubts about Stippo all along. We went back and forth about the true facts of what happened, and everything I had told them and what his family had told them. Finally the agents said, "Kevin is admitting to murder and to extortion and to crimes far exceeding this one. Why would he be arguing about the circumstances of this one crime when he pled guilty to more severe crimes?" Subsequently, based on their investigation and what his family and others said, everything was ultimately corroborated and the situation resolved itself. Stippo had lied.

When I gave up information in 2000, the state police had suspected but didn't know any of the specific details. They knew details based on eyewitness accounts, but they didn't know the inside stories about the Halloran murder or the weapons arsenal. They hadn't known of my involvement in these crimes, but still, they never reacted when I related my accounts.

This was the first time since I was a kid that I didn't have control over my own life. I'd reached a point where my freedom was in other people's hands—in these agents' hands. But during all that time, I never caught them in a lie and was never lied to about anything. It was obvious they all had a hate thing for Stevie. What they detested so much were the women. Stevie had killed a lot of people, but it was the deaths of his girlfriend and his stepdaughter that made him so hated. As for me, I didn't need anyone to hold my hand. I had gotten into this myself. From me, the investigators wanted the connection to the FBI and the state police. They wanted Jimmy and Stevie, the only ones on a large scale who I was involved with, along with Schneiderhan and Connolly, who had become a focus of the investigation before I was arrested. For these investigators, it was the first time they had someone directly involved in all these crimes and the workings of the organization provide testimony.

And I continued to give them every crime I had been involved in over the course of twenty-five years, every single one, the shootings, stabbings, extortions, murders, my involvement with drugs, with loansharking, with gambling, with everything. Before I had been arrested, when I was still on the street, the police had once come to me, given me my rights, and advised me I was the prime suspect in three other murders. Now people were still trying, unsuccessfully, to make a case in those three murders.

The one thing I never did during all my testimony was lie. If I had been caught in even one lie, my credibility would have been gone, my deal would have been gone, and I would have ended up with a life sentence. All I needed to do was tell them exactly what had happened. This was basically the best thing I ever did because now the investigators knew the answers to all their questions. And I knew the information they had received based on their informants. When I was being debriefed, I was given a list of 163 names who were allegedly informants or were allegedly cooperating with law enforcement, and was asked if I recognized any of those names. I did recognize some of them. I knew about the street people who were already arrested, the people who were charged in other crimes, those who had made deals to save their own asses, those who had already given me up. There are people who are on the street now who are walking around like they are standup guys, but in fact I know who they are and what they said. They can fool people around them, but they can't fool me. I know exactly what was said and what was done and who they are.

In May 2002, I was driven to Boston from Allenwood for a few days of testimony in John Connolly's trial for giving the tip-off of the indictments coming down that led to Jimmy fleeing. He'd been named in a five-count federal indictment a month after I was arrested, including falsifying reports about Stevie and Jimmy and funneling $7,000 in payoffs from them to John Morris. He'd been indicted just as the five-year statute of limitations on the tip-off to Jimmy in December 1994 was about to run out. I stayed in a cell at the courthouse for the three days that I was in Boston. During that time, I didn't speak to any lawyers or investigators about the case. No one coached me or told me what to say. I had already been interviewed about Connolly over the course of time. There was no need for me to try to remember any particular details. All I had to do was tell the truth. The two days in the courtroom, there were no surprises for me. I just told them exactly what happened. Each day, I saw Connolly, and as far as I was concerned, he was looking out for himself, as was everybody else. He ended up being convicted of racketeering and sentenced to ten years and one month. Three years later, in Florida, he was indicted for first-degree murder and conspiracy for allegedly providing information that prosecutors said led to John Callahan's death.

I was also brought back to Boston for Schneiderhan's and Michael Flemmi's trials; sometimes I was driven up and other times I was flown there. Schneiderhan was convicted in March 2003 of trying to warn Billy Bulger that his phone was tapped. Six months later, he was sentenced to eighteen months in federal prison for obstruction of justice. Michael Flemmi had been arrested in 2000 and charged with obstruction of justice and perjury, possession of unregistered weapons, and transfer and possession of machine guns, for helping to move the arsenal of weapons from the shed in his parents' backyard. In September 2002, he was sentenced to ten years in prison. Finally, in October 2003, Stevie, then sixty-nine, cooperated with authorities and pled out to ten murders in exchange for a recommended sentence of life in prison to avoid the death penalty for two of the murders, one in Florida and the other in Oklahoma. If Stevie rendered substantial assistance about his own criminal activity and others in a timely fashion, his brother Michael could possibly receive a reduction in sentence.

One of Stevie's sons, Billy Hussey, changed his name to William St. Croix. I think that was a grandparent's name. He testified against his own uncle, Michael Flemmi and, when faced with the possibility of charges against himself, was prepared to testify against his own father. When Stevie pled out, his son did not have to testify against him.

Most of the time, however, the same people I had been with before, the prosecutors, U.S. Attorneys, agents, and members of the Department of Justice Task Force, came to Allenwood to talk to me. I continued to meet with all of them until Stevie pled out guilty to the ten murders.

During one of the flights that I took between Boston and Pennsylvania, the federal marshals brought me to the airport handcuffed and shackled. Of course, the chains limit your movements. You can't scratch your nose or go to the men's room alone. But when the federal marshals marched me on the plane, the flight attendant met us at the door and said, "You can't bring him on like that."

The federal marshals were a little upset and tried to object to removing my shackles and handcuffs, but in the end they had to do it. So they said, "Kevin, do you promise you won't do anything?"

"Yeah," I said, and they removed the handcuffs, waist chains, and shackles. I walked to my seat and went to sleep.

On March 22, 2004, in Boston Federal Court, U.S. District Judge Richard Stearns sentenced me. When I walked into the courtroom, I had no idea what he would give me. All I knew was that it could be anywhere from five to twenty years.

U.S. Attorney Michael Sullivan wanted me to do fifteen years and considered my sentence one of the most distasteful things he had to do. But he did state that you have to deal with violent criminals to get more violent criminals. However, the agents who had been involved with me all that time, along with U.S. Attorneys Brian Kelly, who prosecuted me, and Fred Wyshak, who had worked with me, believed, based on my cooperation, that I deserved less than fifteen years. Kelly and Wyshak spoke on my behalf and kept their word to me, as did Agents Steve Johnson and Dan Doherty.

That day at least twenty agents and prosecutors from Washington and Connecticut and other states came in on my behalf. In the courtroom, they stated that my cooperation was unprecedented, unparalleled in Massachusetts history. All along they had not promised me anything, except that when it came to my sentencing, they would do their best for me. They all kept their word. John Durham from the Justice Department Strike Force, who had prosecuted the case against John Connolly and Richard Schneiderhan, along with Lenny Boyle, another prosecutor, also spoke on my behalf, stating that my cooperation was extraordinary.

There was no victim impact statement, but the lawyer for Michael Donahue's two sons tried to bring up the civil suit. Judge Stearns said that his courtroom wasn't the venue for that case, which would be settled in another court by another judge. He cited that I had given up three bodies with no agreement in place, with no safety net, and, charged with those crimes, I had put myself at peril and placed my faith in the justice system. He also cited that he had seen me testify, that I was very candid and truthful, and that I hadn't hesitated to answer any question posed to me.

I was expecting the worst, but in the end, the judge gave me seventy-two months, including time served. He spoke to me then, saying, "Mr. Weeks, good luck, and I hope I've done the right thing." He also said that the sentence was "one of the most difficult that I have faced as a judge." The whole procedure took about twenty-five minutes.

I spent that night in a holding cell at the courthouse and was driven back to Allenwood the next day. Since they give you fifty-four days a year for good behavior, you usually end up doing 85 percent of your time. I ended up serving a total of sixty-three months.

At Allenwood, I had been put in a prison inside a prison, in the federal inmate witness protection program called WITSEC, a high-security unit for people who were cooperating on cases. Gerald Shur, a federal marshal and one of the original founders of the WITSEC program in 1967, was quoted as saying in front of Congress that doing one day in WITSEC was equivalent to doing three days in regular prison. That's because a WITSEC unit was more confined and there was less to do in it. It housed approximately seventy prisoners, a lot of them involved in high-profile cases from Mafia underbosses down to gangbangers from the Crips and the Bloods.

In our unit, we had Nazi Lowriders, Dirty White Boys, Latin Kings, and traditional organized crime Irish and Italian guys. Occasionally there were fistfights, but it wasn't like being in a regular federal prison in the sense that the chances for violent confrontation were a lot less. Things never really got out of control. Ninety-five percent of the guys who were in there had a chance to get out at some time in their lives, while the other 5 percent were doing life bids and were never getting out.

But if guys got into too many fights, they did get thrown out of the WITSEC unit. While I was there, three guys were thrown out. These guys end up in segregated prison units, where they are locked down twenty-four hours a day, except for three times a week when they're let out for exercise.

While I was there, I had a couple of workout partners, one from Massachusetts and one from Philly, who were real nice guys. Even though you always referred to each other by your first name and last initial, eventually you got to know everybody's name, as well as their background and case. The workout partner I was the closest to was Billy N., who was called "the Hater" by the staff because he didn't associate with a lot of people. He'd been in prison a long time and he could figure out and read people pretty well. My second workout partner, Tommy R., used to cook using the couple of microwaves inside the unit and the three of us would eat together.

I was also close to a few other people in there, guys I would consider friends, fellows from Philly, along with some blacks from DC and New York, and some Spanish guys from Mexico and New York. People ran in different circles and I didn't get along with everyone in there. There were a lot of people you just ignored. They didn't want to be around you and you didn't want to be around them.

While I was there, I read a lot, which was one of the best things you could do there. I received four or five books a week from my brothers, books by Lee Child, Stuart Woods, Lawrence Block, Jack Higgins, Tess

Gerritsen, James Patterson, and Steven Ambrose. I'd read them as soon as they arrived and passed them on to other inmates when I finished them.

I exercised five days a week, lifting weights in the weight room from 9:30 to 10:45 A.M., and on weekends I'd work out with the pull-up bar outside. At night, at six, I'd run on the treadmill for an hour, seven nights a week. And the rest of the time I'd read. Basically, my four years and five months at Allenwood were uneventful. I just read a lot, worked out, and ran.

Time passed pretty quickly as long as you stayed busy. The only thing about being in these WITSEC units was that they didn't have the facilities other prisons had. All they had was a very small yard and no outdoor activities to speak of. There wasn't much for the inmates to do besides reading, working out, and watching TV. No education was available, except for the inmates who were required to get their GED. Since it was too great a security risk to bring in teachers, there were no college courses, no computer classes, no teachers whatsoever. Any time anyone from outside came in to do work, they would put us back in the unit and lock us down. The one big thing that you did have in the WITSEC unit, and which compensated for everything you didn't have, was that eventually, based on seniority, you got a single cell. It took me two and a half years, but I did get my own cell, along with a TV.

We were allowed three hundred minutes a month of phone calls, which was equivalent to twenty fifteen-minute phone calls. In any prison, no one can call you, so you make all the calls. Basically, in WITSEC, you are isolated from everybody. They allow a small list of visitors who have to get clearance from Washington to be on your visiting list. At the beginning, I had visitors, but then I told people not to come. Even my lawyer never came up. I felt it was too long a trip for my family to drive more than seven hours each way just for a visit, but I talked to family and friends once a week. I kept in touch with some good friends on the street who stayed loyal to me, including some people I was involved with when

I was out there. They all understood that after it came out that Jimmy and Stevie were informants, nobody would blame me or anyone else involved in the case for cooperating.

There were two staff members who would go out of their way to help inmates out. Mr. Stork would help an inmate with whatever job he had, while Mr. Fink was the type of guy who would joke with the inmates all day to keep it lighthearted. As long as everything ran smoothly, the unit manager, Mr. Moyer, didn't go out of his way to hassle the inmates. There were a few guards, but not many, who would go out of their way to give you a hard time.

One of my two workout partners and closest friends is still in there. He received a thirteen-year sentence and still has six more to do. My other workout partner was getting out a month or two after me. After my release, there were restrictions on my associations and travel. I have five years of supervised release, which means I can't travel outside the district without permission or associate with any known felons.

Now that I am out, my life is very quiet, with no stress. Coming back, it was strange being around people and adjusting to the freedom of walking into a store and buying something to eat or some clothes for myself. In prison, you're wearing khakis, prison-issued clothes, all the time. When I first got out and came back, I saw that a lot had changed, including the whole dynamics of the city. I don't live in Boston anymore, but I did go back to South Boston and saw family and friends and the people I was involved with. They all understood that I hadn't hurt anyone on the street. To the person, they all came up to me, shook hands, hugged me, and said, "Whatever we can help you with, we will."

The government never gave me any money or anything, so I had to start all over from scratch, except for the support of these friends and family. The one thing the government did do for me was to keep its word and give me my life back.

On February 4, 2005, my oldest brother, Billy, drove down to Allenwood to bring me home. It was a beautiful winter day. We left at eight in the morning and got to Massachusetts at three in the afternoon. When we got to Billy's house, I didn't want a beer or a steak dinner. All I wanted was to go for a walk someplace where there were no walls. I got out of the car and went, by myself, for a long walk.

WHERE ARE THEY NOW?

STEVIE FLEMMI Pled out to ten murders in February 2004 and was sentenced to life in prison with no chance of parole.

JOHN CONNOLLY Convicted in 2002 of one count of racketeering, two counts of obstruction of justice, and one count of making a false statement to the FBI and sentenced to 121 months. Now facing first-degree murder and conspiracy charges in Florida for allegedly providing information that led to the death of former World Jai Alai president John Callahan.

JOHNNY MARTORANO Sentenced to fourteen years in 2004. He'll be out with time served in 2007.

RICHIE SCHNEIDERHAN: Sentenced to eighteen months in 2003 for obstruction of justice and conspiracy.

FORMER FBI AGENT PAUL RICO: Died in an Oklahoma jail in January 2004, at age seventy-eight, while awaiting trial for Roger Wheeler's murder.

FORMER FBI AGENT JOHN MORRIS Retired from the FBI.

KEVIN O'NEIL Home with his family after he did eleven months for racketeering, extortion, and money laundering. Back working in developing and selling real estate.

FRANKIE SALEMME Got out before me but was rearrested on obstruction of justice charge in November 2004.

JIM BULGER Still fine and soaking up the sun.

KEVIN WEEKS Happy to have a second chance in life.

ACKNOWLEDGMENTS

Kevin Weeks

To Herself. Without her constant encouragement and belief in me, this book would never have been written. You are my Angel.

To Sister Superior, who always managed to make me laugh. Imagine a "Nun" in red.

To Phyllis, for putting up with me. No one else would have stuck it out. And to her husband St. Jack. Thank you for always having a kind word.

To my friends who have stood by my side throughout all that has happened: Gerard and Yader, who never wavered in their support of me, Billy, Guy, Charlie, Pat N. and Patty L.

I would like to thank my brothers, Bill and Jack. Their help was always forthcoming, and neither one ever gave a second thought to helping their baby brother.

To Doug Grad, who I liked the first time we met, for constantly giving guidance on this project.

To Helen Rees, who believed in this book before it was even written.

To Judith Regan, who made this book happen.

To Tom Raftery, the Brian Dennehy of the legal world.

ACKNOWLEDGMENTS

To Dennis Kelly and Dave Losier, two of the brightest legal minds in Boston.

To Richie Loiacono and Butch Montoya, two of my close friends from paintball.

To Jay Hurley, my friend since we were kids down O & Third streets.

And to the people of South Boston, a great place to live and grow up in.

Phyllis Karas

Nothing could ever happen without Jack. Nor would I want it to. Yet, there are others who helped in myriad ways. Josh and Chalese and Adam and Amy offered limitless enthusiasm, along with expert editing help. The four of them are the joys of my life, each one a uniquely remarkable person. And the littlest Karas, Jason Brady, made Monday the best day of the week.

Toby and Larry Bondy have always been in my corner, ready to read and provide suggestions and love. Mel and Eddie Karas's knowledge of the subject was another invaluable aid.

For Barbara Ellerin, Karen Madorsky, Arlene Leventhal, Barbara Gilefsky, Ali Freedman, Barbara Schectman, Sheila Braun, and Sharda Jain, my special friends who listen and care, I am especially grateful.

Sherry Perlow and Julie Hoffman, so close and so far away, always managed to be there for me.

No writer cherishes her writers' group more than I do. Nancy Day, Anne Driscoll, Florence Graves, Melissa Ludtke, Judy Stoia, and Pat Thomas never stopped asking the right questions.

Without my brilliant editor Doug Grad, there would be no book. Working with him was a privilege. Not only is he an expert professional, but he always went the extra step to create an important and unique book.

My extraordinary agent Helen Rees used her talents to make certain this book would come to life. Once again, she proved she is the best there is.

The unflappable and ever-helpful Alan M. Thibeault, the chief librarian in the *Boston Herald*'s library, was my knight in shining armor, never hesitating to pore through the files and come up with exactly what we needed.

At ReganBooks, Alison Stoltzfus worked tirelessly and cheerfully, making certain things went smoothly.

Special thanks to the BU School of Journalism, fall of 2005, JO 403B1 Magazine Writing and Editing class, whose unflagging enthusiasm for the project made the semester such a special delight.

But infinite praise must go to Alan Braunstein, the ingenious attorney who put the pieces together in the most original manner imaginable.

And to KJW, my teacher in true crime, who taught me, oh so patiently, more than I will ever need to know, I can only say, "Thanks for a great ride."